When Judaism Began

When Judaism Began

Exploring the Books of Ezra and Nehemiah

STEVEN BOB

WIPF & STOCK · Eugene, Oregon

WHEN JUDAISM BEGAN
Exploring the Books of Ezra and Nehemiah

Wipf & Stock
An Imprint of Wipf and Stock Publishers
199 W. 8th Ave., Suite 3
Eugene, OR 97401

www.wipfandstock.com

PAPERBACK ISBN: 979-8-3852-7123-8
HARDCOVER ISBN: 979-8-3852-7124-5
EBOOK ISBN: 979-8-3852-7125-2

VERSION NUMBER 04/20/26

All English quotations from Talmud, Mikraot Gedolot, and Mishneh Torah follow my own translation of the original Hebrew and Aramaic texts.

I dedicate this book to the memory of my father-in-law, Eric Blaustein, a scholar of ancient Near East and European history and a hero of the Jewish people.

Contents

Acknowledgments xi

Introduction xiii

TORAH

Chapter 1 Sacred History 3

Chapter 2 Torah Rituals 7

Chapter 3 Redaction of the Torah 12

Chapter 4 Who Wrote Ezra/Nehemiah? 16

Chapter 5 When Were Ezra and Nehemiah Written? 20

LANGUAGES

Chapter 6 The Shift to Writing Hebrew in Aramaic Letters 27

Chapter 7 Aramaic, Hebrew, and Judeo-American 31

Chapter 8 Persian Loan Words 36

Chapter 9 How Do You Spell King David's Name? 41

HISTORY

Chapter 10 Our Story in the Much Larger World 49

Chapter 11 Placing Ezra and Nehemiah in Their Historic Context 53

Chapter 12 National Narrative 58

Chapter 13 Taking Possession of the Land 62

Chapter 14 Practical Zionism: The First Aliyah 67

RETURNING HOME

Chapter 15 Cyrus the Great 73
Chapter 16 Political Zionism 78
Chapter 17 Jeremiah's Promise 82
Chapter 18 Babylonian Jews 87
Chapter 19 The First Jew 92

RITUALS

Chapter 20 Understanding the Sukkah 99
Chapter 21 Religious Life During the Exile in Babylonia 105
Chapter 22 Redefining Time 109
Chapter 23 The Right Song 113

JERUSALEM

Chapter 24 Rebuilding the Altar and the Temple 119
Chapter 25 One Temple or Two? 124
Chapter 26 The Walls of Jerusalem 129
Chapter 27 Where Is the Ark? 134
Chapter 28 The Presence of God 139

PEOPLE

Chapter 29 Grouping the Community 147
Chapter 30 Help from Others 152
Chapter 31 What Were Their Names? 157
Chapter 32 Ahasuerus and Ahasuerus 161
Chapter 33 How Do You Say Ahasuerus in Persian? 165
Chapter 34 He Was Wearing a Hat 169
Chapter 35 Foreign Wives 173
Chapter 36 The Davidic Line 178

SELF-RELIANCE

Chapter 37	The Adversaries	185
Chapter 38	The Samaritans	190
Chapter 39	The Letters	195
Chapter 40	Defending Ourselves	200
Chapter 41	Nehemiah's Enemies	204

THE END OF PROPHECY

Chapter 42	Haggai and Zechariah	211
Chapter 43	Already but Not Yet	216
Chapter 44	A Mighty Hand, and an Outstretched Arm	221
Chapter 45	Ezra and Nehemiah in Rabbinic Literature	226
Chapter 46	Lidrosh	231

For Further Reading 235

Bibliography 247

Acknowledgments

As I was searching for a topic for my last year of leading Congregation Etz Chaim's Torah Study Group, I turned to my Talmud Study Buddies for ideas. Rabbi Michael Balinsky suggested that the students and I might enjoy exploring the book of Ezra. That suggestion set me on the path that me led to this book.

I am grateful to friends and relatives who each read a portion of my manuscript and provided helpful suggestions: Rabbi Marc Berkson, Lisa Bob Kaplan, Tammie Bob, Rabbi Norman Cohen, Rabbi Charles Levi, Rabbi Steven Mason, Rabbi Don Rossoff, Rabbi Elliot Strom, Rabbi David Sofian, Rabbi Howard Sommer, David Waksberg, and Rabbi Michael Weinberg.

During the years that I wrote this book I had opportunities to teach Ezra/Nehemiah at Congregation Etz Chaim, the Community Presbyterian Church of Clarendon Hills, North Suburban Synagogue Beth El, Temple Sholom, BJBE, and to the Chalutzim campers and my faculty colleagues at Olin Sang Ruby Union Institute. The questions and comments of my students sharpened my thinking and improved my understanding of Ezra/Nehemiah.

During the process of writing this book I turned to a number of scholars with questions. Their patient answers kept me moving forward on a clear path. I want to thank Dr. Andrew Hill, Dr. Aubrey Buster, Dr. Tamara Eskenazi, Dr. Daniel Master, Dr. Alex Massad, Dr. Jordan Ryan, Dr. Malka Simkovich, and Dr. John Walton.

Dr. Michael Graves has helped me throughout this project. He introduced me to specific source materials. My conversations with him have helped me organize this book.

My partner in life, Tammie, read significant portions of the book at various stages in its creation. Her helpful suggestions guided me on a productive path. She also patiently listened to my enthusiastic description of my progress on this project. Her comments kept me balanced and directed.

The team at Wipf and Stock provided the opportunity for my words to become an actual book. I want to thank Michael Thomson, the acquisitions editor, for his confidence in this project; Matthew Wimer, my editor, for his support; my copyeditor, Hannah Starr, for her helpful suggestions and her deep dedication to this project; Savanah N. Landerholm, for bringing dignity to this volume through her stunning design of the book; and Jonathan Hill, for the beautiful cover.

Introduction

As the "unofficial campus rabbi" at Wheaton College I am regularly invited into Bible classes to explain how Jews read the Hebrew Bible. I tell the evangelical students that Jews are Torah-centric. We do not look at all the sections of the Hebrew Bible as being equally important. I describe the experience of first-time visitors to our synagogue service quickly noticing the special honor that Jews bestow upon the Torah. Only the Torah is kept in the ark. When the ark is opened or the scroll is raised from the reading table, the congregation stands. I explain to the students that Jews read the Torah in an annual cycle, beginning each fall with Gen 1:1.

Synagogue-attending Jews hear sections of the books of the Prophets read as Haftarah portions throughout the year. We read the five Megilloth of festivals: Esther on Purim, Ruth on Shavuot, Lamentations on Tisha Ba'Av, Song of Songs on Passover, and Ecclesiastes on Sukkot. Selected psalms play an important part of Jewish liturgy. Lines from Proverbs appear in Jewish prayers. But Jews do not encounter the books of Ezra and Nehemiah as part of synagogue life, not in our reading of Scripture and not in our prayer books.

Another reason that Jews do not know much about Ezra and Nehemiah is that we do not focus on their time in history. Ezra and Nehemiah mark the beginning of what we generally call the Second Temple period. But most often when we say the phrase "Second Temple Judaism," we tend to refer to the final decades of the Second Temple era, from the beginning of the reign of Herod the Great in 37 BCE to the destruction of the Temple in 70 CE. When we say "the Second Temple" we think the Temple in the time of Herod, not the newly rebuilt Temple of the time of Ezra.

Christian sources also tend to ignore Ezra and Nehemiah. Christian Scripture, often referred to as the New Testament, mentions thirty-nine people from the Hebrew Bible a total of four hundred times. But the twenty-seven books of Christian Scripture do not mention either Ezra or Nehemiah.

As we explore the chapters of these two books, we will see that the era of Ezra and Nehemiah are worthy of our attention. Key foundational elements of Jewish life and other Scripture-based religions emerge from this period. What we call "Hebrew letters" become Hebrew letters. Moses would not be able to read from a Torah scroll because he would not recognize the letters. The Hebrew letters that Ezra and Nehemiah used are the ones we use today.

The public reading of the Torah begins with Ezra reading from the scroll before the community in Jerusalem. The composing and editing of the Torah concludes in the time of Ezra and Nehemiah. In these books we will meet the first people to think of themselves as Jews. The Hebrew Bible does not describe Moses, Miriam, Deborah, or Solomon as Jews. We will see that Nehemiah uses the term *yehudim*, Jews, to describe the people of Jerusalem.

Jewish holidays take shape during the beginning of this period, as does the Jewish calendar. The Torah speaks of the "first month" or the "seventh month." The book of Nehemiah uses the names of the months that we use today, like Elul and Kislev.

The names of these two people describe their role in the life of the community. *Ezra* means help. In Modern Hebrew *ezra rishona* is "first aid." The biblical Ezra comes to the aid of the people. *Nehemiah* means "God comforts." In Isaiah chapters 40–55 the prophet delivers messages of hope to the exiles in Babylon. He begins, *Nachamu, nachamu, ami*, ("Comfort, be comforted, my people"). This leader of the return from exile, Nehemiah, expresses God's support of the people by his deeds and through his name.

As we explore the books of Ezra and Nehemiah we will be reminded of a more recent era in Jewish history. We will see connections between the return from the first exile in Babylonia and the return in the nineteenth/twentieth century from the second exile. Consideration of Zionist texts, ideas, and personalities will be prompted studying Ezra and Nehemiah.

When the exiles returned to Jerusalem from Babylonia, they found other people living in the land. We will look at how Ezra and Nehemiah describe these encounters. The modern Zionists also encountered other people living in the land. Fully exploring the contemporary Israeli/Palestinian conflict is well beyond the scope of this book. To gain a better understanding of the two conflicting ways of looking at the situation I would suggest Adwan, Bar-On, and Naveh's *Side by Side: Parallel Histories of Israel-Palestine*. While I will draw upon the early Zionist movement to illustrate my understanding of Ezra/Nehemiah, I will avoid commenting on the political and military events of the last seventy-five years.

Our journey through Ezra and Nehemiah will be aided by rabbinic literature and academic scholarship. Too often these two approaches remain separate parallel universes. Generally, people who write about the Bible turn only to the rabbis or only to the scholars. I will be drawing on both universes. The reader will regularly see interpretations from Rashi, Ibn Ezra, Malbim, and the Talmud. I draw upon commentaries, articles, and books written by modern academic Bible scholars and upon history, literature, and contemporary culture to illustrate my explanations of Ezra/Nehemiah.

The structure of this book does not follow the sequence of Ezra/Nehemiah. Rather I approach these books thematically. This method allows for a clearer and deeper exploration of the ideas and events in these two biblical books. I have divided the chapters into nine sections: Torah, Languages, History, Returning Home, Rituals, Jerusalem, People, Self-Reliance, and The End of Prophecy. We will begin in the first chapter with a transformative moment in Jewish history: the first public reading of the Torah described in the eighth chapter of Nehemiah.

TORAH

Chapter 1

Sacred History

CIVIC EVENTS AND RELIGIOUS rituals often include a recitation of "sacred history" laying out the past and the purpose of a community. Each spring during our Passover Seder we read a familiar paragraph from the book of Deuteronomy describing the sacred history of the Jewish people:

> "My father was a fugitive Aramean, and he went down to Egypt with meager numbers, and sojourned there; but there he became a great and very populous nation. The Egyptians dealt harshly with us, and oppressed us; they imposed heavy labor upon us. We cried to the ETERNAL, the God of our ancestors, and the ETERNAL heard our plea, and saw our plight, our misery, and our oppression. The ETERNAL freed us from Egypt with a mighty hand, by an outstretched arm and awesome power and by signs, and portents. He brought us into this place, and gave us this land, a land flowing with milk and honey. Wherefore, I now bring the first fruits of the soil, which You, O ETERNAL, have given me." And you shall leave it before the ETERNAL your God, and bow low before the ETERNAL your God.
> (Deut 26:5–10)[1]

The connection of this passage to Passover grows out of its vivid description of the exodus from Egypt. We also encounter this text as part of the annual cycle of Torah readings as the summer turns to fall. It is in the first chapter of the Torah portion Ki Tavo, which we read a few

1. All quotations of the Tanakh throughout follow the 1985 NJPS translation; however, where "LORD" appears in the NJPS, I have adjusted the references to be "ETERNAL."

weeks before Rosh Hashanah. In its original context in Deuteronomy the paragraph is part of the "First Fruits" ceremony. These are the words that we were instructed to recite as we placed the first fruits of the land in the hands of the priests at the Temple in Jerusalem.

We may be so familiar with this version of our sacred history that we do not notice that it omits an important stop on our way from being slaves in Egypt to bringing first fruits to the Temple in Jerusalem. What is missing? Not a minor detail but rather a major foundational event in Jewish history: the revelation of the Torah at Mount Sinai! For the author of the Deuteronomy text, the entire saga of our people leads to bringing sacrifices to the Temple in Jerusalem. From this point of view the bringing of sacrifices to the Temple in Jerusalem is the fulfillment of our destiny.

Chapter 9 of the book of Nehemiah includes another version of our sacred history. It is not part of our annual religious life, so it remains far less well-known. The entire section is thirty verses long, so I will not quote all of it. It begins,

> You are the ETERNAL God, who chose Abram, who brought him out of Ur of the Chaldeans, and changed his name to Abraham. Finding his heart true to You, You made a covenant with him to give him the land of the Canaanite, the Hittite, the Amorite, the Perizzite, the Jebusite and the Girgashite—to give to his descendants. And You kept Your word. (Neh 9:7–8)

The text retells the exodus from Egypt and then continues,

> You came down on Mount Sinai, and spoke with them from heaven; You gave them right rules and true teachings, good laws and commandments. You made known to them Your holy sabbath, and You ordained for them laws, commandments, and Torah through Moses Your servant. (Neh 9:13–14)

This version of our sacred history includes the revelation of the Torah to Moses at Mount Sinai in contrast to the version in Deuteronomy. The earlier versions of the sacred history ignored the revelation at Mount Sinai because when Deuteronomy was written Torah had not yet become a core concern. Torah had not yet become a central means of connecting with God. In the preexilic era, the Temple sacrifices were the single means of expressing connection with God. In contrast, after the return from Babylonian exile, Torah stands as a central focus, as we will see unfold in the books of Ezra and Nehemiah.

The first six chapters of the book of Ezra describe the first two waves of Israelites returning to the land. These first two waves rebuilt the altar in Jerusalem and resumed the offering of sacrifices. In chapter 7 we meet Ezra. The text describes him thus:

> Ezra came up from Babylon, a scribe expert in the Torah of Moses, which the ETERNAL, the God of Israel, had given, whose request the king had granted in entirety, thanks to the benevolence of the ETERNAL toward him. (Ezra 7:6)

Verses 2–5 trace Ezra's lineage back to Aaron, so we know that he is a priest but verse 6, the text that introduces him, emphasizes his connection to the Torah.

Main characters in operas often sing an entrance aria which define their identity. As Figaro comes on stage in Rossini's *The Barber of Seville*, he sings "Largo al factotum," describing his skills as the person who gets things done in Seville. While Ezra is a priest as he "comes on stage," the text describes him as "a teacher well-versed in the Torah of Moses."

The sages in the Talmud (Sanhedrin 24a) point out that the Bible uses the same Hebrew verb, *alah*, to describe Ezra coming up to Jerusalem from Babylon that it used to describe Moses ascending Mount Sinai to receive the Torah in Exod 19:3. This word choice stresses the strength of the connection between Ezra and Moses.

While the eighth chapter of Nehemiah may not be as well-known as the "You shall be holy" section of Lev 19, the binding of Isaac in Gen 22, or Ps 23, it stands as one of the pivotal chapters of the entire Hebrew Bible. It describes the rededication of the people. It begins,

> When the seventh month arrived—the Israelites being [settled] in their towns—the entire people gathered as one man into the square that was before the Water Gate; and they asked Ezra the scribe [Hasofer] to bring the scroll [Sefer] of the Torah of Moses with which the ETERNAL had charged Israel. On the first day of the seventh month, Ezra the priest brought the Torah before the congregation, men and women, and all who could listen with understanding. (Neh 8:1–2)

One might expect that the ceremony of national rededication would take place in the recently rebuilt Temple. But instead, it takes place outside the Temple at the Water Gate. The paragraph mentions that Ezra is a priest, but the ceremony does not feature Ezra putting on the official garments of the priesthood and the offering of a sacrifice. Instead, the ceremony of national rededication features the first public reading of the Torah. Nowhere in the Hebrew Bible is there a record of any of the kings, prophets, or priests of the First Temple period convening the public to hear them read the Torah.

It is no exaggeration to view this moment of Ezra reading the Torah as the beginning of Judaism, as we know it. For Ezra and Nehemiah, the Torah, not animal sacrifice, stands at the center.

In history change generally occurs slowly, but significant turning point moments do emerge. For example, from the beginning of time until the mid-eighteenth century, the only way to convey a message to another person was by speaking it or by writing it down and having it hand delivered. Then in 1844 Samuel Morse sent a telegraph message from the Capitol in Washington to the Mount Claire Depot in Baltimore, proclaiming, "What Hath God Wrought?"[2] In 1876 Alexander Graham Bell used the telephone to summon his assistant from the next room, saying, "Mr. Watson—come here—I want to see you."[3]

The telegraph and the telephone began a process of innovation that led to our current ability to be in contact with anyone anywhere in the world via the smartphone in our pocket or the watch on our wrist. The days on which Morse and Bell sent their first messages are remembered as turning point days in human history. The day on which Ezra read from the Torah at the Water Gate was such a turning point day in Jewish history.

Throughout the Second Temple period our people read Torah and offered sacrifices. We know from Josephus that in the final decades of the Second Temple era some of our people, Sadducees, focused their lives on the sacrifices, and some of our people, the Pharisees, focused their attention on the Torah. The Judaism that guides our lives today grew out of the foundation created by the Pharisees. In reading these verses in Neh 8 we witness the laying of the cornerstone of the foundation of Judaism and the other Scripture-based religions. In the next chapter we will look more closely at the details of this first public reading of the Torah.

2. History Editors, "Samuel Morse."

3. Bruno, "Mr. Watson, Come Here."

Chapter 2

Torah Rituals

IN THE FIRST CHAPTER, I explained the pivotal importance of the public Torah reading described in the eighth chapter of Nehemiah. I want to now turn to the details of the rituals of that event. The text sets the scene:

> And Ezra the scribe stood upon a pulpit of wood, which they had made for the purpose. . . . Ezra opened the scroll in the sight of all the people, for he was above all the people; as he opened it all the people stood up. Ezra blessed the ETERNAL the great God and all the people answered, "Amen, Amen," with hands upraised. Then they bowed their heads and prostrated themselves before the ETERNAL with their faces to the ground.
> (Neh 8:4–6)

Reading this description of the first Torah reading, we see connections to our contemporary Jewish practices. In Ezra, the Torah is read from a raised platform. We read the Torah from a bima. Ezra recited a blessing to which the people responded, "Amen. Amen." In our synagogues, the person called forward for an aliyah recites a blessing to which the people respond.

The sages of Jewish tradition see a strong connection between Ezra's Torah reading and that of their own times. Ralbag, Rabbi Levi ben Gershon (1288–1344), who wrote a commentary to much of the Hebrew Bible, explains the meaning of the phrase "blessed the ETERNAL" in Neh 8:6: "This is the Torah blessing that was recited [by Ezra] before reading from the Torah."

Ralbag sees the blessing recited by Ezra as the same well-known Torah blessing recited in his time and in our time. He sees a straight line connecting Ezra and the Jews of the late Middle Ages. Following Ralbag we can see that line reaching to the early twenty-first century.

Rambam, Moses Maimonides (1138–1204), begins the section on blessings in his Mishneh Torah by explaining the different types of blessing that Jews recite before and after eating, before performing Mitzvot, and as praise and gratitude to God. Then he writes, "The text of all the blessings was ordained by Ezra and his court" (Hilchot Berachot 1:3 and 5).

We can confidently conclude that Rambam sees the blessings before and after the Torah as originating with Ezra and his circle. In the same section of the Mishneh Torah Rambam writes, "Whoever answers *Amen* to a blessing recited by another person is considered as if he recited the blessing himself."

While he does not specifically mention Neh 8:6, he could have been moved by the response of the people to Ezra to formulate his position on the power and the importance of responding *Amen*.

The Babylonian Talmud (BT) traces two rules for Torah reading to Neh 8. In Masechet Sota we learn that one should be quiet during the Torah reading:

> Rava bar Rav Huna says: When you open a Torah scroll one should not speak even about a question of halachah. As Bible text states: "And Ezra opened the book in the sight of all the people, for he was above all the people, and when he opened it, all the people stood up" (Neh 8:5), and the term "standing" in this case refers specifically to silence, as the text states: "And shall I wait, because they do not speak, because they stand still, and answer no more?" (Job 32:16). Offering an alternative proof text, Rabbi Zeira said in the name of Rav Ḥisda: We derive the prohibition against speaking from the verse: "And the ears of all the people were attentive to the book of the law" (Neh 8:3). They did not listen to any other voice. (BT Sota 39a)

Rabbi Zeira quotes Rabbi Hisda's teaching that as the people listened attentively to the first Torah reading, so should Jews throughout the centuries refrain from speaking while the Torah is read.

Masechet Megillah contains the explanation for how many aliyot are read on different days:

> We learned in the Mishnah: On a festival, five people read; on Yom Kippur, six people read; and on Shabbat, seven people read. Ya'akov of Mina said to Rav Yehuda: What is the scriptural basis for establishing six as the number of readers on Yom Kippur? Rav Yehuda answered him: We have six readers to recall the six people who stood to Ezra's right and the six people who stood to his left, as it is stated [in Neh 8:4]: "And Ezra the Scribe stood upon a platform of wood, which they had made for the purpose, and beside him stood Mattithiah, and Shema, and Anaiah, and Uriah, and Hilkiah, and Maaseiah, on his right hand, and on his left hand, Pedaiah, and Mishael, and Malchiah, and Hashum, and Hashbadanah, Zechariah, Meshullam."
>
> The Gemara raise a challenge to this answer: The verse lists seven people standing to Ezra's left not six. The Gemara responds to this challenge: While the Bible lists both Zechariah and Meshullam, we should not take these two names to refer to two separate individuals, rather these are two names for one person. Zechariah is his name and Meshullam is a description of him. Why does the text add this extra name Meshullam? Because he was perfect [*mushlam*] in his deeds. (BT Megillah 23a)

Rabbi Yehuda draws upon the number of people flanking Ezra as he read Torah on Rosh Hashanah to indicate how many aliyot should be read on Yom Kippur. The Stam, the anonymous voice, takes this interpretive opportunity to heap praise on Zechariah while defending this use of the biblical text.

One might be tempted to embrace these claims of the rabbis of late antiquity and the Middle Ages to draw a straight unbroken line from the ceremony described in Neh 8 and our rituals today. But what do we know about the time between Neh 8 and the second century? We do not find much evidence on this topic in the usual sources for the last three centuries before the Common Era.

The Apocrypha does not contain any mention of Torah reading. The only related material in the Apocrypha is in the book of Baruch, which begins with a description of Baruch reading his own book out loud at the time of the destruction of the First Temple.

The Letter of Aristeas describes the creation of the Septuagint, the translation of the Hebrew Bible into Greek in Alexandria around 200 BCE. At the conclusion of the project the new Greek text was read aloud.

> When the work was completed, Demetrius collected together the Jewish population in the place where the translation had been

> made, and read it over to all, in the presence of the translators, who met with a great reception also from the people, because of the great benefits which they had conferred upon them.[1]

This celebratory reading was a onetime event rather an ongoing weekly ritual. So it does not provide us with additional evidence regarding the regular Torah reading.

The writings of Josephus do not include any references to public reading of the Torah during the later Second Temple period. If Josephus had been aware of the custom of weekly Torah reading, he certainly would have mentioned it in one of his comprehensive books about Jewish life. So, while the rabbis draw an unbroken straight line between the first public Torah reading in Neh 8 and the procedures described in rabbinic literature, it would be more prudent to conclude that the rituals in Nehemiah provided the foundation for the later development of the Torah reading ceremonies described by the rabbis.

Before we conclude this chapter, we should consider the meaning of the Torah reading rituals. We can see the public reading of the Torah in Ezra and the public reading of the Torah in our synagogues as a reenacting of Ma'amad Har Sinai, the revelation at Mount Sinai. The Bible describes both Moses and Ezra as "going up." We might think of the wooden platform built for Ezra as a practical means to allow the people to hear and see. But we could also see it as a reminder of Mount Sinai. The synagogue bima inspired by Ezra's wooden platform could also be understood as a reminder of Mount Sinai. We call the act of reciting the blessing an *aliyah*, a going up. The person called to the Torah ascends the bima and recites a blessing praising God "who selected us from among all peoples and gave us the Torah." The ritual of Torah reading calls us to stand again at Mount Sinai. Every time we read the Torah, we renew our self-definition as a people covenanted to God through Torah.

My synagogue's regular Shabbat Torah scroll fits naturally in my bent right arm. As a congregational rabbi I held a Torah scroll in my arms several times every week. In addition to services, I met with the upcoming Bar/Bat Mitzvah students, teaching them the choreography of the service. I enjoyed the opportunity to teach them how to hold the Torah scroll. Many of them started the process fearful that they might not be up to the task. The scroll seemed heavy and awkward to hold. Rachel,

1. Letter of Aristeas 308–9 (Charles).

our tutor, taught them to be confident Torah readers. I helped them to become confident Torah holders.

I led the Congregation Etz Chaim (Tree of Life) for thirty-five years. While I had nothing to do with the choice of name of our congregation, I loved it. I always felt that the name of the congregation describes who we wanted to be as a community. The name comes from a verse in Proverbs that we recite as we return the Torah to the ark: “It is a tree of life to those who hold fast to it and all of her supporters are happy” (Prov 3:18).

When I literally held fast to the Torah scroll, I felt that it defined me and the path of my life. When I publicly read from the Torah, I knew that I was metaphorically standing in Ezra’s footsteps, bringing Torah to the people and the people to Torah.

Chapter 3

Redaction of the Torah

I FIRST HEARD THE song "Book of Love" in a performance by Sha Na Na at the Minnesota State Fair in the Young America's Mind Odyssey Pavilion in the summer of 1970. This song asks an important question about the authorship of the book of love. The protagonist in the song wants to know if love comes from above.

People ask a similar question about the Torah. Traditional sources do assume that the Torah does indeed come from above. They use the term *Torah min hashamaim*, "Torah from the heavens." The academic approach is to search for a human author. Contemporary scholars all agree that the Torah, as it exists today, was not written by a single author or at a single time. Scholars explain that several voices over many years contributed to the text we have today. The classic Documentary Hypothesis teaches that we can see four documents that scholars label E, J, P, and D in the Torah text. This approach began among nineteenth-century German Protestant Bible scholars. Over the past hundred and fifty years many scholars have offered various ideas about how to divide the text into its original documents.

This conversation among scholars continues today. They point out that the Torah contains duplicated stories. In Exod 17:2–7 we read of Moses bringing water out of a rock to save the thirsty people of Israel. The same story reappears in Num 20:2–13. In this second version, Aaron, the high priest, and the tent of meeting are added to the narrative. Scholars recognize these as indicators of the P, or priestly source.

A full explanation of this topic of Torah authorship stands well beyond the scope of this book. If you want to read a full presentation of the documentary hypotheses written for a popular audience, I would suggest *Who Wrote the Bible?* by Richard Elliot Friedman. Here I want to explore where and when the documents became one whole Torah. We call this process *redaction* and the person who did it, the *redactor*.

This redaction of the Torah could not have taken place before the early Second Temple period because the Torah contains some new material written during that period. Nehemiah 8 delineates the preparation for Sukkot. It describes the rituals of building booths and gathering the four species as something new that was not known by earlier generations of Jews.

> And they found written in the Torah, how that the ETERNAL had commanded Moses, that the Israelites must dwell in booths during the festival of the seventh month, and that they must announce and proclaim throughout all their towns, and in Jerusalem, as follows "Go out to the mountains, and bring leafy branches, and branches of olive trees, pine trees and myrtles, palm, and other leafy tress to make booths, as it is written." So the people went out, and brought them, and made themselves booths, on their roofs, in their courtyards, and in the courts of the House of God, and in the square of the Water Gate, and in the square of the gate of Ephraim. The whole community that returned from captivity made booths, and dwelt in the booths—the Israelites had not done so from the days of Joshua the son of Nun to that day—and there was very great gladness.
> (Neh 8:14–17)

Leviticus 23 contains the commandments concerning the various holidays. The section on the holidays begins and ends with a bookend phrase. The section begins in verse 4: "These are the appointed feasts." We then see a paragraph for each of the festivals. Sukkot is described in verses 33–36, but the building of booths and gathering the four species are not mentioned in that paragraph. It describes the length of the festival and the sacrifices to be offered. The section on the festivals concludes with a repetition of the bookend phrase in verse 37: "These are the appointed feasts." Then beginning with verse 39 we find an extra paragraph tacked on which mentions the new Sukkot rituals described in Neh 8:14–17.

> On the first day you shall take the product of the goodly trees, branches of the palm trees, boughs of the leafy trees and the

> willows of the brook and you shall rejoice before the ETERNAL your God seven days. . . . You shall live in Sukkot seven days; all citizens in Israel shall live in Sukkot in order that future generations may know that I made the Israelite people live in Sukkot when I brought them out of the land of Egypt, I the ETERNAL your God. (Lev 23:40, 42–43)

This additional paragraph of Leviticus could not have been written before the time of Ezra and Nehemiah because it contains commandments that were unknown before that time. The fact that these verses are added in after the second bookend verse (37), "These are the appointed feasts," reveals the seam joining the new Sukkot material created during the time of Ezra/Nehemiah to the older preexisting section on the holidays. Since the Torah contains these commandments that were newly received during the public reading of the Torah scroll, described in Neh 8, it could not have been fully edited before the days of Ezra and Nehemiah.

We can also see evidence that it must have been edited by the time of Ezra and Nehemiah. In chapter 8 of the book of Nehemiah, Ezra assembles the people and reads from *Sefer Torat Moshe*, the "Scroll of the Torah of Moses." This marks the Bible's first description of the public reading from a Torah scroll as I explained in chapter 1.

The ritual of public reading requires a fixed text. Or perhaps the act of public reading makes the text a fixed text. The people who hear a text will expect to hear the same text the next time that it is publicly read.

We can see a similar process in the composition of American "sacred" documents. Multiple drafts of the Declaration of Independence were written before the committee agreed on a final draft. While Thomas Jefferson was the principal author of the Declaration, he did not write, "We hold these truths to be self-evident." He wrote, "We hold these truths to be sacred and undeniable." Another member of the committee, Ben Franklin, changed "sacred and undeniable" to the stronger wording "self-evident."[1] The proclamation of the official version of the Declaration of Independence on July 4, 1776, ended the conversation. Jefferson's first draft was largely forgotten. Today many people mistakenly attribute "We hold these truths to be self-evident" to Jefferson.

I think that Torah scrolls, as we know them today, did not exist before the time of Ezra and Nehemiah. The shift to the Aramaic letters and move to writing with a pen/quill during the exile in Babylonia as will be

1. National Archives, "Jefferson's 'Original Rough Draught.'"

explained in chapter 6 made possible the creation of the Torah scrolls we know. The straight letters of the old Paleo-Hebrew alphabet were easily drawn with a stick on a clay tablet or chiseled in to a large stone. But the curved letters of the Aramaic alphabet required a more sophisticated writing technology, such as pen and parchment.

Because the Torah includes Lev 23:40–43 the Torah could not have been redacted before the time of Ezra/Nehemiah. And if we accept my contention that Ezra read from the completed Torah at the ceremony of rededication of the people before the Water Gate on Rosh Hashanah, the redaction must have occurred by the time of Ezra/Nehemiah.

Knowing that this redacting took place in the time of Ezra and Nehemiah leads us to the next question: Who was the redactor? Some people have speculated that it was Ezra himself.

The Hebrew text calls Ezra a *sofer*, which is generally translated as "scribe." Here it may mean much more. Ezra 7:6 describes Ezra as *Sofer mahir b'torat moshe*. The JPS translates the phase as "a scribe expert in the Teaching of Moses," taking the word *mahir* to mean "expert." *Mahir* literally means "quick," like the modern Hebrew word *mahair*. David Kimchi takes the word to mean that Ezra quickly grasped the meaning of the text. Ralbag notices that *sofer* comes from the same three-letter root as the Hebrew verb "to count." He explains that Ezra could "count" or recount all the possible interpretations of each verse.

In modern Hebrew we use the word *sofer* to describe a person who creates sacred objects by copying existing documents. Today a *sofer* copies texts to create parchments for a mezuzah, a set of tefillin, or for a Torah scroll. The commentators agree that Ezra was more than just a scribe who copied preexisting texts.

Ezra has authority, and he had the Torah scroll in his hands. He is a scribe and a priest. I believe that Ezra was not simply "a scribe" but rather "The Scribe." He was able to publicly read from the Torah scroll because he had redacted the Torah. Working with the source material he completed the process of creating the Torah. The Torah scroll from which Ezra read was the first Torah scroll, and he was the first Torah reader.

Chapter 4

Who Wrote Ezra/Nehemiah?

The history books of the Prophets section of the Hebrew Bible move smoothly from one to the other. We can easily see that Joshua, Judges, 1 and 2 Samuel, and 1 and 2 Kings stand as a single unit. Scholars refer to them as the Deuteronomic history, ascribing them to the author of the book of Deuteronomy. The books of the Deuteronomic history seem to all come from the same voice describing adjacent periods of history. They tell an ongoing story in a consistent style.

Traditional sources and modern bible scholars have attempted to connect Ezra/Nehemiah with other books of the Writings section of the Hebrew Bible.

The book of Ezra begins, "And in the . . ." Rashi in his comment on Ezra 1:1 interprets that "and," expressed in Hebrew by the letter *vav*, to present a connection to what comes before it. He argues that Ezra is a continuation of the book of Daniel. He refers to a Talmud passage, Baba Batra 14b, which lists the sequence of the biblical books. In the standard printed Baba Batra text which we have today, we read, "The order of the Writings is: Ruth and the book of Psalms, and Job and Proverbs; Ecclesiastes, Song of Songs, and Lamentations; Daniel and the scroll of Esther; and Ezra and Chronicles." We know that in the centuries in which the Talmud was copied by hand, variations in the text emerged. I imagine that Rashi's version of the Baba Batra text listed Ezra as directly following Daniel. The Hebrew Bible follows the order in Rashi, not the order in the printed Baba Batra.

Daniel is set during the Babylonian exile. Daniel begins with a review of Nebuchadnezzar taking the Judeans into exile. It concludes with

Daniel's vision of the people returning from that exile. So historically, Ezra fits right in place following Daniel. One could say that Ezra follows Daniel as Exodus follows Genesis. Before speaking of the "Pharaoh who knew not Joseph" (Exod 1:8), the book of Exodus begins with a brief recapitulation of the conclusion of the family of Jacob descending into Egypt.

While the period of time in which the events of Ezra/Nehemiah took place does directly follow the period of time in which the events in Daniel took place, the books do not share a narrative voice or common content.

The book of Daniel includes three stories of the dreams/visions of the King Nebuchadnezzar and King Belshazzar which only Daniel can understand and interpret. In the opening chapter of Ezra, King Cyrus appears, but we do not read anything about a dream or its interpretation. Chapter 2 of the book of Daniel tells the story of Shadrach, Meshach, and Abednego miraculously surviving the fiery furnace. Chapter 6 tells the story of Daniel miraculously surviving the lions' den. Ezra and Nehemiah contain no miracle stories. The last six chapters of Daniel contain a lengthy series of apocalyptic visions. Ezra/Nehemiah does not contain any apocalyptic visions.

To paraphrase an old joke, sometimes a vav is just a vav. We should not take the "and" at the beginning of Ezra as a link connecting it to Daniel. It is just part of a very common biblical verb form.

Academic Bible scholars have linked Ezra/Nehemiah to 1 and 2 Chronicles. Some authors have written as if it is a universally accepted fact that the author of Chronicles also wrote Ezra/Nehemiah. Their confidence seems to grow out of the overlap of the conclusion of 2 Chronicles with the beginning Ezra. Second Chronicles 36:22–23 is identical to the opening words of Ezra.

Leopold Zunz of Detmolt, Germany, a founder of the academic study of Judaism, first put forward in 1832 the premise that the Chronicler also wrote Ezra/Nehemiah. For a hundred and fifty years Zunz's position went unchallenged. Numerous scholars, perhaps out of respect for Zunz, accepted his word as the gospel truth. In the last years of the twentieth century Tamara Eskenazi and other scholars began to raise criticism of Zunz's position.

Without getting overly technical we can still understand the position of these more recent scholars. Everyone agrees that J. K. Rowling wrote all seven Harry Potter books. If someone was to challenge the "single author theory" for the Harry Potter books, we could point out that the books share vocabulary, voice, worldview, characters, and values. If the same author wrote 1 and 2 Chronicles and Ezra/Nehemiah we would expect that those books would share vocabulary, voice, worldview, characters, and values.

A close examination of these books provides clear contrasts between Chronicles on one hand and Ezra/Nehemiah on the other hand. Chronicles repeatedly provides the ages of the national leaders. Ezra and Nehemiah never say a word about anybody's age.

Chronicles focuses on King David and the Davidic line. If the Chronicler had written Ezra/Nehemiah we would expect that he would have included mentions of the continuation of the Davidic line in the time of Ezra/Nehemiah or at least would have lamented the absence of a descendant of King David. But Ezra and Nehemiah do not contain a single mention of David or the Davidic line.

Nehemiah uses the "Hebrew" names for the months. None of these months' names appear in Chronicles. Significant sections of Ezra are in Aramaic. None of Chronicles is in Aramaic.

We can see that there is no evidence to conclude that Ezra and Nehemiah were written by the author of Daniel or by the Chronicler. So, who did write these two books? Certainly, more than one person.

The books of Ezra and Nehemiah are clearly not a single document. Many scholars see the two books as composed of four documents.

Ezra does not appear in the book of Ezra until chapter 7. The first six chapters of the book of Ezra, which tell of first waves of return and the rebuilding of the altar and the Temple, are one document. The final verses of chapter 6 read as the conclusion of a biblical book describing the celebration of Passover in the rebuilt Temple:

> They joyfully celebrated the Feast of the Unleavened Bread for seven days for the ETERNAL had given them cause for joy by inclining the heart of the Assyrian [Persian] king toward them so as to give them support in the work of the house of God, the God of Israel. (Ezra 6:22)

The second document is what I think of as the "Ezra Part" of the book of Ezra. Chapters 7–10 describe the events of Ezra's return to Jerusalem from exile.

The third document is almost all of the book of Nehemiah, chapters 1–7 and 9–13. These chapters contain a Nehemiah-centered description of the return. Nehemiah uses distinctive vocabulary. He speaks in the first person. The book opens, "The narrative of Nehemiah: In the month of Kislev of the twentieth year, when I was in the fortress city of Shushan" (Neh 1:1).

In this verse you will also notice he uses "Kislev" as the name of the month. Today all Jews use "Kislev," but the Hebrew Bible generally refers to the months by their number, beginning in the spring with the month of the exodus from Egypt. So, the month that Nehemiah calls "Kislev" would be called the ninth month in other biblical books. We acquired the names we now use for the months during the exile.

Nehemiah focuses on the security and defense of the people rather than on religious life. He decides to go up to Jerusalem because he learns that the people in Jerusalem "are in dire trouble and disgrace; Jerusalem's wall is full of breaches and its gates have been destroyed by fire" (Neh 1:3).

As governor in Jerusalem, Nehemiah leads the rebuilding of the walls and the replacement of the gates while remaining on alert in case of an enemy attack: "Half of my servants held lances and shields, bows and arrows and armor. And the officers stood behind the whole house of Judah who were rebuilding the wall" (Neh 4:10–11).

Chapter 8 of the book of Nehemiah is the fourth document. This is the only portion of Ezra/Nehemiah in which both Ezra and Nehemiah appear. As a child I enjoyed Superman and Batman comic books. My parents did not support my interest in comics, but my friend Ernie had a large collection of both Superman and Batman books. There were a handful of treasured issues in which Superman and Batman appeared together. In chapter 8 of Nehemiah, Ezra and Nehemiah appear together. Some scholars suggest that this chapter 8 of Nehemiah was originally part of the book of Ezra. Ezra has the "leading role" in this chapter, with Nehemiah playing a "supporting role."

I see chapter 8 of Nehemiah as a stand-alone document. It contains important ideas not found elsewhere in Ezra/Nehemiah. In the first chapter of this book, I explained why chapter 8 of Nehemiah is *the* pivotal chapter of the entire Hebrew Bible for the development of Jewish life.

The author of Daniel did not write Ezra/Nehemiah. The author of Chronicles did not write Ezra/Nehemiah. Four authors wrote the four documents that comprise Ezra/Nehemiah. We do not know who wrote each of these four documents. The books Ezra and Nehemiah that we have today are the work of an editor who assembled Ezra/Nehemiah from these four documents. In the next chapter we will look at when Ezra/Nehemiah were written.

Chapter 5

When Were Ezra and Nehemiah Written?

In the movie *His Girl Friday* Walter Burns, played by Cary Grant, "winks" at the audience. He describes Hildy Johnson's fiancé, Bruce Baldwin, by saying, "He looks like that fellow in the movies, you know . . . Ralph Bellamy!"[1] Bruce Baldwin is, of course, played by Ralph Bellamy. Grant again "winks" at the audience by dropping his original name into the dialogue of the film. His character says to the mayor and the sheriff, "Listen, the last man who said that to me was Archie Leach just a week before he cut his throat."[2] Cary Grant counted on audience members knowing that Archie Leach was his real name, and thus being "in" on the joke.

During some lighthearted movies, a character might fully break the fourth wall by turning to the camera to speak directly to the audience. In the Marx Brothers' film *Horse Feathers*, Groucho turns directly to the camera as Chico begins a piano piece and says, "I've got to stay here, but there is no reason you folks can't go out to the lobby until this thing blows over."[3]

While the Bible never actually breaks the fourth wall, many books of the Bible do include material that would not have been known by the characters in that specific story. The narrators give away that they are

1. Hawks, *His Girl Friday*, 50:35.
2. Hawks, *His Girl Friday*, 1:23:50.
3. McLeod, *Horse Feathers*, 37:58.

writing with a later point of view. Seeing "the man behind the curtain" reveals evidence that these books of the Bible were written much later than the events they describe.

Chapter 12 of Genesis tells the story of Abram and Sarai responding to God's call and journeying from their old home to their new home in Canaan. It includes the phrase "And the Canaanites were still in the land" (Gen 12:6). This verse was clearly not written at the time the reported action took place by a contemporary author who saw Abram and Sarai arrive. Rather it must have been composed centuries later after the Canaanites no longer lived in the land.

In 1 Kings' description of the completion of the Temple, we read, "The poles projected so far that the end of the poles were visible in the sanctuary in front of the Shrine, but they could not be seen from outside; and there they remain to this day" (1 Kgs 8:8). The expression "to this day" indicates that many years must have passed between the construction of the Temple and the writing of the text. The words "to this day" demonstrate that this verse must be written before the Temple was destroyed in 586 BCE. From these details, scholars conclude that the text was written at the end of the First Temple era during the reign of King Josiah, when the kingdom of Judah was still strong and independent.

Anachronisms in some biblical stories provide evidence that they were actually written long after the events that the stories describe. As an analogy: Many people visualize Indigenous peoples of the Great Plains on horseback chasing buffalo. But horses were not indigenous to North America. The Spanish brought them to our continent. In a story set before Cortés, Native Americans on horseback would be an anachronism.

The Bible sets the Joseph story about 1450 BCE, but an anachronism proves that it could not have been written by a firsthand witness. The text tells us that after his brothers had thrown Joseph into a pit, "looking up they saw a caravan of Ishmaelites coming from Gilead, their camels bearing gum, balm, and ladanum to be taken to Egypt" (Gen 37:25).

The writer was familiar with camels. They must have become a standard means of transporting goods by the writer's time. But we can find no evidence that camels existed in the land of Canaan in 1450 BCE, the era in which the Joseph story is set. Animal bones are part of the remains of a society which archeologists excavate. If camels had lived in Canaan in 1450 BCE, we would expect that digs of remains from that era would include camel bones. But in truth digs from that time period do not include camel bones.

Archeologists report that camels did not become part of caravans until after 1000 BCE. We can also learn about the domestication of camels by looking at the dating of carved reliefs of camels bearing burdens and people riding camels. In the Joseph story the caravan carries gum, balm, and myrrh. This reflects the Arabian trade of the Assyrian Empire of the seventh and eighth centuries BCE. Scholars conclude that while the story of Joseph going down to Egypt is set in the fifteenth century BCE, it could not have been written before the eighth century BCE.

Another book of the Bible from the Second Temple era includes references to historical events which can be clearly dated. The last three chapters of Daniel are connected to historical events of the Hellenistic period in general and the reign of Antiochus IV Epiphanes in particular. The visions of Daniel in chapters 10, 11, and 12 include descriptions of the wars between the Seleucids in Syria and Ptolemies in Egypt. Many people know of the Seleucid king, Antiochus IV Epiphanes, from the Hanukkah story. The Maccabees rebelled against his rule. Since the author of Daniel describes the oppression instituted by Antiochus but not the victory of the Maccabees in 164 BCE, scholars date these final three chapters to a precise year: 167 BCE.

We can use these tools to help us determine when Ezra and Nehemiah were written. Ezra and Nehemiah do not include any references or subtle allusions to the Ptolemies or to the Seleucids. The writers of Ezra/Nehemiah do not seem to anticipate the arrival of the forces of Alexander the Great in the Middle East. They speak of the Persian Empire as an ongoing enterprise. Nowhere in Ezra/Nehemiah does the text suggest a later point of view by saying, "And the Persians were still in the land."

The stories of the exodus do not include the name of the Egyptian ruler. The texts just refer to him by his title, "Pharaoh." The absence of the name of the pharaoh suggests that there was a significant passage of time between the departure from Egypt and the composition of the book of Exodus. So much time had passed that the name of the pharaoh had been forgotten.

In contrast, when 2 Kgs 23:29 and 2 Chr 35:20–24 tell the story of King Josiah going to Megiddo to battle the ruler of Egypt, the Bible uses his title and his name, Pharaoh Neco. First Kings describes a raid into the land of Israel by another Egyptian ruler: "And it came to pass in the fifth year of King Rehoboam, that Shishak king of Egypt came up against Jerusalem" (1 Kgs 14:25). The military interventions in the land of Israel by both of these pharaohs as described in the Bible match up very closely with what we know from extensive Egyptian sources. This suggests that the biblical material was composed soon after the events took place.

Likewise, the description of the Persian kings in Ezra/Nehemiah matches up well with what other sources tell us about the kings: Cyrus, Darius I, Xerxes I, and Artaxerxes I. Ezra's description of Cyrus's decree allowing the Jews to return to Jerusalem corresponds to what historians know from Persian sources. This suggests that Ezra and Nehemiah were written soon after the events they describe, while the names of the kings were still recalled clearly and accurately.

In chapter 8 I will identify Persian loan words in Ezra/Nehemiah—as one would expect in texts written in a province of the Persian Empire shortly after the return from exile. If the books had been written during the Hellenistic period, we would expect to find Greek loan words. Some of the late biblical books do include Greek loan words. But we do not find any in Ezra/Nehemiah.

Ezra and Nehemiah contain references to Persian political organization. We read of various Persian satraps and governors (Ezra 4:8–10; 5:3, 6; 6:6, 13). The books do not contain any dreams/hopes of an independent kingdom of Judah. They seem to accept the ongoing reality of the Persian Empire.

Chapter 12 of Nehemiah begins by listing the priests and Levites who participated in the first wave of return described in early chapters of Ezra. It continues by listing the next generations of priests and Levites, concluding with, "The Levites and the priests were listed by heads of clans in the days of Eliashib, Joida, Johanan and Jaddua down to the reign of Darius the Persian" (Neh 12:22).

Identifying which Darius this is could help us understand when the book of Nehemiah was written. Three different kings named Darius ruled the Persian Empire. Does this verse refer to Darius the Great, who died in 486 BCE, Darius II, who died in 404 BCE, or Darius III, the last Persian king who died in 330 BCE? Ezra/Nehemiah does not describe any of the Persian kings with a number, like Henry VIII or Elizabeth II. So, we need other sources to figure out to which Darius Nehemiah refers.

The Bible texts list three generations of high priests of the return. This list can help us solve our Darius riddle. We know that the first generation of these priests and Levites came to Jerusalem in 538 BCE with the first wave of returnees during the reign of Cyrus the Great. If we imagine that a generation is twenty-five years, then two generations after the first wave of return in 538 BCE would place the priests of Neh

12:22 in 488 BCE during the reign of Darius the Great, a.k.a. Darius I, who ruled the Persian Empire 521–485 BCE shortly before Nehemiah's arrival in Jerusalem.

We do not find any references in Ezra/Nehemiah to the conquest of the land by the army of Alexander the Great in 330 BCE, of Ptolemies who ruled the land of Israel 323–201 BCE, or the Seleucids who ruled the land of Israel 201–167 BCE. If these books had been written during these years of Hellenistic rule, we would have expected to find some linguistic or historical evidence in the texts.

While I cannot provide a precise year for the composition of Ezra/Nehemiah, I can place it in a narrow window in the years after the completion of Nehemiah's career, 400 BCE, and before the arrival of the armies of Alexander the Great, in 332 BCE.

LANGUAGES

Chapter 6

The Shift to Writing Hebrew in Aramaic Letters

As a child I received a serious Hebrew education at the Minneapolis Talmud Torah. We learned modern spoken Hebrew. We also studied the Torah in Hebrew, and we learned all about the prayer book, prayer by prayer. When we got to the Kaddish, the teacher explained that the Kaddish was in Aramaic but we would have no trouble reading it because Aramaic is written in Hebrew letters. Our teachers repeated this explanation when we read the Aramaic sections of the Passover Haggadah, Halachma Anya and Chad Gadya. We were told these are Aramaic texts but we can read them because Aramaic is written in Hebrew letters. Countless young Hebrew school students and adult Hebrew learners have heard this same explanation from their well-meaning teachers.

I am sure that my Hebrew teachers believed fully and without reflection in the message they conveyed. There is only one problem; it is completely wrong. The real truth is that what we call Hebrew letters are actually Aramaic letters. Genuine Hebrew letters are quite different. Scholars refer to these original Hebrew letters as Paleo-Hebrew. Inscriptions carved in the land of Israel during the First Temple period are all in Paleo-Hebrew. The most widely known example is the Siloam inscription from the water tunnels constructed at the time of King Hezekiah. This inscription can be seen at the Israel Museum in Jerusalem. Other examples include the Gezer calendar, the Tel Dan inscriptions, and the seal of Baruch bullae.

Aramaic was the language of the Babylonian and Persian Empires. As the Babylonian and then the Persian Empires pushed west, the Aramaic language became the "lingua franca" of that part of the world in those days. By the first century of the Common Era, Aramaic had become the everyday language of the Jews living in the land of Israel. This is why some of our prayers were written in Aramaic.

Our people first encountered Aramaic six hundred years earlier during the Babylonian exile. Over those years that our people spent in exile they switched from writing Hebrew in the old Hebrew alphabet and began writing Hebrew words in the Aramaic script.

Physical evidence from the Second Temple period demonstrates the wide acceptance of the Aramaic letters. Inscriptions from the Second Temple period are in the Aramaic letters with which we are familiar. The Dead Sea scrolls are written in the square Aramaic letters.

While the acceptance of the new way of writing Hebrew was widely accepted, there did remain, at least in some quarters, a realization that it was not actual, authentic Hebrew.

Some of the Dead Sea scrolls use the Paleo-Hebrew script for the four-letter name of God. Those scribes understood that the square Aramaic letters were not the authentic Hebrew letters. To render the actual name of God accurately one needed to record it in the genuine original letters, Paleo-Hebrew.

Coins struck during the Bar Kokhba rebellion in the second century CE feature Paleo-Hebrew. Using the original form of the letters expressed the rebels' yearning for the independence of the Jewish people.

Chapter 4 of the book of Ezra contains a letter written by some residents of Judea to the Persian king. The text explicitly says that the text of the letter was "in the Aramaic script and in the Aramaic language" (Ezra 4:7). Why was it necessary for the author to say it was in the "Aramaic script and in the Aramaic language"? Would it not have been sufficient to say that it was written in Aramaic? If I say that I have written a document in Russian I clearly mean that it contains Russian words written in the Russian, Cyrillic, alphabet. The Ezra text says "Aramaic script and in the Aramaic language" because the document could have been written in Aramaic script but in the Hebrew language.

In the time of Ezra, Hebrew was being written in the square Aramaic letters that today we identify as Hebrew letters. We can be confident that the Torah from which Ezra read to people in Jerusalem was written in the square Aramaic letters.

This shift from Paleo-Hebrew to the Aramaic letters took place at the same time as the technological shift from writing with a stick in clay to using a pen/quill to write on papyrus and parchment. If you look at the two alphabets set side by side, you will notice that straight lines dominate the Paleo-Hebrew letters, which could easily be written with a stick on clay. The Aramaic letters feature far more subtle curves, which one could form with pen/quill.

We see the letters of a Torah scroll as sacred, but Moses would not have recognized what we call Hebrew letters. Some midrashim and later mystical teachings assume that our Hebrew letters are the original Hebrew letters. In Menachot 29b we can read the famous midrash of Moses standing at the back of Rabbi Akiva's academy. The story begins with Moses asking God why some of the letters of the Torah include decorative "crowns." God tells Moses that in the future Akiva ben Yosef will explained the meaning of these "crowns." This midrash rests on the assumption that Moses and Akiva read the same Hebrew letters. We know that this was not the case. Writing sacred Hebrew texts the way we write them today began during the Babylonian exile.

The shift in alphabet troubled some of the ancient sages. If the Torah that they had in front of them was not written in the same letters that Moses read, how can they affirm that it is still the same Torah that Moses received from God at Mount Sinai? In order to maintain their confidence in the divine origins of their Torah text they needed to see God's hand involved in the creation of Ezra's Torah text.

The Talmud includes a description of the shift of letters in the time of Ezra:

> Mar Zutra says, but other sources suggest it was Mar Ukava who says, God gave the Torah to the Israelites in the holy language of [Paleo] Hebrew. It was again given to them in the days of Ezra in Aramaic letters and the Aramaic language. The people of Israel chose to use the Aramaic letters and the holy language of Hebrew to write a Torah scroll. (BT Sanhedrin 21b)

This talmudic passage explains how we come to have the Torah written in Hebrew words using Aramaic letters. With the passages of centuries, the Aramaic origin of the Hebrew letters has been largely forgotten. My Hebrew teachers at the Minneapolis Talmud Torah did not intentionally deceive me. The shift to the Aramaic letters took place so long ago that contemporary Hebrew teachers should feel no obligation to refer to Hebrew letters as “new” Hebrew letters.

Chapter 8 of the book of Nehemiah describes Ezra reading from a Torah scroll in public. We can be confident that the Hebrew letters of that Torah scroll were the square Aramaic letters that we read today. I imagine, but I cannot prove, that this reading by Ezra was the first public reading from Torah scroll. It certainly is the first public reading of a Torah scroll that we know about.

Those of us who read from the Torah today could have read from that Torah scroll. It could have been the first such Torah scroll. Our Torah-centered Judaism began that day when Ezra read from that scroll.

Chapter 7

Aramaic, Hebrew, and Judeo-American

Groucho Marx is certainly best known for the madcap movies he made with his brothers in the 1930s and 1940s. In the 1950s he hosted a TV quiz show called *You Bet Your Life*. While Groucho did conduct a quiz game, he mostly kidded around with his guests. Groucho enjoyed asking the contestants on the show trick questions. One of his favorites was, "Who is buried in Grant's tomb?" This appears to be an easy question with an obvious answer: Grant! But in truth the remains of Ulysses and Julia Grant were placed in aboveground tombs. So, who is *buried* in Grant's tomb? No one! Groucho never seemed to tire of asking this trick question. He returned to it again and again.

I have my own trick question: In what language is the Hebrew Bible written? The obvious and incorrect answer would be, "The Hebrew Bible is written in Hebrew." To bring us to a more accurate answer, I will clarify the question: What two languages appear in the Hebrew Bible? The answer is Hebrew and Aramaic. The book of Daniel contains a large section in Aramaic from 2:4 through 7:28. The book of Ezra contains two Aramaic sections, 4:8—6:18 and 7:12–26. An investigation of the Aramaic sections of Daniel are beyond the scope of this book. I will leave them to another time or to another author. Let us turn to the Aramaic sections of Ezra.

The first of these Aramaic sections of Ezra features a letter written to the Persian authorities. The original letter certainly would have been written in the court language of the Persian Empire, Imperial Aramaic.

Including the letter here in Imperial Aramaic strengthens the narrative. It helps the readers believe that this is the actual document.

The second Aramaic section, 7:12–26, contains the letter from the Persian King Artaxerxes granting authority to Ezra. This letter appears in Imperial Aramaic for similar reasons as the first letter; it is in Imperial Aramaic to present the biblical text as the actual original of the letter that Ezra carried with him as he arrived in Jerusalem. In both cases the text switches to Aramaic without introduction or explanation. The author assumes that the reader will recognize the Aramaic and understand it.

While we encountered Aramaic earlier, our people became fully immersed in Aramaic during the exile in Babylonia. Aramaic was the language of the Babylonian Empire. When the Persian Empire conquered the Babylonian Empire it maintained the Aramaic language.

The conquest of the Middle East in 330 BCE by the army of Alexander the Great introduced Greek to the language mix. While Greek became an important language in the land of Israel, Aramaic continued to be spoken every day by regular people. And the people did not forget Hebrew; it remained a language for prayer and study.

Aramaic made its way into the prayer life of the people. The very well-known Kaddish prayer was composed in Aramaic. The traditional Hebrew prayer book contains additional Aramaic sections, such as Bei Ana Racheitz during the Torah service. The Passover Haggadah includes Aramaic sections: Chad Gadya and Halachma Anya.

In the rabbinic period many members of the congregation could not understand the Hebrew Torah text. So, a meturgeman, an official translator, would stand next to the Torah reader during services and translate the text from Hebrew into Aramaic. A written Targum of the Torah, called Targum Onkelos, can be found in a *Mikraot Gedolot*, a "rabbinic Bible," next to the Hebrew text. Scholars differ on exactly where and when it was written. Opinions range from the first to the fifth century CE.

The Babylonian Talmud and the Jerusalem Talmud, written 400 to 600 CE, move back and forth between Hebrew and Aramaic sections without a clear pattern. The editors of both versions of the Talmud assume that the readers would understand Aramaic.

As Late antiquity faded Aramaic became less widely used. In the fourth century, as the Eastern Roman Empire became the Byzantine Empire, Greek became more prominent. With the rise and spread of Islam in the seventh century, Arabic replaced Aramaic as the "lingua franca" in the Middle East and North Africa. Living in twelfth-century Egypt,

Maimonides wrote his great philosophic work, *Guide for the Perplexed*, in Arabic, not in Hebrew and not in Aramaic.

As Jews moved into Europe, they did not maintain Aramaic as a spoken language. In his commentary to these Aramaic sections in Ezra, Rashi translated them into Hebrew. He assumed that the Jews of his time could not comprehend the Aramaic text. At times in his Bible commentaries, Rashi translated a difficult-to-understand Hebrew word into the vernacular of his time and his community, Old French.

In the rabbinic period, the Hebrew text was translated into Aramaic so that people could understand it. But many Jews of the Middle Ages did not understand Aramaic! The languages of our people are constantly in flux. Jews of Eastern Europe spoke Yiddish as their everyday language. No one invented Yiddish. It developed through a folk process over time.

Jews came to communities in the Rhine valley, Mainz, Worms, and Speyer, in the tenth century. The Yiddish that developed drew on the German of that time, Hebrew, and words from other languages. This original Yiddish is often called Western Yiddish. As Jews moved east over the centuries to what is now Lithuania, Poland, Belarus, Russia, and Ukraine, Eastern Yiddish developed. It drew on the existing Western Yiddish and added words from the local languages. Yiddish experts can easily distinguish between the various versions of Yiddish.

Sephardic communities, established by the Jews expelled from Spain, carried with them Ladino, also known as Judeo-Spanish. Various versions evolved in each of the new Sephardic communities, incorporating words from the host cultures.

In the Ashkenazic and Sephardic communities of the "old world," Jews mostly lived in defined enclaves, geographically and culturally. In the United States, today Jews are much fuller participants in the communal and cultural life of the host society. Acceptance is so full that many people would be surprised to find me using the phrase "host society" to describe American life. They would say America is not our "host"; it is our home!

Yiddish and Hebrew words have become part of accepted American spoken vocabulary, including *chutzpah*, *tush*, *schlepping*, *schmaltzy*, and *maven*. Sometimes American society uses Hebrew/Yiddish words in new ways. In English, "You are my rabbi" does not have to include any religious meaning. It is used more broadly to refer to a mentor. We often hear it in movies and television programs set in police departments. The young officer works with a more senior officer who he or she describes as "my rabbi."

Similarly in English the word *kosher* can be used to describe anything that is proper. In English the word *kosher* is also used to convey that something is Jewish. I recall a restaurant in Cincinnati promoting its "Kosher Reuben Sandwich," which featured Swiss cheese on top of nonkosher meat. It was not at all kosher by Jewish religious standards.

Some Yiddish words have become so much a part of English that their Yiddish origin has been forgotten by some people who use them. My congregant Gerry worked at the Spiegel Catalogue company in what was formally called the Tchotchke Department. A gentile coworker once asked him, "Is there a Jewish word for tchotchke?" My wife, Tammie, taught English as a Second Language (ESL) at our local community college. Once on the first day of class a Vietnamese student introduced herself by saying, "My American name is Yentl." In recent years professional football teams have in short-yardage situations been using a play called the "Tush Push."

Contemporary spoken Hebrew includes many words borrowed from English: *radio*, *televisia*, *jeep*. Hebrew applies Hebrew grammar to these borrowed words. So the plural of *jeep* becomes *jeepim*.

I also see the creation of a new language that I call Judeo-American. As words move from Hebrew to Judeo-American the accent shifts forward from the end of the word. In Hebrew we say "ketu*bah*." In Judeo-American we say "*ket*ubah." The Hebrew word "mitz*vah*" becomes the Judeo-American word "*mitz*vah." The phrase Hebrew "ma*zal* tov" becomes the Judeo-American "*ma*zel tov"! The Hebrew "chutz*pah*" becomes "*chutz*pah" in Judeo-American.

The meaning of words may shift as they move from Hebrew into Judeo-American. The Hebrew word *shiva* describes the seven-day mourning period following burial. It grows out of the Hebrew word for seven, *sheva*. So if a person says, "I am sitting shiva," we understand that they are in this seven-day period of mourning. Today, in America, less traditional Jews can be heard to say, "I am sitting shiva for three days." They are not using the Hebrew word *shiva* referring to the initial seven-day period of mourning but rather the Judeo-American word, which refers to the initial period of mourning no matter what its length. The Hebrew word "mitz*vah*" means commandment, while the Judeo-American word "*mitz*vah" means good deed.

In Hebrew *tikun olam* (mending of the world) has been a term in mysticism describing the repair of the vessels which held divine light at the moment of creation of the world. In contemporary Judeo-American, the term describes social action projects to repair the real world in which we live. In 1982 Emil Fackenheim published a book titled *To Mend the World*. He may have been the first to apply this mystical term to real-world projects.

When words move from Hebrew into Judeo-American, English grammar rules are followed. So the plural of the Judeo-American word *mitzvah* becomes *mitzvahs*. Judeo-American breaks apart two-word Hebrew expressions in the construct form to use one word on its own. So the Hebrew *Birkat Hamazon* becomes the Judeo-American *Birkat*. And the Hebrew *Oneg Shabbat* becomes Judeo-American *Oneg*. And the plural form becomes "Oneg*s*," as in "Who will host the Oneg*s* in July?" The Hebrew/Aramaic noun *Bar Mitzvah* becomes a Judeo-American past tense verb: "I was Bar Mitzvah*ed* in Chicago."

The languages of the Jewish people are constantly evolving. We do not find Aramaic in the earlier biblical books. In the Babylonian and Persian periods Jews knew Hebrew and Aramaic. As we will see in the next chapter, the Hebrew of the Second Temple period also incorporated Persian words that earlier generations of Jews would not have understood.

Chapter 8

Persian Loan Words

YEARS AGO, I AGREED to attend an opera to be a good husband. Much to my surprise, I enjoyed it a great deal. We quickly became subscribers to Chicago's Lyric Opera. I am no expert, but I look forward to the opera performances. One evening during an intermission, we ran into my friend Jan, a professional tenor, who sang at our synagogue. Jan asked me what I thought of that evening's presentation. I told Jan that I was enjoying the opera. I spoke of the costumes and the sets. I asked Jan what he thought. He scowled and told me that the tenor had missed many key notes during the first act. Jan, the professional tenor, clearly heard details that my untrained ears had not noticed.

Many people who read the Bible miss details because their untrained eyes do not notice them. People who read the Bible in English cannot see details contained in the original Hebrew but obscured by the translator's desire to produce a smooth text. I comfortably read the text in the original Hebrew. As I spend more and more time focusing in on a specific text, I keep noticing subtleties that eluded me on previous readings. An analogy from computer maps will help us understand this process.

On computer maps we can zoom in to see the details or quickly zoom out to see more area. People who zoom out and read the Bible in an English translation will cover more text, but they will miss details that those who zoom in and read the text in the original Hebrew will be able to see. Zooming in more tightly, through repeated readings, I notice details that earlier escaped my eye.

This approach led me to a greater appreciation of a word in the book of Ezra's description of the presentation of the Temple vessels to the Israelites who were about to return to Jerusalem:

> King Cyrus also brought out the articles belonging to the House of the ETERNAL that Nebuchadnezzar had carried away from Jerusalem and placed in the temple of his gods. Cyrus king of Persia had brought them out of the hand of Mithredat, the treasurer [hagizbar], who counted them out to Sheshbazzar, the prince of Judah. (Ezra 1:7–8)

The text describes Mithredat as "the treasurer." The original Hebrew word is *hagizbar*. Because I know this word *gizbar* from Modern Hebrew, I had casually read it as a Hebrew word. I learned this word before I really knew Hebrew. In Habonim Labor Zionist Youth the gizbar took care of the money. My brother, Ken, served as gizbar, the treasurer, of Kibbutz Gezer.

Upon further review, I have learned much more about the word *gizbar*. It is not found in the pre-return books of the Hebrew Bible. *Gizbar* appears in the Hebrew Bible only once, here in Ezra 1:8. Scholars use the Greek term *hapax legomenon* to describe these words that are used only once in the biblical text.

We can see two sources of evidence that *gizbar* is not a Hebrew word. First, the vast majority of Hebrew words have a three-letter root. *Gizbar* has a four-letter root. Secondly, *gizbar* does not fit the patterns of Hebrew profession terms. For example, Deut 29:11 use *chotaiv* to describe the "hewer of wood" and *sho'aiv* to describe the "drawer of water." Following this vowel pattern, we would expect the Hebrew word used to describe the person who oversees the money to be *kosaif* from the three-letter root, K-S-F, for the word for money, *kesef*.

The other common vowel pattern for profession words in the Hebrew Bible uses an "ah"/"ah" vowel pattern, like *dayag* for a fisherman or *tzayad* for hunter (Jer 16:16). *Gizbar* does not follow this vowel pattern.

Twenty-five hundred years ago, *gizbar* was a new Hebrew word borrowed from existing Persian words. It comes from two Persian words: *ganaz*, "treasury," and *bara*, "have responsibility for." *Ganzabara* can be found in Persian texts and in archeological inscriptions at Persepolis, the ancient Persian capital.

Another example of a new Second Temple era word is *dat*. It occurs only twelve times in the Hebrew Bible, appearing just in Ezra and Daniel. All five of the Ezra occurrences are in chapter 7 in verses 12, 14, 21, 25, and 26. Generally it is translated as "law." In modern Hebrew the word means "religion." A religious Jew is described as *dati*. Lisbeth Fried explains that the word *dat* comes from the Persian word *data*, which "typically was used to refer to the word of the Achaemenid kings or their god Ahuramazda."[1]

A final example of a new Second Temple era word is *igeret*. It only appears in the books of the Bible from after the return from the exile. It occurs in the Hebrew Bible a total of only ten times: six in Nehemiah, twice in Esther, and twice in 2 Chronicles. An Aramaic equivalent also occurs in Ezra.

The 1882 English edition of William Gesenius's dictionary of Biblical Hebrew and Aramaic defines *igeret* as,

> Most probably the word comes from an obsolete form of אגר, Agar one hired, specifically a letter carrier or courier. It may derive from a Persian word *engariden* denoting "to paint" or "to write" hence *engareh* any writing.[2]

Igeret remains a part of modern spoken Hebrew, but it is not used for a letter. Modern Hebrew uses the word *michtav* to refer to a letter. It comes directly from the root word for "write," *kotaiv*. *Igeret* emerged in modern Hebrew to refer to an aerogram. In the pre-email era, ultralight aerograms were used for international airmail letters. In those days people had a choice to send a letter "surface" or "airmail." When writing from Israel to one's parents in the States, "surface" meant by ship—a slow, lengthy trip from one country to another.

The Minnesota election official sent me my absentee ballot for the November 1972 election by "surface" mail. I received it in Jerusalem in January of 1973. Airmail rates were calculated by the half ounce. So, limiting the weight of an international letter was quite desirable. This led to the creation of the aerogram. An aerogram was a flat, thin piece of paper that you wrote on and then folded into the shape of an envelope. In Hebrew, speakers called the aerogram an *igeret*. Today in Modern Hebrew, Israelis use the term *igeret* to refer to a newsletter or a bulletin.

The rise of Modern Hebrew beginning with the efforts of Eliezer Ben Yehuda (1858–1922) involved creating many new terms to meet the needs of an ever-changing society. Gideon Remez provides one example:

1. Fried, *Ezra*, 309.
2. Gesenius, *Hebrew and English Lexicon*, s.v. "אִגֶּרֶת."

> David Remez, as minister of communications in the first Israeli cabinet, devised dozens of Hebrew terms that the revived language still lacked for 20th century items in his purview. . . . Many of his neologisms were accepted so fast and widely that not many realize today what inspired innovations they were at the time.
>
> He may have indulged in a bit of vanity by incorporating our surname in one such invention: "traffic light" is for any Hebrew speaker "ramzor"—a portmanteau, as Alice's Humpty Dumpty would call it, of "remez" (signal) and "or" (light).[3]

Some people incorrectly imagine that Hebrew existed in two stages: a monolithic Biblical Hebrew, and then after twenty centuries of being a static worship language it emerged in the twentieth century as Modern Hebrew. In truth, Hebrew has been an ever-changing language.

In this study we can see the shift from early Biblical Hebrew to late Biblical Hebrew. People speak of rabbinic Hebrew, but if we look more closely, we can also see a shift from early to late rabbinic Hebrew. In the Middle Ages, Hebrew continued to change as new situations created the need for new words. For example, Samuel Ibn Tibon created new Hebrew philosophic terms to translate Moses Maimonides's *Guide for the Perplexed* from its original Arabic into Hebrew.

Many speakers of Modern Hebrew cannot easily sort Hebrew words into categories of early Bible, late Bible, rabbinic, and modern. When we read the Hebrew Bible slowly and carefully, we will notice details that most people miss.

Ezra and Nehemiah contain other Persian loan words, including *hattirsata*, "the governor" (Ezra 2:63, Neh 7:65), and *pitgama*, "answer" (Ezra 4:17, 5:7, 5:11). How did Persian words enter Hebrew during the Babylonian exile? I can offer two explanations. First, all the Jews in exile did not return to Jerusalem in response to the decree of Cyrus. Cyrus issued his decree of return in the first year after the Persians conquered the Babylonians. As we will see in future chapters, Ezra and Nehemiah tell of waves of return taking place over many years. Participants in the later wave of returnees lived for years in the Persian-controlled Tigris/Euphrates valley. Secondly, the reestablished Judea did not become an independent Jewish state. It remained a province of the Persian Empire until the armies of Alexander the Great arrived in the Middle East in 332 BCE. So Persian words could have become part of everyday Hebrew

3. Remez, "Alas, Poor El Al."

vocabulary among the Jews who came to Jerusalem in later waves, or they could have been adopted by the Jews in Jerusalem as a result of conversations with Persian officials.

In a similar ways English words entered Modern Hebrew during the years of the British Mandate, 1918–1948. The Hebrew word *patent*, with the accent on the second syllable, means "a plan." It clearly was borrowed from the similar English word pronounced with the accent on the first syllable, which has a related but slightly different meaning.

Reading the Bible slowly and carefully in its original language allows us to captures its subtleties and nuances. The origins of the words in the Hebrew Bible can help us understand when and where the specific books were written.

Chapter 9

How Do You Spell King David's Name?

When I ask students, "Who is the central human figure in the Hebrew Bible?" Jews tend to respond, "Moses." That would be the correct response if I had asked about the five books of the Torah. But if we consider the entire Hebrew Bible, the correct response would be David. The Hebrew Bible mentions David more often than any other person, in a total of 1,023 verses. Moses appears in only 770 verses. In the preexilic books that tell the David story or that refer to his descendants, 1 and 2 Samuel and 1 and 2 Kings, his name is spelled *dalet-vav-dalet*. The major prophetic books of the preexilic era, Isaiah and Jeremiah, maintain this spelling. The three-letter spelling also occurs in Psalms, Proverbs, Ruth, and Ecclesiastes.

But Ezra, Nehemiah, and other postexilic books add a *yod*. The three-letter *dalet-vav-dalet* becomes the four-letter *dalet-vav-yod-dalet*. This four-letter version of the name appears eight times in Ezra/Nehemiah: Ezra 3:10; 8:2, 20; Neh 3:16; 12:24, 36, 45, and 46. And in 1 and 2 Chronicles, which retell the history of David and the Davidic line, we find his name with the four-letter spelling almost a hundred times.

We do not know for certain what caused this change. We see a similar change in other Hebrew names in the Second Temple period where a *yod* or a *vav* is added to help express the sound of a vowel. For example, Jacob is written *yod-ayin-qoph-vet* in preexilic texts.[1] But in Second Temple texts a *vav* is added between the *qoph* and the *vet* to clarify the last vowel sound. We might consider the possibility that it was the result

1. With *vet* being a variation of *bet*.

of an exposure to the languages our people encountered during the exile: Persian and Imperial Aramaic. The reason for the change may be lost to us. Often the original reason behind a change becomes obscure.

To help us unravel this mystery of the added *yod*, we can turn to other examples of complicated origin stories. During World War I, many German supply trucks featured paintings of Wagnerian war maidens, known as Valkyrie. In response, the French cartoonist Benjamin Rabier painted a picture of a laughing cow on the trucks in which he brought food to French soldiers at the front. In the bilingual wordplay, Rabier took the German *Valkyrie* and transformed it into the French *vache qui rit*, or "laughing cow," to express a disdain for the Germans.

After the war, Rabier's friend Léon Bel used that image of the laughing cow on the packaging for his new cheese company. The first generation of customers may have connected the cheese products to the food trucks of World War I. Over the decades as time passed and the Bel company expanded, they maintained the logo of the laughing cow. But the origins of that laughing cow have been largely forgotten. Today's purchasers of Bel products have no understanding of why a laughing cow adorns the package.[2]

A similar dynamic can be seen in the name of a London neighborhood called the Elephant and Castle, which includes a well-known pub of the same name. The name has been connected to this area south of the Thames for centuries. Shakespeare mentioned an inn called the Elephant in his play *Twelfth Night*. Some people believe that the name Elephant and Castle is a corruption of the Spanish phrase *La Infanta de Castille*, describing Catherine of Aragon before her marriage to Henry VIII, or Eleanor of Castile before her marriage to Edward I.

The New York City restaurant named The Elephant and Castle suggests a different Spanish princess:

> Two years before acceding to the throne of Great Britain and Ireland in 1625, Charles I made an incognito visit to Spain in an attempt to conclude a marriage treaty with a young languorous Spanish princess, the Enfanta de Castile. The mission failed because Charles refused conversion to Roman Catholicism, a condition imposed by the Spanish government. This romantic setback so angered the young prince that it helped to trigger war against Spain a few months later.

2. Wikipedia, "Laughing Cow."

> In London, however, the journey was marked by the opening of a publick house (pub) appropriately named Enfanta de Castile.[3]

Albert Jack, in his *The Old Dog and Duck: The Secret Meanings of Pub Names*, provides a different approach. He explains that the corner at the center of the Elephant and Castle was once the location of a cutlery center. The symbol of the guild of cutlers was an elephant with a howdah, a carriage for passengers, on its back. The cutlers used the symbol of an elephant because they made knife handles from ivory. One could imagine the howdah being described as a castle, which could lead to the name Elephant and Castle.[4]

We cannot know which of these narratives contains the genuine origin of the name of this neighborhood south of the Thames. Similarly, while we have not established why postexilic biblical texts spell *David* with a *yod*, we do know that the extra *yod* in *David* marks a text as being composed during the postexilic age.

The four-letter spelling of *David* can be seen in some prophetic books. It is not a surprise to find it in Zechariah, where it occurs three times: 12:7, 12:8, and 13:1. Many scholars see the book of Zechariah as the work of two authors, referred to as First Zechariah (chs. 1–6) and Second Zechariah (chs. 7–14). All scholars agree that all of the book of Zechariah was written in Judah during the postexilic period. I will delve more deeply into the book of Zechariah in chapter 42.

It is more curious to find the "long" spelling of David in Amos and Hosea, two of the Twelve "Minor" Prophets. Both Amos and Hosea lived during the preexilic period. They both preached in the Northern Kingdom of Israel in the eighth century BCE. So, one would expect that both books would spell *David* with only three letters. But it appears with four letters in Amos 6:5 and 9:11 and in Hos 3:5 and 6:5.

Noted scholar Professor David Noel Friedman explains, "The examples of the longer spelling in Amos and Hosea, while technically anachronistic nevertheless reflect the date of publication of the composite work (the twelve minor prophets.)"[5] We know that several of the Twelve Minor Prophets—Zechariah, Haggai, Malachi, Joel—lived during the postexilic period. The "Book of the Twelve Minor Prophets" could

3. Elephant and Castle, "Story."
4. Jack, *Old Dog and Duck*, 80–82.
5. Friedman, "Spelling of the Name David," 100.

not have reached its final form until after the death of the last of these prophets—Malachi—in the fifth century BCE, approximately 430 BCE.

While the Hebrew Bible and the Protestant Old Testament contain the same texts, the two communities organize them differently. The Hebrew Bible considers the Twelve Minor Prophets to be one book. Christians view them as twelve separate books. The Jewish view of the twelve as one book is assumed in Professor Friedman's analysis.

I can offer a possible explanation for the added *yod* in David's name in postexilic texts. Rather than looking for outside cultural sources for the shift in spelling, we can see it as tool to help the people of the postexilic period with proper Hebrew pronunciation.

The vowel marks which are so familiar to us did not yet exist at that time. They would be created by the Masoretes around 1000 CE, fifteen hundred years after the days of Ezra/Nehemiah. Before the Masoretes, pronouncing Hebrew words correctly grew out of the community's mastery of vowel patterns and knowledge of specific words and names.

In this case, without the *yod* one could apply standard Hebrew vowel patterns to the letters *dalet-vav-dalet* and pronounce the name Davad or Deved. The extra *yod* is a device that clearly signals that the vowel sound connected to the *vav* is an "ee" sound, not an "ah" or an "eh." I think that someone added the *yod* to help the postexilic readers properly pronounce the word.

This dynamic is similar to providing a pronunciation guide to Americans for a non-English name. American leaders and diplomats receive coaching on correct pronunciation of foreign leaders' names.

The Los Angeles Times explained,

> And despite being U.N. secretary-general for well over a year now, Ban Ki-moon still gets addressed as Mr. Ki-moon or Mr. Moon, prompting his chief of staff to send out an e-mail in March on the correct way to refer to the South Korean diplomat. As in many East Asian languages, the U.N. chief's first name is his surname. Thus, his correct title is Secretary-General Ban, and it "is pronounced Baahn, as in 'Autobahn.'"[6]

The extra *yod* in David's name in postexilic texts is twenty-five-hundred-year-old pronunciation guide. The authors and editors of postexilic texts did not trust the people of their era to know enough to correctly pronounce King David's name. They believed that the people of their era

6. Beehner, "Pronunciation Protocol."

did not know as much as the people of the previous era. While the need for the extra *yod* has disappeared, the dynamic of seeing one's own generation as less knowledgeable than previous generations abides. Today's traditional Torah sages view the Torah sages of one hundred years go as more authoritative than the rabbis of today. Some operagoers prefer the nineteenth-century operas to those of the twenty-first century. While we do embrace modern medicine and communications and computers, some of us may feel that the rabbis, composers, writers, artists, or musicians of an earlier era were superior to our own.

HISTORY

Chapter 10

Our Story in the Much Larger World

Ezra/Nehemiah and the rest of the Hebrew Bible tell the story of the ancient past with Israel at the center of the narrative. "Our" story is presented as "the" story. A broader view of the history of the world would present the events in Israel and Jerusalem as being at the fringes of other major events. The Hebrew Bible is not interested in this broader view of history. The Hebrew Bible establishes the land of Israel and the city of Jerusalem as the central locations in "the" story. We have seen maps and works of art that place various cities as the focus of all that exists.

Orbis Habitabilis, drawn by Pomponius Mela in 43 BCE, depicts Rome as the center of the world. The March 29, 1976, cover of *The New Yorker* features a drawing by Saul Steinberg called *A View of the World from Ninth Avenue*. Steinberg depicts this street in Manhattan in detail and the rest of America as insignificant. In a similar way, the Bible tells its story with the Israelites as the star, with the Egyptians, Assyrians, Babylonians, and Persians playing supporting roles.

How were the Israelites able to move into the spotlight? The key events in "our" story, the exodus from Egypt, the revelation at Sinai, the establishment of the Davidic kingdom, and the construction of the Temple in Jerusalem, took place during what ancient Near East historians call a "Dark Age."

Historian Eric Cline explains,

> As I see it, all of these groups were able to really "set up shop," as it were, in the regions of Canaan from which the Egyptians

> and Hittites had both just withdrawn—especially in what is now modern Israel, Lebanon, and Syria. To put it in modern terms, I think that the Israelites, Phoenicians, Aramaeans, and Philistines benefited from the "power vacuum" that was created in this area when the Great Powers were laid low. There was no way that any of them could have established a foothold in this area if the Egyptians, Hittites, and Canaanites had still been as powerful as they were even in the 13th century BC. The calamitous events at the beginning of the 12th century BC made all the difference.[1]

While I cannot take time to explore the decline of all these major powers, I will briefly examine highlights of Egyptian history as an example of this decline. The rulers of the Old Kingdom, who built the large pyramids of Giza and the Great Sphinx, reigned over Egypt at the dawn of recorded history, 2750–2150 BCE.

The New Kingdom, 1570–1069 BCE, included the most well-known rulers of Egypt: Pharaoh Ramesses II, Queen Nefertiti, and Pharaoh Tutankhamen, a.k.a. King Tut. During the height of the New Kingdom, the Egyptian empire included modern Sudan, Israel, Lebanon, and the coastal portions of Syria. These pharaohs controlled the copper mines at Timna in Canaan just north of modern Eilat. The biblical stories of slavery and the exodus are set during this period. But by the conclusion of the New Kingdom era, the Egyptian empire had collapsed in on itself, to the point that it included only the Nile Delta and the Nile valley within the borders of modern Egypt.

King David came to the throne of Israel and Judah around 1000 BCE, after the decline of Egypt and the other empires. The united monarchy was able to establish itself because of the vacuum created by the collapse of the large empires of the previous age.

At an opera house, as the time for the opera approaches, sometimes a member of the staff emerges from behind the curtain. The audience sighs in response to seeing her. We know that she has come forward to announce that a member of the cast is sick and that their place will be taken by an understudy. We will see and hear a young up-and-coming opera performer rather than the established star we had expected. Very often at the conclusion of the opera the understudy will receive the loudest applause. The last-minute opportunity to sing on the big stage has launched the careers of a number of opera stars.

1. Cline, *1177 BC*, 145.

In the history of the Middle East, the Israelites can be seen as the "understudies" who make their way on stage only when the Egyptian, Assyrian, and Babylonian "stars" have taken ill, all at the same time.

The Bible explains the downfall of the Northern Kingdom of Israel and later the Southern Kingdom of Judah as being God's punishment for a multitude of sins. Secular historians would point to the return to power of the Assyrian and then the Babylonian Empires. We tend to speak of the empire that destroyed the Northern Kingdom of Israel as the Assyrian Empire. Historians call it the Neo-Assyrian Empire. Likewise, we speak of the Babylonian Empire conquering Jerusalem and destroying the Temple; historians refer to it as the Neo-Babylonian Empire. Historians see these two empires as revived versions of old empires that held sway in a previous age before the establishment of the Davidic monarchy. Both of these revived empires come into contact with the people of Israel because the land of Israel forms the land bridge between Asia and Africa. For the Assyrians, the broad flat Valley of Jezreel provided a path to the coastal road on their way to attack Egypt.

Later, the Southern Kingdom of Judah gets caught up in the much larger struggle between Egypt and the Babylonians. The last kings of Judah allied themselves with Egypt. As part of their reconquest of Egypt, the Babylonians took full control of Judah. The Babylonians under the leadership of Nebuchadnezzar destroyed the Temple and led the leadership of the people of Judah into exile in 586 BCE.

Tom Stoppard reimagined the Hamlet story by taking two minor characters and placing them at the center of the action in his play *Rosencrantz and Guildenstern Are Dead*. In more recent decades many other writers have followed Stoppard's model. Professor Jeremy Rosen has reflected on this genre of literature in his recent book *Minor Characters Have Their Day*. The Bible reimagines the history of the Middle East by taking minor characters, the Israelites, and placing them at the center of the story.

This dynamic continues in Ezra/Nehemiah, which begins with a mention of King Cyrus of Persia. For the Bible, Cyrus was the Persian king who allowed the people of Judah to return to Jerusalem. For historians, this King Cyrus is Cyrus the Great who created the Persian Empire. In chapter 6 of Ezra, we read of the steps King Darius took which led to the resumption of the rebuilding of the Temple. Enemies of the Jews had caused the rebuilding of the Temple to be halted by allegations that Cyrus had not issued a decree:

> Thereupon, at the order of King Darius, they searched the archives where the treasures were stored in Babylon. But it was in the citadel of Ecbatana, in the province of Media, that a scroll was found in which the following was written; Memorandum: In the first year of King Cyrus . . . (Ezra 6:1–3)

After the discovery of the original decree of Cyrus, Darius issued his own decree for the rebuilding of the Temple to resume and to continue uninterrupted:

> Allow the work of the Jews and the elders of the Jews to rebuild this House of God on its site. . . . May the God who established His name there cause the downfall of any king or nation that undertakes to alter or damage that House of God in Jerusalem. I, Darius have issued the decree; let it be carried out with dispatch. (Ezra 6:7, 12)

Students of history know Darius as Darius the Great, who led the Persian Empire to a growth of its power and size. He extended the reach of the empire in Europe and in Africa. He built the Nile River / Lake Suez Canal, which connected the Mediterranean Sea with the Red Sea. He led the Persian forces at the Battle of Marathon in Greece. The Bible does not mention any of these major events in human history because they do not directly impact the stars of the Bible's narrative, the Jews.

I admit that I see myself as the "star" of the story of my life. I am not the only player in my story. I know that the story of my life intersects with the stories of many other people's lives. In some of those stories I am an important supporting character: grandpa, friend. In other stories I might be a secondary character: rabbi, teacher. And in still other stories I am just an extra: the old man with a big white dog.

I tend to see the events of the contemporary world through Jewish eyes, but I also realize that Jews are not at the center of everybody's world. I have met some members of the Jewish community who seem to take the biblical approach, imagining Jews standing at the center of all that exists. They speak of the population of America consisting only of Jews and non-Jews. I know that regular Americans do not think of themselves as non-Jews. "How does it affect the Jews?" is not the only question to ask about current events. We should be concerned about the well-being of our people. We should try to recruit others to be concerned about the well-being of the Jewish people, but we should not expect that everybody will see the world through Jewish eyes.

Chapter 11

Placing Ezra and Nehemiah in Their Historic Context

A FEW YEARS AGO, I attended my fiftieth year high school reunion. I grew up in Minnesota, but I have lived my entire adult life in Illinois. So, I had not seen many of my classmates since our graduation. The conversations included catching up and recalling our shared youthful experiences. One of my classmates reminded me that she sat across from me in our eighth-grade Communication class. I knew why she recalled that particular class from 1963. We shared a very clear memory of hearing the PA announcement that President Kennedy had been assassinated and then watching as our teacher began to cry.

We can all place major historical events in the context of our individual lives. My mother remembered hearing the news of the attack on Pearl Harbor. I recall watching the first moon landing at Habonim Camp Tavor in Michigan. I was driving my twins to high school when we heard the first report of the 9/11 terrorist attacks.

Many people want to place the stories from the Bible in the context of the history we know from other sources. We look to Egyptian and Assyrian records and other archeological data to find mentions of biblical persons and events. This is a difficult to impossible task for the first books of the Bible.

The earliest mention of Israelites in Egyptian sources is engraved on a stele describing a campaign of Pharaoh Merneptah, son of Ramesses II, who ruled Egypt from 1279 BCE to 1213 BCE. The stele reports Merneptah's defeat of Israel in Canaan.

In the stories of 2 Kings, the Bible mentions specific Egyptian pharaohs, Assyrian kings, and other rulers that we know about from sources beyond the Bible. These details help us begin the process of establishing dates for the Bible stories.

Clear connections between history and the Bible emerge during the reign of King Hezekiah. We have multiple sources for data from this period. The Bible, Assyrian court history, and archeology overlap in painting a picture of King Hezekiah, who ruled Judah from 715 BCE to 687 BCE. When Hezekiah came to power, Judah was a vassal state to the Assyrian Empire. Hezekiah rebelled. He instituted religious and political reforms. He eliminated the offering of sacrifices at the rural high places and removed images of the Assyrian gods from the Temple in Jerusalem. He stopped paying tribute to the Assyrian Empire. He extended the border to the north to include part of the area of the recently destroyed kingdom of Israel.

King Sennacherib and the Assyrian army responded by attacking Judah. They plundered most of the country. They laid siege to Jerusalem but failed to conquer it. Second Kings chapter 19 describes these events in detail. The story of the siege can also be found on the Sennacherib Prism, a six-sided prism found in Nineveh in 1830. The Sennacherib Prism is now on display at the Institute for the Study of Ancient Cultures in Hyde Park in Chicago.

The British Museum in London has a full room devoted to the Lachish reliefs, which depict the Assyrian destruction of the Judean city of Lachish in 701 BCE. Second Chronicles 32:9 describes the same events depicted in the reliefs.

We know from Egyptian sources that Pharaoh Neco II ruled 610–595 BCE. The Bible tells us about the death of King Josiah: "In his days Pharaoh Neco king of Egypt went up against the king of Assyria to the river Euphrates; and King Josiah went against him; and he slew him at Megiddo, when he had seen him" (2 Kgs 23:29).

With this background we can turn to the question of Ezra and Nehemiah. The book of Ezra begins, "In the first year of King Cyrus of Persia, When the word of the ETERNAL spoken by Jeremiah was fulfilled, the ETERNAL roused the spirit of King Cyrus of Persia to issue a proclamation throughout his realm" (Ezra 1:1). The "first year" refers to the first year after Cyrus's conquest of Babylonia, not his first year as king of Persia. He could not have freed any resident of Babylon until he controlled Babylon. We know from a variety of historical sources that this is 538 BCE. The participants in this first wave of return, led by Sheshbazzar, made their way to Jerusalem. Jeshua and Zerubbabel begin the rebuilding of the altar and the Temple (Ezra 2).

Local enemies caused an interruption in the construction. The prophets, Haggai and Zechariah, inspired people to resume the construction of the Temple. "The house was finished on the third of the month of Adar in the sixth year of the reign of King Darius" (Ezra 6:15). We know about the reign of King Darius from a variety of historical and archeological sources. We can confidently conclude that the "sixth year of the reign of King Darius" was 515 BCE.

In chapter 7 of the book of Ezra we read that Ezra arrived in Jerusalem in the seventh year of King Artaxerxes. Among scholars, the standard approach is to assume that this Artaxerxes is Artaxerxes I, who ruled from 465 BCE to 625 BCE. So that would put Ezra's arrival in Jerusalem 458 BCE, fifty-seven years after the completion of the Temple.

The Bible tells us that Nehemiah arrived in Jerusalem in the twentieth year of Artaxerxes (Neh 1:1). If we assume that this Artaxerxes is again Artaxerxes I it would put Nehemiah's arrival in Jerusalem in 445 BCE.

While this remains the most straightforward way to understand the dates, some scholars do hold to an alternative approach. They argue that if one reads the text closely one will see evidence that Ezra arrived in Jerusalem after Nehemiah, not before him. They point to Ezra 9:9:

> For slaves we are, though even in our bondage God has not forsaken us, but has disposed the king of Persia favorably toward us, to furnish us with sustenance and to raise again the House of God, repairing its ruins and giving us a hold in Judah and in Jerusalem.

The Bible clearly reports that the walls of Jerusalem were rebuilt under Nehemiah's leadership. Some scholars argue that Ezra could not have spoken these words if he was the first to arrive in Jerusalem.

The second key verse used to support this alternative position is Ezra 10:1, which describes a large population in Jerusalem: "Now while Ezra was praying and making confession, weeping and prostrating himself before the house of God, a very large assembly, men, women and children, gathered to him from Israel; for the people wept bitterly."

This contrasts with Neh 7:4, which speaks of the small population of Jerusalem: "Now the city was large and spacious, but the people in it were few and the houses were not built."

These scholars argue that it is very unlikely that the population was large and then became small. The opposite is much more likely—that the population of Jerusalem grew over time.

The scholars supporting this alternative position then argue that Ezra did not arrive in Jerusalem during the reign of Artaxerxes I but rather Artaxerxes II, who reigned from 405 BCE to 359 BCE. The seventh year of King Artaxerxes II would have been 398 BCE. This reworking of the dates places Ezra's arrival in Jerusalem 117 years after the completion of the Temple and 57 years after the arrival of Nehemiah.

Those who hold to this position have to deal with the eighth chapter of Nehemiah, which describes Nehemiah and Ezra appearing together before the assembled people in Jerusalem. They have to contend that the eighth chapter of Nehemiah was artificially created to put Ezra and Nehemiah "on stage" together. Most people holding to this position argue that chapter 8 of Nehemiah was actually part of the book of Ezra placed within Nehemiah. And then Nehemiah was "photoshopped" into verse 9.

Personally, the "alternative" scholarly position does not convince me. I see it as building a large argument on a weak foundation of a narrow reading of a few verses. First, it depends on taking a poetic image literally. These scholars take the mention of a wall in Ezra 9:9 literally as testimony to the existence of fully rebuilt actual wall; I see it as a metaphor for the rebuilt Jewish people. The second foundation stone for this position is contrasting "large" in Ezra 10:1 and "few" in Neh 7:4. We should understand the size of a group of people depends on context. I could say, "This year we had a small crowd for Rosh Hashanah," to describe a gathering of 800 people. And I could say, "We had a huge congregation last Friday night," to describe 175 people.

A second challenge to the standard approach can be found in traditional Jewish sources. Traditional Jewish texts do not look to academic history or archeology for evidence. Traditional sources from the Talmud and Rashi to contemporary Artscroll volumes depend on Seder Olam, an early rabbinic history of the world, for all dates. The Talmud (Yebamot 82b and Nedarim 46b) attributes Seder Olam to Rabbi Yosi ben Halafta in the mid-second century. Seder Olam creates a timeline for history from the creation of the world to Ezra/Nehemiah based entirely on details contained in the Bible. The last two chapters of Seder Olam deal with the time period of Ezra/Nehemiah.

According to Seder Olam the Babylonians conquered Jerusalem in 3319 (451 BCE) and destroyed the Temple in 3338 (423 BCE). Seventy years after the conquest of Jerusalem, in 3390 (371 BCE), Cyrus launched the first wave of return. And the rebuilding of the Temple is resumed in 3408 (353 BCE), seventy years after the destruction of the First Temple, and completed in 3412.

Chapter 7 of the book of Ezra describes Ezra's ascent to Jerusalem. Ezra 7:7 says that it took place during the seventh year of King Artachshast. In his comment to 7:7, Rashi says that King Artachshast is Darius and that *bishnat sheva*, was "seven years after the completion of the Temple." Which would be 3415 (348 BCE) or 3413 (346 BCE).

Nehemiah arrived in Jerusalem in the twentieth year of King Artachshast, still understood by Rashi to be Darius, which would be 3426 (335 BCE).

The gap in the dating between the traditional Jewish sources and the Western academic approach is significant. Alexander the Great's forces arrived in the land of Israel in 332 BCE. The dating from traditional sources makes Nehemiah a contemporary of Alexander.

Living in the Rhine valley a thousand years ago, Rashi did not have access to modern academic knowledge. Rashi had a full mastery of the Jewish sources, but he knew very little about the ancient Near East. I do not find fault with Rashi for his embrace of Seder Olam. But for us to continue to use the dates in Seder Olam and the Talmud means rejecting the scientific method and the modern acquisition of knowledge. We should read the Bible from the context of everything else we know from a wide variety of sources.

Throughout this book I will use the standard approach to dating the events described in Ezra/Nehemiah.

Chapter 12

National Narrative

In the late sixties the *Minneapolis Star* published a feature story about the Habonim Israeli Dance group of which I was a member. The story included my explanation of Zionism. I told the reporter, with the moral certainty of a sixteen-year-old, that "as a Jew living in the United States, I feel that I am living in exile!" This public pronouncement surprised my parents.

Today most Jews in America feel fully American. We feel part of American history, American society, and American culture. The America narrative is our narrative. At the same time, we can feel fully Jewish.

My great-grandparents, living in nineteenth-century Lithuania, understood that they were Jews who happen to be living in Lithuania, not Lithuanians who happened to be Jewish. If they ever forgot this, the real Lithuanians regularly reminded them. My great-grandparents did not feel that the Lithuanian national narrative was their story.

In the context of this study, we can ask, How did the people see themselves while in Babylonian exile? Did they think of Babylonia as their new home? Or did they understand it to be a temporary residence? Did they see themselves as Jews who happened to be living in Babylonia? Or as Babylonians who happened to be Jewish?

The initial period of the exile between our arrival in Babylonia and the first wave of return was brief, forty-eight to seventy years, depending on how you count. But we know that not everybody took advantage of the first opportunity to return to Jerusalem. The Bible tells of three waves of returning: Zerubbabel led the first wave, Ezra led a second wave, and Nehemiah led the third wave.

Both Ezra 2:1 and Neh 7:6 include the phrase "These are the people of the province who came up among the captives." Some of the people chose to return, while others stayed in Babylonia. This departure was not like the exodus from Egypt when everybody left all at once in the middle of the night. The book of Exodus does not have to list the people who left Egypt. Everybody left. Here in our story everybody did not leave. Even after three waves of returning, a sizable population of Jews remained in Babylonia.

Why did some of the people choose to remain in Babylonia? The text does not explain their motives. Generally, the Bible does not include anybody's thought process. It tells what happened, rather than why. The traditional commentators often explain the motivations of the people in the Bible. But these commentators do not address this question of why some of the people returned to Jerusalem while others stayed in Babylonia. Their silence leaves us room to speculate.

It could have been an issue of religious devotion. We could imagine that the more religiously focused of the people wanted to return to Jerusalem to rebuild the Temple and the city. They wanted to be closer to God.

Or we could think of this issue in more national terms. Some of people maintained a stronger sense of Jewish national identity, while others had more fully settled in, becoming assimilated into Babylonian life. Jews remained in Babylonia for twenty-five hundred years, from 586 BCE until the modern Iraqi Jewish community left for the infant State of Israel in 1951.

The individual stories we tell express our personal sense of identity. The first step in community organizing is to sit in a conversation with one other person and say, "Tell me your story." The stories we share express our group identity. Families, congregations, sports teams all have famous stories which explain their group. Nations do as well.

In Washington, DC, one sees the Lincoln Memorial, the Jefferson Memorial, and the Washington Monument. In Edinburgh, Scotland, one does not see tributes to national political leaders but rather the two-hundred-foot-high memorial to the writer Sir Walter Scott. It dominates the main boulevard, Princes Street, adjacent to the Waverley Train Station, which is named for Scott's Waverley novels. Sir Walter Scott was not a hero of Scottish military or political history but rather a writer of the great Scottish historical novels. His books include *Waverley*, *Rob Roy*, and *Ivanhoe*. Many people see Scott as the nineteenth-century reviver of the Scottish national narrative.

Following the Acts of Union in 1707 and the collapse of Bonnie Prince Charlie's rebellion, Scottish national identity had been on the wane. The Dress Act of 1746 made the wearing of Highland dress, the kilt, illegal. A significant expression of Scottish national identity had been outlawed. Through his novels Scott helped revived popular enthusiasm for Scottish national identity.

In 1822 King George IV became the first reigning British monarch to visit Scotland in two hundred years. Sir Walter Scott played a key role in orchestrating the visit. For the main event of the visit, Scott had the king dress in a full Highland outfit to greet the leaders of Scotland at Edinburgh's Holyrood Palace. David Wilkie's painting of King George IV, showing him in a kilt, provides a lasting image of that moment, suggesting that one can be both Scottish and British. Residents of Scotland continue to waver between these two poles of identity: Scottish and British.

Winston Churchill wrote a four-volume work called *A History of English-Speaking Peoples*. He began the project in the mid-1930s, but he did not complete it until the mid-1950s. He was otherwise engaged during many of those years. Churchill saw a common narrative and destiny uniting the people of the far-flung British Commonwealth and the United States. Many people think that he invented this category of human beings, called "English-speaking people," by writing these books. I think that Americans continue to feel a special connection to the United Kingdom and certainly to Canada. The shared language and the partially shared history create the means of having a partially shared popular culture.

On one level I know that Neil Young, Joni Mitchell, and Michael J. Fox are all Canadians, but I think of them as part of a cultural "us" rather a cultural "them," into which I would place Korean, Czech, or French entertainers. For me a "foreign film" is one that requires subtitles.

In *War and Peace* Leo Tolstoy told the story of Russia's wars with Napoleon through the lives of a few families. Tolstoy's novel also expresses his version of the Russian national narrative. While the novel is set in the first decades of the nineteenth century, Tolstoy is more interested in explaining what it means to be a Russian in his own time, the late nineteenth century.

Over the centuries Jews have wavered between two identities. Jews have seen themselves as Jews and as members of the society in which they dwelled. Often the external factor of hostility from the majority culture has helped Jews maintain a national identity.

The rise of Zionism in the late nineteenth century grew out of an increasing sense of Jewish national identity. We felt connected to the Jewish national story. This reflected the growing nationalism during that period in many countries in which we dwelled. Italy and Germany became countries for the first time in the late nineteenth century. Political leaders expressed this identity in speeches and pamphlets. Writers and composers also gave moving expression to national identity.

In 1896 Theodor Herzl wrote *The Jewish State*. He originally called it, *Address to the Rothschilds*, referring to the Rothschild family banking dynasty. Herzl intended to speak to members of the Rothschild family. Their support would have given significant status to his project of lobbying European leaders to support the creation of a Jewish state. But Baron Edmond de Rothschild, leader of the French branch of this banking family, rejected Herzl's plan to create a Jewish state. Baron Rothschild saw himself as a Frenchman, not a member of the Jewish people. But other Jews did rally to Herzl's call. Fifty-two years later on May 14, 1948, in an art museum in Tel Aviv, David ben Gurion declared the independence of the State of Israel.

We can imagine that those who joined Zerubbabel, Ezra, and Nehemiah in returning to Jerusalem embraced the Jewish national narrative. In chapter 18, we will look more closely at the fate of the people who chose to remain in Babylonia. In the next chapter we will begin to look at practical steps taken by the people who returned from exile.

Chapter 13

Taking Possession of the Land

THE MISHNAH DESCRIBES HOW people demonstrate ownership of several categories of objects:

> One acquires large animals by leading them from one place to another and small animals by lifting them up, according to Rabbi Meir and Rabbi Elazar. But the sages say: small animals are also acquired by being led. The rightful ownership of property can be secured though the payment of money, the completion of a document or the performance of a proprietary act.
> (Mishnah Brachot 1:4–5)

Today in America people acquire ownership of land through money and signing a few documents. But there was a time during which a "proprietary act" played a key part role in land acquisition in the United States.

The United States Congress passed the Homestead Act in 1862 to accelerate the settlement of the Western territory by granting adult heads of families 160 acres of surveyed public lands for a minimal filing fee and five years of continuous residence on the land. As a child I learned about homesteading from Laura Ingalls Wilder's series of *Little House* books, which told the story of her family's pioneering years in the Midwest in the late nineteenth century. In *By the Shores of Silver Lake*, Laura describes the process of establishing the family's homestead in South Dakota.

Early in the book Pa explains his plan to his wife: "'Listen to reason Caroline,' Pa pleaded. 'We can get a hundred and sixty acres out west just by living on it.'"[1] After the family moves to South Dakota it takes Pa some months to find the right land. When he does, he pays $14 to file a claim.

> "I've bet Uncle Sam fourteen dollars against a hundred and sixty acres of land that we can make out to live on the claim for five years. Going to help me win that bet?"
> "Oh, yes, Pa!" Carrie said eagerly, and Mary said, "Yes, Pa!" gladly, and Laura promised soberly, "Yes, Pa."[2]

Near the conclusion of *By the Shores of Silver Lake* Charles reflects on their new life in their "claim shanty." "'Now we are all snug,' Pa said, 'Bring me my fiddle, Laura, and we will have some music.'"[3]

I was six years old when the Bob family came to Minneapolis, Minnesota, seventy-six years after the Ingalls had arrived in the Walnut Grove, Minnesota. I enjoyed the *Little House* books as a child. My sister, brother, and I identified with Laura's family's adventures. A generation later Tammie and I read the books to our children. Our children are now sharing these stories with their own children. Tammie and I have visited many of the *Little House* sites during our driving trips.

On a driving trip to LA we made what we thought would be a brief stop at the Laura Ingalls Wilder Home/Museum in Mansfield, Missouri. We spent half a day looking at artifacts from the Ingalls family's pioneer life. We saw many "sacred objects" from the Ingalls family including Pa's actual fiddle. Looking at the fiddle hanging on the wall, I could imagine Pa playing it for his family in their South Dakota claim shanty.

How did the people returning from exile in Babylon acquire ownership of the land? They had a legal document, the proclamation of Cyrus the Great, but they needed to perform a "proprietary act" to feel themselves as owning the land. The people asserted their ownership of the land by rebuilding the altar. Shortly after the first wave of returnees arrived back in the land they begin to rebuild:

> When the seventh month arrived—the Israelites being settled in their towns—the entire people assembled as one person in Jerusalem. Then Jeshua son of Jozadak and his brother priests and Zerubbabel son Shealtiel and his brothers set to and built the altar of the God of Israel to offer burnt offerings upon it as is written in the Torah of Moses, the man of God. (Ezra 3:1–2)

1. Wilder, *By the Shores*, 4.
2. Wilder, *By the Shores*, 237.
3. Wilder, *By the Shores*, 297.

The first wave of the returnees followed in the footsteps of the first members of our people to acquire the land. In Gen 12 God told Abram and Sarai to go, to leave all they knew in Haran and go to the new land. Later in the Torah God commissions the people in the wilderness to enter the land that had been given to the matriarchs and the patriarchs. We read, "See, I place the land at your disposal. Go, take possession of the land that the ETERNAL swore to your fathers, Abraham, Isaac, and Jacob, to assign to them and to their heirs after them" (Deut 1:8).

The rabbis explain that the patriarchs each performed a "proprietary act" to demonstrate that they owned the land. In the Sifre on this Deuteronomy verse we read,

> A parable: A king gave a specific undeveloped field his servant as a present. The servant went to work to develop the field, saying, "What I currently have is only an undeveloped field in the same state in which it was given to me." He planted a vineyard in it, saying again, "What I have taken full ownership of the field that was given."
>
> So also when the Holy One, of blessing gave Abraham the land, He gave it to him undeveloped as the text says, "Arise, walk through the land in the length of it and in the breadth of it; for unto thee will I give it" (Gen 13:17). Abraham then went to work to develop the land, as it is said, And Abraham planted a tamarisk tree in Beer-sheba (Gen 21:33). In a similar manner, Isaac went to work to develop the land, as it is said, And Isaac sowed in that land, and found in the same year a hundredfold (Gen 26:12). Jacob also went to work develop, as it is said, And he bought the parcel of ground (Gen 33:19).
> (Sifrei Piska 8)

One of the first projects of the modern Zionist movement was the creation of the Jewish National Fund in 1901 to purchase parcels of land from Ottoman landowners for Jews to build new homes and villages. The process continued during the years of the British Mandate.

Between 1936 and 1947 the Jewish Nation Fund sought to settle the land that it had purchased, establishing facts on the ground. During that dangerous and difficult time they built 118 *chomah umigdal*, "watchtower and stockade," settlements "overnight" using an old Ottoman law which prohibited the demolition of completed settlements. Hundreds of volunteers worked together to quickly assemble the community from prefabricated parts.

As the Zionist pioneers took possession of portions of the land at the end of the nineteenth century and during first decades of twentieth century, the other people living on the land, the Palestinians, became dispossessed. On November 29, 1947, the United Nations voted to partition Palestine into a Jewish state and an Arab state. David Ben Gurion and Zionist leaders accepted the Partition Plan, knowing that the Palestinians and the neighboring Arab states would reject it and turn to war. What Jews call Israel's War of Independence is known among Palestinians as the Nakba, "the catastrophe." The ceasefire, agreed to after months of fighting, left more of Palestine in Jewish hands than had been allotted to the Jewish state by the original Partition Plan.

The modern Zionist Chalutzim (pioneers) also planted trees as part of the Jewish people's ongoing acquisition and development of the land. It was for them a "proprietary act." In the mid-twentieth century, Jewish children brought dimes to Hebrew schools. The dimes went into blue-and-white cardboard holders of the Jewish National Fund. Each folder had room for twenty dimes. When the folder was filled, we had the two dollars to purchase a tree to be planted in Israel. Bringing those dimes to Hebrew school was our "proprietary act." We felt that in our own modest way, we were helping to rebuild the Jewish homeland.

One of the ways in which I have tried to continue to do my part in the ongoing work of building the Jewish state has been to lead groups from the congregation to Israel. Every three years I took a group of Etz Chaim high school students. In 1991 we visited Yad Lakashish, Lifeline for the Old, in Jerusalem for the first time. In welcoming the teens and me, the director, Nava Ein Mor, said to me, "I see you are from Chicago. Do you know Rabbi Mark Shapiro? He is a dedicated supporter of ours."

Nava asked a pretty straightforward question of Jewish geography, but it touched me deeply. Where in Israel would someone say to a visitor, "I see you are from Chicago. Do you know Rabbi Steven Bob?"

I understood that I had allowed myself to be too passive a supporter of Israel. I wanted to become a more active, self-directed participant in the life of Israel. I needed to perform ongoing "proprietary acts" to express my connection to Israel.

I became a dedicated worker in support of the Lifeline sheltered workshop for the elderly of Jerusalem. I volunteered for Lifeline by running the booth at a series of national Jewish education conferences. A main stream of support for Lifeline comes from the sale in Jerusalem of the handiworks created in its workshops. I helped Congregation Etz

Chaim to become a Midwestern hub promoting a broader sales effort. By promoting the efforts of Lifeline, I did my modest part to participate in the life of the State of Israel.

At the conclusion of the Passover Seder we say, "Next year in Jerusalem." When we say these words, we are not speaking of Jerusalem as it is; we imagine returning to the "rebuilt Jerusalem." The first wave of our people returning from exile in Babylonia did their part to rebuild Jerusalem. The Chalutzim of the Zionist movement did their part to rebuild Jerusalem. In 1967, songwriter Naomi Shemer described Jerusalem in "Yerushalayim Shel Zahav," "Jerusalem of Gold." Her song became a celebration of the reunification of Jerusalem, expressing the spirit of that era. In our own time, there remains much work for us to do to rebuild Jerusalem. It is not yet the city we hope it will be.

Chapter 14

Practical Zionism: The First Aliyah

We use the term "Political Zionism" to describe the efforts of Theodor Herzl, Chaim Weizmann, and others who lobbied the heads of nations and later the United Nations to support the creation of a Jewish state in the land of Israel. The accomplishments of modern "Political Zionism" include the Balfour Declaration of 1917 and the United Nations' approval of the Partition Plan on November 29, 1947. In the process of returning from the exile in Babylonia, we can see the decree of Cyrus and the later letter of Darius as acts of Political Zionism.

These political acts are important but not sufficient. Proclamations alone do not build a homeland or a state. The real-world grassroots efforts of Practical Zionism transformed the Zionist idea into the State of Israel. Even after the November 29, 1947, United Nations vote, practical on-the-ground deeds moved the Partition Plan into a real-world country. While we generally use the term "Practical Zionism" to describe these efforts of the Jewish people in the nineteenth and twentieth century, the term can also apply to the people returning to the land of Israel twenty-five hundred years ago.

The book of Exodus tells us that the entire people left Egypt in one night. While the Egyptians were reeling from the tenth plague the entire community of Israelites departed. Cyrus's proclamation launched the process of the return of the exiles to Jerusalem, but the entire community of exiles did not leave Babylonia all at once. Ezra and Nehemiah tell of waves of return. Chapter 2 of Ezra describes Zerubbabel leading the first wave of returnees. In chapter 8 we read of a second wave of returnees led by Ezra. We can imagine that a third wave of returnees went to Jerusalem with Nehemiah. Each of these waves had their own concerns and their own tasks. The first wave rebuilt the altar and started to rebuild the Temple. The second wave contributed to building the religious life of the society. The third wave rebuilt the walls and gates of Jerusalem.

The modern Zionist return to the land also came in waves. The First Aliyah, the first major wave of Jews returning to the land of Israel, was triggered by the assassination of Czar Alexander II in 1881. Or, more precisely, the response to that assassination motivated Russian Jews to seek new options. Russian authorities blamed the death of Alexander II on "the Jews" and launched pogroms in many Russian towns. The subsequent May Laws added new restrictions to the lives of Russian Jews. Many Jews responded to the difficulty of their lives in Russia by leaving for America. Advances in steamship technology and construction in the 1880s opened new possibilities of immigration for poor Russian Jews. A smaller group of immigrant Russian Jews came to the land of Israel, establishing new communities including Rishon Letziyon, Rosh Pina, and Zichron Ya'akov. Thirty-five thousand Jews came to the land of Israel during the First Aliyah from 1882 to 1904 as members of Hibbat Ziyon and Bilu.

The first wave of returnees in 536 BCE needed financial assistance to successfully begin their new lives in the land of Israel. Cyrus's proclamation included a call for financial support for the returnees. He did not distribute small blue boxes, but he did say, "And whoever stays behind, wherever he be living, let the people of his place assist him with silver, gold, goods and livestock besides the freewill offering to the House of God that is in Jerusalem" (Ezra 1:4).

Rashi understands this to be a description of gentile Babylonians helping poor Jews going up to Jerusalem. He understands the phrase *kol hanishar*, "whoever stays behind," to refer to "all of the Jews who remain in their place [in Babylonia] because they have no wealth," who will receive help from the Babylonians. Rashi explains that *y'nasuhu*, "assist him," expresses that:

> I [Cyrus] direct the gentile peoples of those place to provide silver, gold and supplies so that the poor Jews will be able to go up to Jerusalem with the contributions that the people of their places have freely given them to rebuild the Temple. (Rashi on Ezra 1:4)

Rashi's understanding of the text would make this event parallel to the exodus from Egypt. There, the Egyptians bestowed gifts of gold and silver on the departing Israelites (Exod 12:35–36).

The academic Bible scholars are divided as to whether this sentence refers to gentile or Israelite supporters of the returnees. Some of them follow Rashi, viewing the supporters as gentiles. Others see the supporters as the Jews who do not participate in the first wave. In her commentary on Ezra, Lisbeth Fried writes, "The verse is ambiguous because of several pronouns without clear antecedents."[1] I read the verse as referring to Jews of Babylonia who did not themselves go up to Jerusalem. They saw the participants in the first waves as their representatives.

The Jews of the modern waves of immigration also received help from people who remained in "exile." We can see the name of the key supporter of the First Aliyah on street signs in many Israeli cities.

My first trip to Israel was in the summer of 1968. I participated in an exchange program sponsored by the Minneapolis JCC and the city of Rishon L'Tziyon, one of the communities established during the First Aliyah. Six teenagers from Minneapolis spent the summer in Rishon living with families and working in the summer camps of the city of Rishon. And six teenagers from Rishon spent the summer in Minnesota living with American Jewish families and working in the camps of the JCC. Today Rishon is a large city of two hundred and fifty thousand and part of the Tel Aviv metropolitan area. But in 1968, Rishon was a small town of twenty-five thousand with one main street, Rothschild Street.

Many Israeli cities have a street named Rothschild. Rothschild Boulevard, one of Tel Aviv's oldest streets, remains a main thoroughfare. In Jerusalem, Rothschild Street runs next to the Supreme Court building. In Haifa the Rothschild name adorns the cultural center. These streets and buildings honor Baron Edmund de Rothschild, of the French branch of that famous family.

Baron Edmund de Rothschild funded many of the key projects in Rishon during the First Aliyah period. He paid for the all-important activity of drilling wells for water. He provided the backing for the founding of the Carmel Mizrachi winery. Today Israel has many wineries offering a wide variety of wines; but for the first seventy-five years of the twentieth century if you bought a bottle of Israeli wine, it was Carmel Mizrachi wine.

1. Fried, *Ezra*, 61.

On the first day of our trip, we were taken on a "grand tour" of the small city. The winery was the first stop. The manager showed us how they made the wine, and then they gave us samples. We were teenagers away from our parents on the first day of our first ever international trip. No one had ever given us free-flowing wine. I suppose that we could have demonstrated good judgment and maturity beyond our years. But instead, we drank too much. It was the morning in Israel in the summer; the weather got hotter as the day went on. The next stop was a razor blade factory. We wilted in the summer heat. The refrain of an old Zionist song that I learned at Habonim camp proclaims, "When we die bury us in the winery of Rishon L'Tziyon." We thought it was going to come true that July morning.

Baron Edmund de Rothschild was also the patron of Zichron Yaakov in northern Israel on the Carmel just south of Haifa. It is named in honor of the baron's father, James (Yaakov). Carmel-Mizrahi also built a winery in Zichron Yaakov. Just south of Zichron one finds Ramat Hanadiv, a large park/garden in honor of *hanadiv*, "the benefactor," Baron Rothschild. The main street in Zichron is called Hanadiv.

Baron Edmund de Rothschild provided the essential support to the first wave of practical Zionists, but he did not support the political Zionism of Theodor Herzl. Rothschild supported Jewish settlements in the land of Israel to provide a refuge for Jews fleeing anti-Semitism in Czarist Russia. But Herzl's call for a Jewish state did not move him. Rothschild saw himself as a fully French citizen of the French state. He believed that the Russian Jews needed a refuge, but he did not think that the Jews needed a state. He expected that Palestine would continue to be part of the Ottoman Empire.

The first wave of the returnees from Babylonia led by Zerubbabel were not going to Jerusalem to create a Jewish state. They would be living in the Persian province of Judea. The journey back to Jerusalem was a return to the people living in their own land, bringing offerings to the rebuilt Temple. But it was not the recreation of the Davidic monarchy. We will explore the topic of the Davidic monarchy more fully in chapter 36.

The complimentary interaction between the Political Zionism and Practical Zionism continues today. We can see expressions of Political Zionism in the work of pro-Israel activists lobbying American congressmen. We can observe Practical Zionism in the grassroots work of the Jewish Agency integrating new immigrants into Israeli society. The work of Practical Zionism was ongoing for the generations of those who returned from the first exile twenty-five hundred years ago and for those who have returned from the second exile in our own time.

RETURNING HOME

Chapter 15

Cyrus the Great

The text of the book of Ezra begins,

> The Eternal roused the spirit of King Cyrus to issue a proclamation throughout his realm by word of mouth and in writing as follows. Thus said King Cyrus of Persia: The Eternal God of Heaven has given me all the kingdoms of the earth and has charged me with building Him a house in Jerusalem, which is in Judah. Anyone of you of all His people—may his God be with him, and let him go up to Jerusalem that is in Judah and build the House of the Eternal God of Israel, the God that is in Jerusalem. (Ezra 1:1–3)

Cyrus the Great, the Persian king, became a vehicle through which God worked in the world. Throughout the Bible God uses a wide variety of objects and people as agents. For example, in the book of Jonah, God designates a big fish, a kikayon plant, and a worm to act in the world as agents of the divine will. But here in Ezra God uses a human being as the divine agent. One might read the Ezra text to say that God spoke directly to Cyrus, thus making the gentile king of the Persians a prophet. This possibility bothered Rashi. So, he provides Cyrus's explanation:

> He commanded me through Isaiah the prophet to build for Him the Temple in Jerusalem as it says in the book of Isaiah (44:28–45:1) "He is My shepherd / He shall fulfill all my purposes / He shall say of Jerusalem, 'She shall be rebuilt' / And to the Temple: 'You shall be founded again.' Thus said the Eternal to Cyrus, his anointed one— / Whose right hand he has grasped."

> This had already been conveyed through prophecy by Isaiah. (Rashi on Ezra 1:2)

Rashi's position is to demote Cyrus from prophet to agent of God. Cyrus merely carries out the will of God as expressed in the words of Isaiah, an actual prophet. Even if we do not think of Cyrus as a prophet, nevertheless he should have special status. As God's agent he launches the return from exile. But organized Jewish religious life does include a means to honor Cyrus. We do not have a Cyrus day or a Cyrus prayer. We do not even have a Cyrus sweet. Haman, the villain of the Purim story, gets the Hamentaschen, but Cyrus, a very positive figure, gets nothing.

Often, during our holidays we recount the major events of Jewish history. We mention the names of those who tried to destroy us in ancient days and throughout the centuries. We often connect the dots between the leaders of various nations who expelled us or sought to destroy. We do not give sufficient attention to prominent people in history who aided the Jewish people. We bitterly recall that Ferdinand and Isabella expelled the Jews from Spain in 1492. But do we often think of the leaders of the nations who gave refuge to these expelled Jews?

Many of the Jews who left Spain found refuge in the Ottoman Empire. Most contemporary Jews have never even heard the name of Beyazid II, the Ottoman sultan who welcomed the fleeing Jews from Spain. He is said to have taunted the rulers of Spain saying, "You venture to call Ferdinand a wise ruler, . . . he who has impoverished his own country and enriched mine!"[1] How many contemporary Jews know that Oliver Cromwell welcomed Jews back to England in 1653? Jews had been absent from England since they had been expelled in 1290 by King Edward I. Too often in recounting Jewish history, we emphasize what was done to us by those who sought to harm us, rather than raising up what was done for us by those who sought to help us.

On Tisha Ba'Av we recall the destruction of both the Temples in Jerusalem. We remember being driven into exile by Nebuchadnezzar. But we do not have a companion holiday to celebrate the return from Babylonian exile. Cyrus the Great has received some Jewish honors. Journalist Meir Javendanfer writes,

> King Cyrus is considered as one of the saviors of the Jewish people, and for this, he is one of the most respected and loved foreign Kings in Jewish history. This also explains why he has so

1. Danon, "Bajazet II."

> many streets named after him in Israel. Here is one street named after him . . . in Jerusalem. Its right near the old city, near the city center. There are also streets named after King Cyrus in Tel Aviv, Haifa, Rishon Le-Tzion, Petakh Tikva, Pardes Hana and Afula.[2]

Cyrus is called Koresh in Hebrew, so the streets named for him in Israel are called Koresh Street.

President Harry Truman saw the connection between the return from the first exile and the return from the second exile. He understood the connection between the biblical account of the first return and the second return that took place before his eyes.

> In November 1953, just a few months after leaving the presidency of the United States, Harry S. Truman was brought to the Jewish Theological Seminary in New York to meet a group of Jewish dignitaries. Accompanying him was his good friend Eddie Jacobson, a comrade from his Army days and former business partner in a short-lived men's haberdashery 30 years earlier. Jacobson introduced his friend to the assembled theologians: "This is the man who helped create the State of Israel." Truman retorted, "What do you mean, 'helped to create'? I am Cyrus. I am Cyrus."
>
> Truman's self-identification with Cyrus had nothing to do with self-glorification. It followed from his understanding of history and of the Bible. His Sunday School teachers had taught him that someone, someday, would be called upon to be a second Cyrus.[3]

Harry Truman became president of the United States on April 12, 1945, following the death of Franklin Delano Roosevelt. Truman immediately faced serious challenges with long-lasting implications, including concluding World War II, rebuilding a shattered world, and confronting the Soviet Union. In the spring of 1947 Truman had to steer the American response to the United Nations' proposal to partition Palestine into a Jewish state and an Arab state. He received intense advice from many quarters and ultimately had the American representative to the United Nations vote in favor of the Partition Plan on November 29, 1947. Truman's support made the passage of the Partition Plan possible. Israel declared its independence on May 14, 1948. Eleven minutes after that

2. Javedanfar, "King Cyrus."
3. Merkley, "I Am Cyrus."

declaration, President Truman recognized the State of Israel. Harry Truman earned the right to think of himself as a modern-day Cyrus.

Tisha Ba'Av has come to recall both exiles: the first following the destruction of the First Temple by the Babylonians in 586 BCE, and the second following the destruction of the Second Temple by the Romans in 70 CE. We do have a Jewish holiday celebrating a return from the second exile, Israel's Independence Day. We should add to that day a celebration of the return from the first exile. Israel's Independence Day is a national holiday of the State of Israel. Many American Jewish communities have Yom Ha'atzmaut programs. Some modern Orthodox synagogues add Hallel to their daily service on Yom Ha'atzmaut. But Yom Ha'atzmaut has not yet become a broadly observed religious holiday for American Jews.

We could imagine a new Jewish religious holiday of return, recalling both returns—a holiday with prayers and ritual honoring both returns. We would connect the parallels between the two stories: the declaration of Cyrus and the Balfour Declaration, the waves of immigration in both returns, Nehemiah's rebuilding of the walls and gates of Jerusalem and the building of the wall and tower communities of the 1930s and 1940s, which I described in chapter 14.

We could create new holiday treats. I imagine a pastry in a Persian style which could be named *Keter Koresh*, Cyrus's Crown. My friend and baking expert, Dr. Kathy Schwartz, suggests our starting point could be a "Persian Love Cake featuring cardamon, almonds and rosewater that baked in a Bundt pan would look like a crown."[4]

I have consulted cantors and song leaders, and none of them know any Jewish songs about Ezra and Nehemiah. We could commission the composition of songs about Ezra and Nehemiah to become part of our celebration of the return from exile.

A service could include Ps 126. This psalm, which begins, *Shir hama'alot*, is well-known as the paragraph that we add to Birkat Hamazon after meals on Shabbat and holidays.

> A song of ascents.
> When the Eternal restores the fortunes of Zion
> we see it as in a dream
> our mouths shall be filled with laughter,
> our tongues, with songs of joy.
> Then shall they say among the nations,
> "The Eternal has done great things for them!"

4. Kathy Schwartz, email message to author, July 21, 2023.

> The ETERNAL will do great things for us
> and we shall rejoice.
> Restore our fortunes, O ETERNAL,
> like watercourses in the Negeb.
> They who sow in tears
> shall reap with songs of joy.
> Though he goes along weeping,
> carrying the seed-bag,
> he shall come back with songs of joy,
> carrying his sheaves.

We could draw on the plural form of the last word of verse 3 and call this holiday *Yom S'meichim*, "The Day of Rejoicings," referring to the return from the first exile and the more recent return from the second exile.

The Jewish calendar includes holidays recalling many important moments in the Jewish past. We remember high points and low points in the long history of our people. Creating the new holiday of Yom S'meichim would add the joy of returning from Babylonian exile to annual reexperiencing of the Jewish past.

Chapter 16

Political Zionism

THE BOOK OF EZRA begins with Cyrus the Great's proclamation that we read in the last chapter. The Bible describes Cyrus's declaration specifically affecting the Judean exiles. The Cyrus Cylinder, a clay artifact from Babylonia now housed in the British Museum in London, tells a broader story. It explains that Cyrus freed all the foreign leadership cohorts that the Babylonians had carried into exile to return home. In general, the Bible places the story of the Children of Israel at the center of the narrative. It does so here as well. The biblical authors are not interested in sharing a history of the world but rather the story of one people, with all other peoples serving as supporting characters.

This political act by a major ruling power sets in motion the step-by-step return of the Jewish people to the land of Israel. The practical steps of returning and rebuilding would be taken by the members of the Jewish people. But the grassroots efforts of the people themselves could not have begun without the charter from the Persian ruler.

Cyrus the Great's proclamation stands as one in series of other similar moments in Jewish history. While several of the proclamations come from powerful human beings, our relationship with the land began with a call directly from God. According to the Bible, God calls Abram:

> Now the ETERNAL said unto Abram: "Go forth from your native land and from your father's house to the land that I will show you. I will make of you a great nation, and I will bless you; I will make your name great. And you shall be a blessing. I will bless

> those who bless you. And curse the one who curses you; And all the families of the earth shall bless themselves by you."
> (Gen 12:1–3)

Abram does not ask God any questions about the nature of the land or the challenges he will face. Abram responds with deeds not words. The text of Genesis tells us,

> Abram went forth as ETERNAL had commanded him, and Lot went with him. Abram was seventy-five years old when he left Haran. Abram took his wife Sarai and his brother's son Lot, and all the wealth that they had amassed, and the persons that they had acquired in Haran; and they set out for the land of Canaan. Abram passed through the land as far as the site of Shechem, at the terebinth of Moreh. The Canaanites were then in the land.
> (Gen 12:4–6)

In this new land, then known as Canaan, Abram and Sarai would become Abraham and Sarah. God lengthened their names to express their participation in the divine plan, linking their descendants to the land.

The second proclamation to go to the land came from a major gentile ruler, the pharaoh of Egypt. According to the Bible, Pharaoh does God's will to send the Children of Israel on their way back to the land of Israel. After the tenth plague at the conclusion of 430 years of slavery in Egypt, Pharaoh tells Moses and Aaron to take the people of Israel out of Egypt. "And he summoned Moses and Aaron in the night and said: 'Up, depart from among my people, you and the Israelites with you! Go, worship the ETERNAL, as you have said!" (Exod 31:12). Pharaoh's words release the people to begin their forty-year journey back to the land where they would dwell until the Babylonian exile.

The proclamation of Cyrus marked the third movement of the people toward the land. The fourth movement of our people back to the land included a proclamation from a government acting in the name of yet another gentile king, King George V of the United Kingdom. The British government issued the Balfour Proclamation in 1917 in response to a request from the Zionist movement.

Theodore Herzl brought organization to the Zionist Movement by summoning Zionist leaders to Basel, Switzerland, in 1897 for the first World Zionist Congress. Who gave Herzl the authority to issue such a call? Herzl! He had established himself as a promoter of Zionism through the publication of his book *The Jewish State* in 1896. The First

Zionist Congress elected Herzl to be the president of the World Zionist Organization.

Theodore Herzl devoted himself to seeking endorsement of the Zionist project from major governments. He sought out the sultan of the Ottoman Empire, Kaiser Wilhelm II of Germany, and Russian Minister of the Interior Viacheslav Plehve. The seeking of a charter for the Zionist Movement is generally called Political Zionism. We can apply the term to Cyrus the Great's decree as well. Cyrus gave an international license to the Jewish people to return to their homeland.

Theodore Herzl did not live to see the granting of a Zionist charter by a major world power. He died young, at the age of forty-four, without reaching that goal. Chaim Weizmann took up the effort. Weizmann was born in Russia in 1874. He moved to Germany then on to Switzerland, pursuing advanced studies in organic chemistry. In 1904 he moved to England to accept an academic position. While living in Germany, Weizmann became part of a circle of Zionist thinkers and activists. While growing in stature in his scientific field, his position in the Zionist movement was also elevated.

Weizmann's work in developing explosives for the British war effort during World War I brought him into contact with prominent British politicians. He took that opportunity to seek the support of the British government for the Zionist project of creating a Jewish state. After many meetings and much conversation, Weizmann succeeded in persuading the British government to act.

On November 2, 1917, the United Kingdom's foreign secretary, Arthur James Balfour, sent a letter to Lord Rothschild, a leader of the British Jewish community, for transmission to the Zionist Federation of Great Britain and Ireland. It proclaimed,

> His Majesty's government view with favour the establishment in Palestine of a national home for the Jewish people, and will use their best endeavours to facilitate the achievement of this object, it being clearly understood that nothing shall be done which may prejudice the civil and religious rights of existing non-Jewish communities in Palestine, or the rights and political status enjoyed by Jews in any other country.[1]

At that time Palestine was still part of the Ottoman Empire. The British government had no power to act in support of its Balfour Declaration.

1. Balfour, "Balfour Declaration."

But four weeks later, the British military forces led by General Edmund Allenby defeated the Ottoman troops and took possession of Palestine on behalf of the British Empire. In 1922 the League of Nations entrusted the British with the Mandate of Palestine.

In 1947 the British turned to the brand-new international organization of the United Nations to determine the long-term future of Palestine. On November 29, 1947, the United Nations approved the Palestine Partition Plan, also known as Resolution 181. The vote was thirty-three countries in favor, thirteen countries opposed, and ten countries abstaining. The resolution to create two states received the required support from two-thirds of the countries voting yes or no.

This resolution was the international charter that the advocates of Political Zionism had been seeking since the days of Herzl. We can see a direct line from the proclamation of King Cyrus that created the second Jewish commonwealth in the land of Israel to the UN resolution that created the third Jewish commonwealth.

Chapter 17

Jeremiah's Promise

THE PROPHET JEREMIAH ESCAPED to Egypt before the destruction of Jerusalem. So, he was not carried off to Babylon. From Egypt, Jeremiah sent a letter to the exiles in Babylon to reassure them that the covenant that God established with Abraham and Sarah still held. He wrote, "For thus says the ETERNAL: When Babylon's seventy years are over, I will take note of you and I will fulfill to you My promise of favor-to bring you back to this place" (Jer 29:10).

Jeremiah wanted the exiles to be certain to understand that their exile would be temporary, not permanent. He explained to them that even though the Temple had been destroyed, God's covenant was unbreakable.

When I read Jeremiah's promise of seventy years, I imagine that he is speaking poetically about a medium length of time, longer than the common biblical "forty years" but not a time without end. Jeremiah draws on another biblical image: "The span of our life is seventy years" (Ps 90:10). Some of the commentators take the number—seventy years—more literally, which creates a math problem. The destruction of the Temple took place in 586 BCE according to academic scholars. Scholars date Cyrus's proclamation to 538 BCE, only forty-eight years later. Rabbinic sources count the years between the destruction of the Temple and the proclamation of Cyrus slightly differently. They see the gap as fifty-two years, still eighteen years less than Jeremiah's promise. Rashi offers a solution in his comment to Ezra 1:1:

> And this is the accounting of how Israel returned to their land and built the foundation of the Temple even though they did not complete the construction in this time. We have found that it was fifty-two years from the exile of Zedkiah at which time the Temple was destroyed until the first year of the reign of Cyrus as king of Persia. And it was eighteen years after the first year of Cyrus that came the second year of Darius as king of Persia. This fulfilled the seventy years from the destruction of the Temple and the exile of Zedkiah until the second year of the reign of Darius when Israel resumed the construction of the Temple and completed it. And thus, it is explained in Seder Olam in Massechect Megilah and in this book as I have explained.

Other rabbinic sources offer slightly different ways of solving the math problem by counting not from the destruction of the Temple but from the earlier date of the Babylonians' conquest of Jerusalem. While I understand that the sages want to defend the literal truth of Jeremiah's promise, I believe that the exact math is not the heart of Jeremiah's message to the people as the exile begins.

Jeremiah's confident declaration that the people will return after seventy years in exile is the gift of hope. Jeremiah tells them that the destruction of the Temple in Jerusalem and the exile in Babylon is not the end of the story of the Jewish people. The prophetic messages of Ezekiel and Second Isaiah (chs. 40–55) center on the possibility of returning to the land of Israel. Using moving poetic images, Ezekiel and Second Isaiah inspired the exiles to imagine their future return. The most well-known of these messages is the vision of the valley of dry bones in Ezekiel:

> The hand of the ETERNAL came upon me. He took me out by the spirit of the ETERNAL and set me down in the valley. It was full of bones. . . . He said to me, "O mortal, can these bones live again?" I replied, "O ETERNAL God, only You know." Thus said the ETERNAL God to these bones: "I will cause breath to enter you and you shall live again. I will lay sinews upon you, and cover you with flesh, and form skin over you. And I will put breath into you, and you shall live again. And you shall know that I am the ETERNAL!" I prophesied as I had been commanded. And while I was prophesying, suddenly there was a sound of rattling, and the bones came together, bone to matching bone.
>
> I prophesied as He commanded me. The breath entered them, and they came to life and stood up on their feet, a vast multitude. And He said to me, "O mortal, these bones are the whole House of Israel. They say, 'Our bones are dried up, our hope is gone; we

> are doomed.' Prophesy, therefore, and say to them: Thus said the ETERNAL God: I am going to open your graves and lift you out of the graves, O My people, and bring you to the land of Israel." (Ezek 37:1, 3–12)

We find countless expressions of hope in popular culture. The classic 1972 disaster movie *The Poseidon Adventure* features Maureen McGovern confidently singing "The Morning After." The grand musical films produced during the Great Depression included upbeat visions of a better world to come expressed in songs such as "Pennies from Heaven." In the 1977 musical *Annie*, set in the depths of the Great Depression, Annie sings the very optimistic anthem "Tomorrow."

Hope provides the strength to continue to battle against "the slings and arrows of outrageous fortune."[1] The alternative to embracing hope is becoming a passive victim waiting to be consumed.

We know very little about the life of the people during the forty-eight years of the exile. We do know that they dreamed of returning to Jerusalem. Psalm 137 eloquently expresses the ongoing connection the people felt to the land of Israel:

> By the rivers of Babylon we sat and wept when we thought of Zion.
> There on the poplars we hung our lyres,
> our captors asked there us for songs,
> our tormentors for amusement
> "Sing us one of the songs of Zion!"
> How can we sing the songs of the ETERNAL while on alien soil?
> If I forget you, Jerusalem, let my right hand wither.
> let my tongue stick to my palate
> if I do not keep Jerusalem in memory, even at my happiest hour.
> (Ps 137:1–6)

We can see a parallel to this biblical expression of hope in Theodor Herzl's reflection on the First Zionist Congress, which took place in Basel, Switzerland, in 1897:

> Were I to sum up the Basel Congress in a word—which I shall guard against pronouncing publicly—it would be this: At Basel, I founded the Jewish State. If I said this out loud today, I would be answered by universal laughter. Perhaps in five years, certainly in fifty, everyone will know it.[2]

1. Shakespeare, *Hamlet*, act 3, scene 1, line 66.
2. Herzl, *Complete Diaries*, 224 (entry for Sept. 3, 1897).

Fifty years later, on November 29, 1947, the United Nations General Assembly voted to approve the Partition Plan to divide Palestine into two states. I certainly am not claiming that Herzl was a prophet predicting the future. But we think of him as a visionary. The State of Israel refers to him as *Chozeh Hamedinah*, "The Visionary of the State." The chamber of the Israeli Knesset contains a picture of only one person: Theodor Herzl.

What did the people in exile mean when they spoke of returning to Jerusalem? What did the exiles in Babylon mean twenty-five hundred years ago? What did the nineteenth- and twentieth-century Zionists mean? Did they express a wish to again live in the land of Israel, the place where their ancestors lived? Or were they expressing a more political wish to live again under Jewish government? Or were they expressing a wish to bring offerings to a rebuilt Temple in Jerusalem?

For the exiles in Babylonia, we have only one source: the Bible. The book of Ezra tells us that the returnees rebuilt the altar and the Temple to renew the offering of sacrifices. The book of Nehemiah describes rebuilding the walls and gates of Jerusalem to provide security. Full political independence was not a possibility. Judea was a small province of the powerful Persian Empire.

For the modern Zionists, we have many sources describing their dreams, thoughts, ideologies, and plans. Many hoped to create new Jews in the homeland. Only a small segment of the Zionists thought about rebuilding the Temple. They had a greater focus on returning to our homeland and creating a Jewish state. Hatikvah, the national anthem of Israel, proclaims, *Lihiyot am chofshi b'artzeinu*, "To be a free people in our land."

Naftali Hertz Imber wrote a nine-stanza poem, "Tikvatenu" (Our Hope), in 1878 in the town of Zolochiv, in what was then the Austro-Hungarian Empire (today it is in Ukraine). A few years later he made aliyah. In Palestine he recited his poem of hopeful yearning to the residents of the new Jewish towns. In 1887, a resident of Rishon L'Tziyon, Shmuel Cohen, put the words to a melody he knew from his childhood in Romania. Many people recognize the melody from a piece by Czech composer Bedrich Smetana. But Smetana did not create the melody line; he took it from a folk melody. As is often the case with folk melodies, it is difficult to say with complete confidence who actually created it.

In 1901, the Fifth World Zionist Congress concluded with the singing of Hatikva, making it the anthem of the movement. With small adjustments, Hatikva became the anthem of the State of Israel. It continues to express the hopes of the Jews to live securely in a state of their own.

In the coming chapters, we will continue to explore the story of the people returning from the Babylonian exile. Genuine political sovereignty was not a possibility. They would remain part of the Persian Empire. But the leaders of that empire provided many avenues for them to be a free people in their land in fulfillment of Jeremiah's promise.

Chapter 18

Babylonian Jews

The book of Ezra begins dramatically with the proclamation of the Persian king, Cyrus the Great, announcing to the exiled Judeans that they may return to their homes in Jerusalem. In Ezra 1:3 Cyrus declares, "Let anyone among you of His entire people, may his God be with him, go up to Jerusalem." Chapter 2 of Ezra lists the families that participated in this first wave of return. But all the exiled Judeans did not "as one arise" to go up to Jerusalem. Some portion of the people remained behind in Babylonia. Ezra and Nehemiah describe waves of the people returning to Jerusalem. After each wave of return, a portion of the people remained in exile.

What happened to the people who did not return? Did they assimilate into Babylonian society? Was their fate similar to the "Ten Lost Tribes" exiled from the Northern Kingdom?

After the death of King Solomon, the united kingdom of Israel divided into a Northern Kingdom of the ten tribes led by King Jeroboam and a Southern Kingdom of two tribes led by Solomon's son King Rehoboam. The two kingdoms existed as separate entities until the Assyrian Empire conquered that Northern Kingdom in 722 BCE.

In keeping with standard Assyrian empire building practice, the entire population of the Northern Kingdom was removed and replaced by peoples from elsewhere in the Assyrian Empire. As the Bible explains, "And the king of Assyria did carry away Israel unto Assyria, and put them in Halah and in Habor by the river of Gozan, and in the cities of the Medes" (2 Kgs 18:11).

We read additional details in another passage: "The king of Assyria brought people from Babylon, Kuthah, Avva, Hamath and Sepharvaim and settled them in the towns of Samaria to replace the Israelites. They took over Samaria and lived in its towns" (2 Kgs 17:24).

The members of these ten tribes disappeared into the populations of the places in which they were resettled. The term often used to describe them, "the ten lost tribes," is a misnomer. That term suggests that the tribes continued to exist but could not be found. This image has led to a variety of highly creative theories of discovering the "lost tribes." Writers have suggested that the "ten lost tribes" are the ancestors of the Maori of New Zealand, the Navajo of North America, and Bnei Menashe of India. While these origin stories may be entertaining, the truth is that the members of these ten tribes assimilated into the cultures and societies of the nations where they had been resettled. These tribes ceased to exist as a definable group.

The Babylonians took a different approach to creating empires than did the Assyrians. The Babylonians did not spread the exiles out. They maintained them in a clustered setting. As a result, the Judeans did not assimilate into Babylonian/Persian society. In fact, the community lasted for twenty-five hundred years. Throughout the Second Temple period a sizable Jewish community remained in Babylonia. After the destruction of the Second Temple the importance of this community increased. During the difficult Roman period some Jews fled east seeking safety and security. Eventually Babylonia became the center of Jewish life.

The history of the area on the banks of the Tigris and Euphrates Rivers is long and complex. In the era of Ezra/Nehemiah, Babylonia had been conquered by the Persians in 539 BCE, led by Cyrus the Great. The Persians ruled there until the arrival of Alexander the Great's army. Following the death of Alexander the Great, in 321 BCE, his empire split into four parts, each led by one of Alexander's generals. The portion including the Tigris and Euphrates valleys came under the control of Seleucus I Nicator. This territory that he and his successors led became known as the Seleucid Empire.

In 141 BCE the Parthians led by King Mithridates I conquered the eastern portion of the Seleucid Empire, the area that had been Babylonia. The Romans conquered the western portion of the Seleucid Empire, including the land of Israel in 63 BCE. Regular border wars continued between the Romans and the Parthians, but the Romans were never able to establish a long-term border beyond the lands along the Mediterranean

Sea. The Jews living in the Tigris and Euphrates valleys remained beyond the reach of the Roman Empire.

In 224 CE the Sasanian Empire replaced the Parthians as the rulers of the area under discussion. As the Eastern Roman Empire transformed into the Christian Byzantine Empire, the Sasanian army continued to maintain the border separating their lands from the territories under Roman-Byzantine control. Thus, these eastern Jews did not face the pressure to accept Christianity that the western Jews did. The Sasanians maintained their hold until the rise of the Islamic Empire in 651 CE.

The Abbasid Caliphate, which replaced the Umayyad Caliphate in 750 CE, built Baghdad on the banks of the Tigris River near the location of ancient Babylon to become the center of the Islamic world. While the political power of the Abbasid Caliphate declined over time with the rise of independent caliphates in the west, it remained the religious and cultural center until the arrival of the Mongols in 1258. The Mamluk Caliphate in Cairo became the power until the establishment of the Ottoman Empire in the 1500s. It is not a coincidence that while Baghdad was the center of Islamic society, it was also the center of Jewish life and learning. During the height of the Abbasid Caliphate, Jews saw the Geonim of the Baghdad area as the most respected sages of their time.

My son-in-law's father, Tzadok, who was born in Mosul, Iraq, told me that unlike European Jews who sat on their suitcases always ready to move from place to place, the Jews of Iraq arrived in there in 586 BCE and remained in place until 1951. His family all came to Israel in 1951 together with almost all of the Iraqi Jewish community. In the first three years of the state, 120,000 Jews came to Israel from Iraq.

The big question which all this history raises is this: Why didn't all the exiled Judeans come back to the land of Israel in the waves of return described in Ezra/Nehemiah? And why in the subsequent centuries did the Jewish population of the Tigris and Euphrates valleys grow? To answer these questions, we can look at more recent events.

The assassination of Russian Czar Alexander II in 1881 triggered a series of pogroms which motivated a mass movement of Jews to leave the Russian Empire. From 1881 until the beginning of World War I in 1914, about three million Eastern European Jews came to America. During the same time period 65,000 Eastern European Jews immigrated to Palestine, then under Ottoman control. Since the establishment of the State of Israel in 1948 some American Jews have moved there, but the vast majority have chosen to remain in the United States. Currently about

190,000 American citizens live in Israel while six million American Jews choose to remain in the United States.

Why did millions of Eastern European Jews go to America 1881–1914, while only thousands came to Eretz Yisrael? The immigrants saw America as the land of economic opportunity, a perfect place to build a new, prosperous life. In contrast, the Ottoman-controlled land of Israel seemed dangerous and economically backwards. Why do American Jews remain in the United States? We feel comfortable and secure here. We have had economic success, and we feel at home in the "land of the free and the home of the brave." I do not feel like an outsider in America. As I have indicated in other chapters I feel profound connections to the land, people, and State of Israel. But I also feel fully American.

I feel connected to American history, including events which happened before my family came to his country. For a number of years, I read book after book about the Civil War. Some years ago, my son Gideon was in Virginia with his wife, Molly, and Molly's parents for her graduation from the FBI Academy. One day Gideon and Molly's parents visited the Chancellorsville Battlefield. Gideon called me, and I was able to guide them by cell phone as they walked, explaining how the battle took place. I have not yet been there myself, but I knew the battle so well I could visualize where they were standing and what they were seeing.

I am very engaged in community and political life. We have held events in our home in support of candidates for office. We hosted Jeanne Simon, the wife of Senator Paul Simon, in support of his reelection campaign. We hosted Dick Durbin in his first campaign to become a US Senator. In 1992 I was on the ballot to be a delegate to the Democratic National Convention pledged to Senator Tom Harkin. In 2008 I was a founder of Rabbis for Obama. In more recent years I have been active on the local level as a leader of DuPage United, working to build affordable and accessible supportive housing in our community.

I have comfortable places to sit where I feel at home. I love going with my son Gideon to Wrigley Field via the Blue and Red Lines of the El to sit in seats 5 and 6 of the second row of section 421R to watch the Chicago Cubs. In retirement from my synagogue position, I have become the "unofficial campus rabbi" of Wheaton College. I have an office in Billy Graham Hall. I enjoy sitting in the lodge at Olin-Sang-Ruby Union-Institute in Wisconsin, playing American folk songs on my banjo.

I feel deep bonds to the people, land, and State of Israel, but I have chosen to remain in America. I imagine that a similar dynamic moved the

Babylonian Jews of Ezra's and Nehemiah's time to remain on the banks of the Tigris and Euphrates Rivers. They had created new lives in Babylonia. The generations that had been born there felt secure and at home. Sitting in my home in Illinois I understand why Jews of Ezra's and Nehemiah's time chose to remain sitting in their homes in Babylonia.

Chapter 19

The First Jew

IF I WERE TO ask a Jewish group of adults or children, "Who was the first Jew?" They would respond, "Abraham," or, "Abraham and Sarah." No one would give me any other answer. So, this response must be correct, right? No! It is most certainly wrong. Abraham and Sarah were not Jews. The term *Jew*, or in Hebrew *yehudi*, comes from the name of one of their great-grandchildren, Judah (*Yehudah*).

The Torah tells us about many generations of our people who lived after Judah. Would they have known that they were Jews, *yehudim*? No! The Torah never uses the term *yehudim* to describe the people. The Torah generally uses *bnei yisrael*, translated as "Children of Israel" or "Israelites," to label the entire nation. The alternative is *ivrim*, translated as "Hebrews." Early in the book of Exodus Moses sees two members of our people struggling. The text describes them as *ivrim*, "Hebrews" (Exod 2:13).

None of the people we meet in the Torah would have thought of themselves as Jews. If you had asked Moses or Miriam if they were *yehudim*, perhaps they might have understood you to be asking them about their tribal identity. They might respond that they were members of the tribe of Levi, not of the tribe of Judah.

After the conquest of the land in the time of Joshua, the term *Judah* became a geographic title for the area in which the tribe of Judah settled. Some texts describing the events of King David's reign use the term *Judah* to label the southern portion of his kingdom. For example,

> David was thirty years old when he became king, and he reigned forty years. In Hebron he reigned over Judah seven years and six months, and in Jerusalem he reigned over all Israel and Judah thirty-three years. (2 Sam 5:4–5)

Following the death of King Solomon, the united kingdom divided into two: the Northern Kingdom of ten tribes known as Israel, and the Southern Kingdom of two tribes known as Judah. The Hebrew Bible does not use the term *Jew/yehudi* to describe anybody during this period.

In the book of Jonah, during the big storm the sailors ask Jonah, "Tell us, you who have brought this misfortune upon us, what is your business? Where have you come from? What is your country, and of what people are you?" (Jon 1:8). Jonah does not identify himself as a *yehudi*. He does not say, *Yehudi anochi*, "I am a Jew." Rather he says, *Ivri anochi*, "I am a Hebrew" (Jon 1:9).

The term *yehudi* does appear in Nehemiah in its plural form. "There was a great outcry by the common folk and their wives raised against their brother [*hayehudim*]" (Neh 5:1). The JPS and NRSV both translate the term *hayehudim* in Nehemiah as *Jews*. But it probably should be translated as *Judeans* and understood as a geographic term, as people of the Persian province of Judea. It could also be understood as a tribal designation: members of the tribe of Judah.

The term *yehudim*, in various forms, appears in the Hebrew Bible a total of seventy-two times. All of these occurrences are in texts that we can confidently claim were written during the Second Temple period after the return from the exile. I see the use of the word *yehudim* as a marker that a text was written after the return from the exile.

The later chapters of Jeremiah often use the term (e.g., Jer 32:12). The JPS translates it there as *Judeans*. Similarly, the later chapters of 2 Kings use the term a few times (e.g., 2 Kgs 25:25). The JPS translates it there as *Judeans*. Scholars agree that these late chapters of Jeremiah and 2 Kings were written during the Second Temple period. They include other words and linguistic forms typical of texts of that period.

Of the seventy-two times the word *yehudi* appears in the Hebrew Bible, forty-eight of the appearances are in the book of Esther. Let's look at the first time *yehudi* appears there in the book of Esther.

> In the fortress Shushan lived a Jew [*ish yehudi*], by the name of Mordecai son of Jair, son of Shimei, son of Kish a Benjaminite. (Esth 2:5)

Here the term *yehudi* cannot be a geographic term, describing where Mordecai lived. The sentence begins by telling us he lived in Shushan. Also, the term cannot be conveying his tribal origin because the verse explicitly states that Mordecai was from the tribe of Benjamin. I believe that the use of the term *yehudi* here in Esther conveys more or less the same meaning as the term does today. The text is telling us that Mordecai was a member of the Jewish people who followed Jewish religious practices. So, while it might be an overstatement to claim that Mordecai was the first Jew, I can confidently state that Mordecai is the first person that the Hebrew Bible identifies as a Jew.

This term, *yehudi*, develops out of our experience in exile. Waves of our people went up to Jerusalem from Babylonian exile, but some remained in exile. The Esther story grows out of the experiences of those Jews who chose to remain in exile. Translating *hayehudim* in Neh 5:1 to mean "Jews" would be an anachronism. The concept of using the term *yehudim* to identify Jews as a religious group had not yet fully formed at the time the book of Nehemiah was written.

Often people use words imprecisely. After I retired from my longtime pulpit, I spent the high holidays leading services for a very small congregation in the modest central Illinois city of Decatur. The day after Yom Kippur the first part of my drive home was on a two-lane country road past farms of the Illinois prairie. It was a bright, sunny fall day. The cornfields had been harvested, but the stalks of the plants had not yet been cut down. I was in a good mood. I felt positive about having helped the small congregation maintain its ability to function. I felt good about the opportunity to still be a rabbi. As I watched the corn stalks move with the breeze. I saw them as amber waves of grain. Driving home from Decatur after Yom Kippur I felt I was driving through "America the Beautiful."

Later it was pointed out to me that when Katherine Lee Bates composed "America the Beautiful" she was thinking of the Kansas wheat fields that she had seen on her 1893 train trip from Boston to Pikes Peak in Colorado Springs, not Illinois cornfields. I had gotten carried away by my enthusiasm to blur the meaning of the phrase "amber waves of grain."

Recently a minister friend of mine called to consult on the precise meaning of the word *kosher*. She asked how her church could purchase kosher food. She explained to me that a new member of her staff had advertised that their Vacation Bible School would be serving kosher and halal meals so that everybody could attend. My friend wanted to know what would be involved for them to fulfill the promise of kosher food.

While I did explain to my friend how they could secure kosher food, I began by telling her that I was quite sure that no family who kept kosher would enroll their children in her church's Vacation Bible School. The church's young staff member, in his enthusiasm to promote the church's gracious hospitality, had used terms from other religions in an odd manner. In translating words from one language or context to another we should strive to be accurate.

This challenge of translating *yehudim* also emerges in Christian texts. The Gospel of John uses the Greek word *Ioudaia* (Ιουδαια). While it is generally translated as "Jews," a careful examination of the context of each use of this word yields varying meanings. In John 7:1 the text states, "After this Jesus went about in Galilee; he would not go about in Judea, because the [*Ioudaia*] sought to kill him." The term here could not mean "Jews," for the people in Galilee were also Jews. In John 7:1 the word *Ioudaia* must have the geographic meaning of "Judeans."

The use of the word *yehudim* in Neh 5:1 is an early appearance of the word. Its meaning shifted between the time in which the book of Nehemiah was written and the later composition of the book of Esther. The book of Nehemiah extols the virtues of those who returned from exile. Professor Elsie Stern explains, "Esther is a cautionary tale about life in the diaspora."[1] While contemporary Jews have great fun reading this Megillah each Purim, the original meaning of the book of Esther was a summons to the Jews who stubbornly remained in Babylonia to return to Jerusalem, where they could safely live as Judeans.

1. Stern, "Megillat Esther."

RITUALS

Chapter 20

Understanding the Sukkah

In the first chapter of this book, we discussed the importance of the public Torah reading found in the eighth chapter of Nehemiah. After that public reading of the Torah scroll, the people began to study the scroll's contents. They discovered a commandment to build sukkot (booths):

> They found written in the Torah that the Eternal had commanded Moses that the Israelites must dwell in booths during the festival of the seventh month. . . . The whole community that returned from captivity made booths, and dwelt in the booths—the Israelites had not done so from the days of Joshua the son of Nun to that day. And there was very great gladness. (Neh 8:14, 17)

These verses seem to say that building a sukkah was a new ritual created in the time of Ezra and Nehemiah by the generation that had returned from exile. These verses suggest that the judges and the kings—Deborah, Gideon, David, and Solomon—had not built sukkot. These verses imply that all the prophets of the First Temple period from Elijah and Elisha to Isaiah and Jeremiah had never entered a sukkah. Could this be true? Is it possible that this verse means exactly what it says?

Over the centuries many voices have been raised to argue that this verse should not be taken literally. They insist that it could not be possible for the construction of the sukkah to be something new in the time of Ezra and Nehemiah. Accepting the plain meaning of this verse would upset their method of understanding the Bible. We find this type of response in rabbinic sources and among modern Bible scholars. We will look first at rabbinic authorities.

The sages address this question in the Babylonian Talmud Masechet Arachin 32b. The Talmud explains that we should not take Neh 8:17 to be talking specifically about who built a sukkah. It contends that the reference to Joshua in the Nehemiah verse reflects the dedication of the land of Israel to God as holy by Joshua. This dedication ceased to be in effect when the Babylonians destroyed the First Temple. Now through the efforts of Ezra and Nehemiah the land was once again dedicated to God.

As often is the case in the Talmud, a second voice objects to this first opinion. This second voice says that the holiness of the land endured even after the destruction of the Temple. The change expressed in the Nehemiah verse is that during the First Temple period the people regularly gave in to the temptation to engage in idolatry. But by the Second Temple period this problem had disappeared. The Talmud argues that the description of Ezra and his followers dwelling in sukkot should be understood as metaphoric language expressing that they remained loyal to the One God of Israel; they did not serve other gods, as did the previous generations.

The Talmud points out that in the Nehemiah verse Joshua's name is spelled without a *he*. It is rendered *yeishua* rather than the typical spelling *yehoshua*. The removal of the *he* in this context is to express Joshua's lack of full devotion to God in that he allowed idolatry to continue to exist in the land. The letter *he* is one of the four letters in the divine name. Its inclusion in a person's name often expresses that person's deep devotion to God.[1]

While the later rabbinic authorities—Ralbag, Metzudat David, and Malbim—each followed their own creative path in explaining away this apparent addition of new ritual created at the time of the return from exile, they all began with the assumption that the verse could not be literally true.

Some modern academic Bible scholars have also wrestled with this verse in a similar way. I will share two examples from prominent authorities.

H. G. H. Williamson wrote,

1. The names of many people in the Bible express their relationship to God. In Gen 17:5 God add a *he* to Abram's name. His new name, Abraham, expresses his closeness to God.

> Even if booths were erected at the festival before Ezra's time, they were merely part of the harvest aspect of the festival. . . . Now, however, the significance of the booths in terms of Israel's history were introduced. For the first time in centuries, they were erected in Jerusalem as a reminder of the wilderness wanderings.[2]

Joseph Blenkinsopp wrote,

> If, therefore, we are to look for any historical innovation, it is not in the celebration of the festival itself, which already was well established or even in the dwelling in booths implied in the very name of the festival but in the use of the species to construct and cover the *sukkah*.[3]

Both Williamson and Blenkinsopp create arguments to avoid taking Neh 8:17 at face value. The scholarly discourse and the rabbinic tradition both work hard to reject the point the Nehemiah text proclaims.

I see this key verse in Nehemiah in a completely different way. I have no problem accepting Neh 8:17 as it is written. I read the verse as an accurate reporting of the creation of this new ritual of building sukkot, never before performed in Jerusalem.

We have known the meaning of a sukkah since we were children. To understand what is truly going on here I have to ask you to set side those childhood lessons and follow my explanation of the creation of the ritual.

STEP ONE: BEFORE NEHEMIAH, NOBODY IN THE BIBLE ACTUALLY BUILT A SUKKAH

Deuteronomy 16 mentions the festival, calling it the festival of Sukkot, but it does not mention anybody dwelling in a sukkah:

> After the ingathering from your threshing floor and your vat, you shall hold the Feast of Booths for seven days. You shall rejoice in your festival your son and your daughter, your male and your female slaves, the Levite, the stranger, the fatherless, and the widow in your communities. You shall hold the festival for the ETERNAL your God in the place that the ETERNAL will choose [Jerusalem]; for the ETERNAL your God will bless all

2. Williamson, *Ezra-Nehemiah*, 296.
3. Blenkinsopp, *Ezra-Nehemiah*, 292.

> your crops and all your undertakings and you shall have nothing but joy. (Deut 16:13–15)

Judges 21:19 attests to the celebration of *chag*, "festival," but does not mention the construction of actual booths. First Samuel 1:3 describes Elkanah making an annual pilgrimage to Shiloh to offer sacrifices. Most readers assume that this refers to Sukkot, but the text does not specifically mention *chag*. Nowhere does this story describe the construction of actual booths.

The only place the Hebrew Bible mentions the actual construction of a sukkah on Sukkot is Neh 8:17 and Lev 23:42–43, which is based on the Nehemiah verse as I explained earlier in chapter 3.

The entire Hebrew Bible describes only one person actually dwelling in a sukkah. In the fourth chapter of the book of Jonah, the prophet builds a sukkah to protect himself from the sun. This event has nothing to do with the festival.

So why doesn't the Bible mention anyone building a sukkah to celebrate Sukkot before the exile? The ritual did not yet exist.

STEP TWO: THE BIBLE STRESSES THE CONNECTIONS BETWEEN THE TEMPLE AND SUKKOT

King Solomon dedicated the First Temple on the festival of Sukkot:

> Then Solomon convoked the elders of Israel—all the heads of the tribes and the ancestral chieftains of the Israelites—before King Solomon in Jerusalem, to bring up the Ark of the Covenant of the ETERNAL from the city of David, that is Zion. All the men of Israel gathered before King Solomon at the Feast [of Booths] in the month Ethanim—that is the seventh month. (1 Kgs 8:1–2)

When the Maccabees cleansed the Temple they wanted to follow King Solomon's example and rededicate it on Sukkot, but it was not ready in time. So, they created a "second Sukkot" later in the fall, patterned on Sukkot:

> They rededicated the Temple on the twenty-fifth day of the month of Kislev, the same day of the same month on which the Temple had been desecrated by the Gentiles. The happy celebration lasted eight days, like the Festival of Booths, and the people remembered how only a short time before, they had spent the

> Festival of Booths wandering like wild animals in the mountains and living in caves. But now, carrying green palm branches and sticks decorated with ivy, they paraded around, singing grateful praises to Him who had brought about the purification of His own Temple. Everyone agreed that the entire Jewish nation should celebrate this festival each year. (2 Macc 10:5–8)

Many Jews today do not know that Hanukkah grows out of Sukkot. But it is clear from these two stories of the dedication of the Temple and the rededication of the Temple that we should see the close connection of the Temple and the festival of Sukkot.

STEP THREE: THE MEANING OF LIVING IN BOOTHS IN THE WILDERNESS

The section of Lev 23 which I have identified as having been composed in the time of Nehemiah includes a reference to the forty years in the wilderness:

> You shall live in booths seven days; all the citizens in Israel shall live in booths; in order that future generations may know that I made the Israelite people live in booths when I brought them out of the land of Egypt, I am The ETERNAL your God. (Lev 23:42–43)

I do not understand this verse to be referring only to the years the Israelites lived in the wilderness following the exodus from Egypt. I think that it is referring to the years in exile in the "wilderness" of Babylonia.

Why did the custom of build sukkot arise during the exile? I believe that during the years in Babylonian exile, the people built booths on the festival of Sukkot to recall the destroyed Temple which had originally been dedicated on that festival by King Solomon. The booths were a *zeicher l'mikdash*, a "memorial for the Temple." Building a sukkah each fall for the festival of Sukkot helped the exiles maintain their religious identity in Babylonia.

When the people returned from exile, they continued this ritual that they had begun in Babylonia. They read into it the additional meaning of the earlier forty years in the wilderness. This connection between the two periods in the wilderness served to create a useful way of understanding their recent suffering in Babylonia.

During the years in Babylonia the sukkah reminded the people of the Temple they hoped to rebuild when they would return to Jerusalem. Once they returned to the land and rebuilt the Temple, they continued to annually construct a sukkah and began to dwell in it to remind them of their years in exile in Babylon and the forty years in the wilderness.

The meaning of the sukkah has shifted over the centuries. With the passage of years, the sense of connection to the first exile in Babylon has diminished. Because of the length of the second exile and the level of suffering we experienced in Europe, we no longer identify with Babylonian exile. When we speak of the forty years in the wilderness, we imagine the Sinai Peninsula. We do not connect that term with Babylon in the way that the people of the early Second Temple era did. As a result, we have lost the ability to see the sukkah as a reminder of the destroyed Temple.

Chapter 21

Religious Life During the Exile in Babylonia

As we saw in chapter 13 the first wave of returnees to Jerusalem quickly set about the task of rebuilding the altar in Jerusalem on the foundation of the old altar in order to resume offering sacrifices to the One God. What had been their religious life during the exile in Babylon? Did the exiles offer sacrifices in Babylon?

In the early biblical period, the patriarchs offered sacrifices in various locations. After the conquest of the land led by Joshua, the tabernacle was placed at Shiloh, but sacrifices were not limited to that location. Levites continued to offer sacrifices at rural high places even after the construction of the Temple in Jerusalem. This practice continued until the reign of King Josiah.

The Bible in 2 Kgs 22:3–13 tells the story of the discovery of a scroll in the walls of the Temple during the reign of King Josiah. After reading the contents of this new book King Josiah orders the destruction of the rural high places where the people had been bringing their sacrifices. Most scholars see this "discovered" text as the book of Deuteronomy. That book of the Torah returns time and again to the commandment that sacrifices can only be brought in the one spot that God will designate. Josiah's reformation put an end to offering sacrifices outside of the Temple in Jerusalem.

Following this Deuteronomic approach one could conclude that no sacrifices could have been offered anywhere during the years between the destruction of the Temple and its rebuilding. So, it is surprising to learn that

Judean exiles in Egypt did offer sacrifices. In response to the destruction of the Temple in 586 BCE some of the people fled the Babylonians by going to Egypt. Scholars have evidence from papyrus documents of a community of Judean exiles who built a temple on the island of Elephantine in the Nile River in southern Egypt. Subsequent archeological excavations have confirmed the existence of a Jewish temple as the documents describe.

This discovery in Egypt raises the question, Did the Judeans in exile in Babylonia build a similar Temple? We have no evidence that they did. Scholars have not discovered any written record of such a Temple. Also there have been no excavations yielding evidence of a Judean Temple in Babylon. One might respond by saying papyrus documents were exclusively an Egyptian phenomenon and that there has been much more archeological work done in Egypt than in modern Iraq, ancient Babylon. The Babylonian exile did produce a source lacking in Egypt of that period, biblical books.

The biblical book of Isaiah contains the words of three different prophets, generally called First Isaiah (chs. 1–39), Second Isaiah (chs. 40–55), and Third Isaiah (chs. 56–66). The prophecies of First Isaiah contain harsh criticism of the leaders and the people during the last years of the First Temple period. Third Isaiah was written after the return from exile. The prophet we call Second Isaiah spoke to the people in exile in Babylonia to bring a message of hope. This prophet reassures the people that as they turn to God, so God will return to them.

If we carefully look at the chapters of the book of Isaiah designated as Second Isaiah we do not find any mention of the people offering sacrifices in Babylonia. Ezekiel was also a prophet who carried God's message of hope to the people in exile. His most well-known image is that of the valley of dry bones. Ezekiel also does not mention the people offering sacrifices in Babylonia.

Psalm 137, which I will explore in more detail in the next chapter, specifically responds to the question of worshiping the One God of Israel in Babylonian exile. In that psalm the Babylonians taunt the exiled Judeans saying, "Sing us one of the songs of Zion" (verse 3). The people respond, "How can we sing the ETERNAL's song in a strange land?" (verse 4). We might expect a different response if the people were engaged in regularly bringing offerings to the ETERNAL at a temple in Babylonia. While I cannot say with 100 percent confidence that there was no Jewish Temple in Babylonia during the exile, the complete lack of evidence for its existence leads me to conclude that it probably did not exist.

So, how did the exiles express their connection to the One God of Israel? A quick response would be to say that they must have done something. We know that they maintained their religious/national identity. I have argued in chapter 20 that they built temporary booths on the festival of Sukkot in remembrance of the Temple in Jerusalem. Some scholars imagine that they may have gathered to study or worship in what might be described as proto-synagogues. We should limit our speculative imagination to say that we do not really know how they expressed their day-to-day religious selves.

We do know that a portion of the people engaged in an important step in the development of the Torah as we know it. They spent their time in exile composing literature which we now know of as the P source. The Documentary Hypothesis explains that the Torah is composed of four documents: the E document, written in the Northern Kingdom of Israel before its destruction in 722 BCE; the J document, written in the Southern Kingdom of Judah during the same time period (the E and J documents make up most of the books of Genesis, Exodus, and Numbers); the D document is the book of Deuteronomy, composed during the reign of King Josiah.

I believe that the P document was written during the Babylonian exile. It includes all of Leviticus and portions of Genesis, Exodus, and Numbers. In the P source God is more transcendent. The P source contains no blatant anthropomorphisms. We do not hear of God's hand or God's back in the P source. P does not include stories of talking animals or angels.

The P source presents the priests as intermediaries between God and the people. In the P source, there are no sacrifices until Aaron is consecrated as the high priest. P elevates the status of Aaron. J and E texts report God speaking to Moses. In the P source, God speaks to Moses and Aaron. In the P source the tent of meeting becomes a key location. According to the P source proper sacrifices brought to a proper priest will free you from your sins.

The first sixteen chapters of Leviticus describe in great detail the proper way to bring a whole range of sacrifices. I and many scholars believe that these texts were written in exile as a response to the destruction of the First Temple. These sixteen chapters of Leviticus lay out how the people will properly bring sacrifices if they are allowed to return. It seems to me that the text acknowledges that during the latter years of the First Temple period, sacrifices were offered improperly. The P source says to God, "If you give us a second chance, we will get it right."

We refer to chapters 17–26 of Leviticus as the Holiness Code. The scholars that I find persuasive see the Holiness Code as a subsection of the P source, also written during the Babylonian exile. The most well-known chapter of this section is Lev 19, which begins with God's call: "Holy you shall be because I the ETERNAL your God am Holy" (verse 2). It continues with examples of how to lead a holy life: avoiding stealing, gossiping, standing idle while your neighbor suffers. It urges us to "love your neighbor as yourself."

These moral instructions can also be understood as a response to the destruction of the First Temple. Isaiah, Hosea, and Jeremiah proclaimed that the amoral behavior of the people during the last decades of the First Temple period would bring great suffering to the people. Sitting in exile the people proclaim through the Holiness Code, "If we are allowed to return, we will lead better lives."

Often when people survive difficult moments in their lives, they make changes to avoid repeating the trouble. Living in the Midwest, thunderstorms are a part of every summer. While we know enough to come in out of the rain, few people have taken the precaution to add lightning rods to their homes. Some years ago, lightning struck the home of one of the families in the congregation, setting it on fire. When they rebuilt their home, they placed lightning rods on the high points of their home. Other families in the congregation followed their lead.

The generation that been carried into exile by the Babylonians felt they had been struck by the lightning of God's anger punishing them for leading corrupt lives and offering improper sacrifices. They composed the P source to express their commitment to hewing to God's will in their religious and personal lives.

The P source adds to the holidays mentioned in the earlier sources. It presents the fall holidays of Rosh Hashanah and Yom Kippur as an opportunity for the people to express atonement for sin. Dwelling in exile, the people accepted responsibility for the wayward behavior that so angered God in the final years of the First Temple period. The people do not cry out in anger to God saying, "How could you do this to us?" Rather they humbly say, "Because of our sins we were exiled from our land." This humility coupled with the commitment to offer proper sacrifices and lead proper lives as described in the newly written P documents provides the foundation for a successful return from exile.

Chapter 22

Redefining Time

EVERY SOCIETY DIVIDES AND labels time. Communities within societies have their own ways of counting time. The manner in which we mark time defines who we are and how we see ourselves.

Sports writer Tom Boswell's excellent book of essays about baseball, *Why Time Begins on Opening Day*, resonates with me. As a baseball fan I greatly appreciate the title of Boswell's book.

During my Minnesota childhood I remember my father going up north each spring with friends from work for the May 15 opening of the walleyed pike fishing season. They wanted to be on the lake as the season began at dawn. It was, for them, the first day of the year.

I have seen signs in bars counting down the days to St. Patrick's Day. I know young people who spend the winter counting down the days to the beginning of the next session of summer camp.

In Western society we count our birthdays. Birthday parties become major events in the lives of children. In the age of Facebook, adults receive birthday greetings from a wide circle of friends. My daughter Abby refers to February as "our family's birthday month." Two of her daughters and her husband's birthdays fall within a few weeks in February. Neither the Hebrew Bible nor the Christian Greek Scripture mention a single person celebrating their birthday. Newspapers often identify a person through mentioning their age. The Bible rarely does so.

The Jewish counting of years comes from Seder Olam, which is attributed to Rabbi Yosi ben Halafta, a second-century sage from the land of Israel. Scholars agree that in truth Seder Olam was written centuries later and attached to the name of Yosi ben Halafta to give it greater authority. This is a common dynamic in medieval Jewish texts. The most well-known example is attributing the Zohar to Simon bar Yohai of second-century Galilee even though it was in truth written by Moses de Leon in thirteenth-century Spain.

The Hebrew Bible has its methods for counting time. The Bible does not use the traditional Jewish calendar method for counting years. It only refers the years between events, such as the 430 years between the arrival in Egypt and the exodus.

Almost all of the Hebrew Bible refers to the months by number, not by the names familiar to us. The Bible counts the month of the exodus from Egypt as the first month. So, in Lev 23:5–6 we read, "In the first month, on the fourteenth day of the month at twilight there will be a Passover offering to the ETERNAL and on the fifteenth day of that month the ETERNAL's Feast of Unleavened Bread."

The book of Numbers begins, "On the first day of the second month . . ." In chapter 10, verse 12, of Numbers we read, "In the second year, on the twentieth day of the second month . . ."

The now familiar Hebrew names of the months appear in the Bible for the first time in Ezra/Nehemiah. The opening verse of Nehemiah states, "The words of Nehemiah son of Hacaliah: 'In the month of Kislev in the twentieth year, while I was in the citadel of Susa . . .'" (Neh 1:1).

The Bible uses Kislev only here and in Zechariah, a late prophet. The next chapter of Nehemiah describes the events which led to Nehemiah going up to Jerusalem. "In the month of Nisan in the twentieth year of King Artaxerxes, when wine was brought for him, I took the wine and gave it to the king" (Neh 2:1–5). The Bible uses Nisan only here and in Esther, a later Second Temple text. A few chapters later we read of Nehemiah's success in Jerusalem: "So, the wall was completed on the twenty-fifth of Elul, in fifty-two days" (Neh 6:15).

This is the only use of Elul in the entire Hebrew Bible. The book of Ezra describes the completion of the rebuilding of the Temple: "The House was finished on the third day of the month of Adar in the sixth year of the reign of King Darius" (Ezra 6:15). The Bible mentions Adar only here and in the book of Esther.

Ezra and Nehemiah do not explain or introduce their use of these new names of the months. The authors seem to assume that their readers will recognize and understand the new terminology. I imagine that by the time of Ezra/Nehemiah these month names were no longer new. By

Nehemiah's time these months must have already have been fully integrated into the thinking and vocabulary of our people. While each of these month names derives from Assyrian/Akkadian month names, I am not aware of any source objecting to these month names as not Jewish. Jews do not see these month names as foreign words. We embrace the names as the authentic Jewish names of the months.

We do not view customs and culture brought back from Babylon as foreign. They have been fully incorporated into Jewish life. We properly want to zealously protect Jewish identity. But we should understand that much of what we consider authentically Jewish once was new and borrowed in from other cultures.

What many of us think of as "Jewish food" was not actually created by Jews. The delicacies treasured by Ashkenazi Jews—blintzes, borscht, kugel, and brisket—are in truth Eastern European food.

I enjoy Israeli food. I have a favorite hummus spot in Haifa, Hummus Eliezer. It is around the corner from my daughter's home in Ramat Allon near the Technion. It is small hole-in-the-wall with a few tables inside and a few more outside. What do they serve? Hummus!

I have a favorite falafel place in Jerusalem. It is at the corner of King George Street and Agripas Street in the center of the city. I am not claiming it is the best, simply my favorite. Certainly, one of the reasons I enjoy eating there is that this falafel spot has not changed since my student days fifty years ago. I also have a favorite shawarma place in Rehovot where I stop for lunch with groups after visiting Machon Ayalon, the underground ammunition factory.

Are all of these Israeli foods actually Israeli? We know that they are Middle Eastern foods. Jews who live far from Israel eat them as "Jewish foods." Jewish summer camps in North America serve these Middle Eastern culinary treats as Israeli food. Synagogues include them as authentic Jewish food. Because the process of their adoption by Jews is still recent, we remain aware of their origin. We can easily trace the process of their becoming part of Jewish life.

The process of choosing what elements of host cultures to incorporate into our lives continues. We can see this process in how time is labeled and measured in Israel today. In many ways the country runs on Jewish time. The Jewish Shabbat is the day of rest for the country. As sundown on Friday approaches business and public transportation begins to shut down. On Fridays, flower sellers can be seen on many street corners offering their wares for Shabbat dinner tables.

Jewish holidays impact the life of the Israeli society. Evidence of Purim, Hanukkah, Tu Bishvat can be seen in the streets and the stores. During Hanukkah sufganiyot (donuts) stands pop up all over the country. On Yom Kippur even fully secular Israelis leave their cars at home. The streets in Israel on Yom Kippur are taken over by children riding bicycles.

On Israel's Memorial Day a siren sounds at ten o'clock in the morning. People stop right where they are standing. Drivers stop their cars and get out and stand. The same ritual takes place the week before on the Yom Hashoah, the Holocaust Memorial Day.

But in other ways Israel operates on the Western calendar. The school year follows the Western calendar. Schools open in Israel each fall on September 1, not on the first day of the Hebrew month of Cheshvan one week after the conclusion of the fall holidays. Israelis get their paychecks by the Western months and pay their taxes in Israel by the Western calendar year.

The role of the Jewish calendar varies widely among North American Jews. There was a period during my youthful romantic Zionist period when I kept my watch set to Israeli time. I have calmed down, but I am always aware of the eight-hour time difference between Chicago and Haifa. American cultural realities have been incorporated into Jewish religious life. Many Jewish families exchange Hanukkah gifts. American guitar melodies have been accepted as authentic Jewish expressions. The cantorial school of the Reform movement is named in memory of Debbie Friedman, the pioneer of guitar-accompanied Jewish worship music.

We generally view Ezra and Nehemiah as a single unit. I regularly use "Ezra/Nehemiah" to refer to them. But in their style of referring to the months we can see a distinct contrast. In all but one case, the book of Ezra uses the "old-fashioned" numerical biblical method of counting months. The book of Nehemiah includes only the "new" method of using the Babylonian names for the months. I imagine that as an officer of the Persian court, Nehemiah was more fully acculturated to the Persian world. In these two books we can see the "seam" in the garment of Jewish history. Jewish culture is not fixed and unchanging. It is always adjusting to new realities and influences. The shift in the naming of months is another way in which Ezra and Nehemiah mark a pivot point in the development of Jewish life.

Chapter 23

The Right Song

CHAPTER 3 OF EZRA describes the rebuilding of the altar in Jerusalem and the laying of the foundation of the Temple. The text says, "They sang songs extolling and praising the ETERNAL, 'For God is good, the divine steadfast love is everlasting'" (Ezra 3:11).

What were the people singing? Rashi tells us, "They sang the psalms of David." The excerpt included in the text of Ezra is very similar to a well-known verse from Psalms: "Praise the ETERNAL who is good, whose steadfast love is everlasting" (Ps 106:1).

Readers may recognize this verse in Hebrew from the Hallel prayers. During services on the festivals, we sing, *Hodo l'adonia ki tov, ki l'olam chasdo*. The Ezra verse in the original Hebrew reads, *B'halleil uv'hodot l'adonia ki tov, ki l'olam chasdo*. The verses are almost identical. The phrase *ki l'olam chasdo*, "whose steadfast love is everlasting," occurs several times in Psalms: 107:1; 118:1, 29; 136:1. We should not be surprised by the similarity of the words in Ezra and the words in the psalms' verses.

What else would they sing? They sang the official Temple songs, the psalms that had been part of the Temple rituals before the exile. It seems that during the exile they had not sung these Temple songs. Psalm 137 describes how the Babylonians taunted the people in exile:

> By the rivers of Babylon,
> There we sat down, yea, we wept,
> When we remembered Zion.
> Upon the willows in the midst thereof
> We hanged up our harps.

For there they that led us captive asked of us words of song,
And our tormentors asked of us mirth:
"Sing us one of the songs of Zion."
How shall we sing the ETERNAL's song in a foreign land?
(Ps 137:1–4)

Now that they have returned to their land and rebuilt the altar, they can resume singing the "ETERNAL's song." Despite the years of exile, they still knew the Temple ritual. They knew the right songs even if they had not sung them aloud at public rituals during the exile. They saw the rebuilding of the altar as a demonstration of God's everlasting love.

Another well-known psalm also proclaims that despite the years of exile God had not forsaken the people. Jews sing Shir Hama'alot, Ps 126, as a prelude to Birkat Hamazon after meals on Shabbat and festivals. This psalm describes the returnees to Jerusalem singing:

A song of ascents.
When the ETERNAL restores the fortunes of Zion
we see it as in a dream
our mouths shall be filled with laughter,
our tongues, with songs of joy.
Then shall they say among the nations,
"The ETERNAL has done great things for them!"
The ETERNAL will do great things for us
and we shall rejoice.
Restore our fortunes, O ETERNAL,
like watercourses in the Negeb.
They who sow in tears
shall reap with songs of joy.
Though he goes along weeping,
carrying the seed-bag,
he shall come back with songs of joy,
carrying his sheaves.

Following the destruction of the Second Temple by the Romans in 70 CE, the sages began to create the worship services that we continue to use today. This was not done by a single person on a single day. It took time, and many people contributed to the process. The sages did draw on the structure and content of Temple ritual to create the "script" of synagogue worship. One clear example is the use of psalms. We know from Ezra and other sources that psalms played an important role in the Temple ritual.

Psalms can be found in many places in the Jewish prayer book. We find psalms in the morning services, in the Kabbalat Shabbat on Friday evening, in the Hallel recited on festivals, and in Birkat Hamazon, the Grace After Meals. We recite psalms at funerals and in private prayers at times of personal need. When we sing or recite psalms today, we can feel connected through time to Jews throughout history who have recited psalms. We can feel connected through space to Jews around the world today who recite or sing the psalms today.

We want to sing the "right song." Chad Gad Ya and Maoz Tzur are both fine songs. But they each have their specific place in our ritual life. Chad Gad Ya is for Passover. Maoz Tzur is for Hanukkah. Nowhere in Jewish community would you hear Chad Gad Ya on Hanukkah or Maoz Tzur on Passover.

The songs that we sing express who we are. Secular ritual also features singing the right song at the right time. Right before a Cubs game begins, the stadium announcer will ask people to rise for the national anthem. Everybody knows what to sing. At a hockey game at the United Center, "national anthem" will become "national anthems" if the visiting team is from Canada.

In 1918, Irving Berlin wrote "God Bless America" while serving in the American armed forces during World War I. He revived and revised the song in the late 1939 as World War II began. It was featured in a patriotic musical *This Is the Army* in 1943. Following September 11, 2001, "God Bless America" became a regular part of athletic and public events.

Some people did not fully embrace "God Bless America." In 1940 in response to the jingoism of "God Bless America," Woody Guthrie wrote a song he sarcastically called "God Blessed America for Me." He adjusted the last line of the chorus and retitled it "This Land Is Your Land." In the sixties some summer camps sang "This Land Is Your Land" in place of "The Star Spangled Banner" at the daily flag-raising ceremony. At Labor Zionist Habonim Camp Tavor, we thought that "This Land" was too soft. We sang Phil Ochs's more assertive song "Power and Glory." On occasion in place of "Hatikvah," we sang a musical setting of Hayim Nachman Bialik's "Tehezakna," which affirmed our commitment to strengthen the hands of our brothers and sisters renewing the soil of our land.

During the Civil War the South sang "Dixie" written in the 1850s. The North sang the "Battle Hymn of the Republic" using the melody of "John Brown's Body." The soldiers sang these songs. And the people at home sang these songs.

When the news of Robert E. Lee's surrender, signaling the end of the war, reached Washington, a large crowd gathered outside the White House. They called upon President Abraham Lincoln to come out and share his reflections on this historic moment. The president explained that the moment of celebration was an occasion to bind up the wounds. He noticed that the crowd included a few bands. He suggested a song to conclude the impromptu celebration. People may have expected the President to request the "Battle Hymn of the Republic." He did not. President Lincoln said, "Let the band play 'Dixie.'" President Lincoln understood that the moment called for a message of reconciliation, not triumph.[1]

The songs we choose to sing express group cohesiveness. The fans of the Chicago Cubs know that after a victory at Wrigley Field, we will join in singing "Go Cubs Go." When I sit with my friends at camp playing my banjo while my buddy Mike plays his guitar, we do not have a list of songs. Mike will have ideas. I will have ideas. The other people who are singing with us that evening in the Lodge meeting room will have ideas. First timers might imagine that we will sing new songs. But the veterans of these music evenings know to expect old folk songs and really old folk songs.

The key moment of Yom Kippur is the chanting of Kol Nidre. The meaning of Kol Nidre for the members of the congregation does not grow out of the manifest meaning of the Aramaic words. The heart of the experience is the haunting melody. As Yom Kippur begins, chanting Kol Nidre expresses that we are the right people, in the right place, at the right time, singing the right melody.

The book of Lamentations mourns the destruction of the First Temple. It begins by describing desolated Jerusalem left empty by the people marching into exile. But the tone of the book shifts dramatically at the very end. It concludes, "Return us, O ETERNAL, and we shall return. / Renew our days as of old!" (Lam 5:23)

When the Jews, returning from Babylonian exile, stood at the base of the reconstructed altar singing the lines from the psalms, they knew that the they were the right people, in the right place, at the right time, singing the right words. That experience filled the singers with a strong sense of identity and purpose. They understood that God had brought them back home, renewing their days as of old. They sang, "Praise the ETERNAL who is good, whose steadfast love is everlasting" (Ps 106:1).

1. Lincoln, *Collected Words*, 393.

JERUSALEM

Chapter 24

Rebuilding the Altar and the Temple

In 1961, when I was eleven years old, the Washington Senators moved to the Land of Ten Thousand Lakes to become the Minnesota Twins. A child's dream was fulfilled. Our Midwestern town had become a major-league city. I became a big fan of the Twins. My childhood heroes included Harmon Killebrew and Tony Oliva.

When I moved to Cincinnati for rabbinic school, I wanted to become a full citizen of my new hometown. So I gave up my connection to the Twins and became a supporter of the Big Red Machine, featuring Johnny Bench, Pete Rose, Tony Perez, and Joe Morgan. After rabbinic school I settled in Chicago and became a die-hard fan of the Chicago Cubs.

One March a few years ago we were visiting friends in Florida. My buddy Gary said, "Let's go to a spring training baseball game." We drove to the Twins spring training facility in Fort Myers. The Twins were playing the archenemy of the Cubs, the St. Louis Cardinals. I expected that I would spend the afternoon joyfully rooting against the Cardinals. I did not expect that I would feel any emotional attachment to the twenty-first-century version of the Minnesota Twins.

When we stopped to buy lunch, we saw the concession stand featured a special Twins beverage, Killebrew Root Beer, "with that Hall of Fame taste." I had to have one. The can included Harmon's unique autograph. When Harmon appeared at baseball card shows, the line to get his autograph moved slowly because Harmon signed carefully. I am told that Harmon was so concerned about fans he practiced signing his autograph, making sure every letter was legible. Killebrew coached young players to improve their signatures. Killebrew believed that the fan who waits for a player's autograph, and then treasures it, should be able to read it. The walls of my study include a photograph of Harmon Killebrew with that ultra-clear autograph.

Right before the game began the public address system played the Twins' song, which much to my surprise was the "We're Gonna Win Twins" song that I lovingly recall from my childhood. They have continued to play the same song at home games since 1961.

Because we were in a small spring training stadium, I could see into the Twins' dugout. I noticed one of the players was wearing a 6 on the back of his uniform. I was shocked. How could the Twins let some rookie wear Hall of Famer Tony Oliva's number? Then he turned around. I knew right away this was no rookie. This was Tony Oliva, *batzmo uch'vodo*, "in all his personal glory." He had been invited to spring training to tutor the young Twins hitters.

On one level I was still sitting in Fort Myers, Florida, with my friend Gary. On another level I had drifted back over time and space, returning to Metropolitan Stadium in Bloomington, Minnesota, in the early sixties, sitting with my parents, my brother, Ken, and my sister, Ellen.

During the return from exile the people also drifted over time and space. The book of Ezra tells that after settling in Jerusalem, the people begin to rebuild the altar of the God of Israel.

> When the seventh month arrived—the Israelites being settled in their towns—the entire people assembled as a body in Jerusalem. Then Jeshua son of Jozadak and his brother priests and Zerubbabel son of Shealtiel and his brothers set to and built the altar of the God of Israel to offer burnt offerings upon it as is written in the Torah of Moses, the man of God. They set up the altar on its foundation because they were in fear of the peoples of the land and they offered burnt offerings on it to the ETERNAL, burnt offerings each morning and evening. (Ezra 3:1–3)

The text does not describe the project as new construction. They did not build a new altar or a new Temple. They rebuilt what the Babylonians had destroyed. The text emphasizes that they built the altar on "its foundation," which remained from the earlier Temple.

Jewish tradition imagines that this is "the" spot on earth on which to build an altar. According to tradition Solomon built the altar on the same spot on which Abraham had built the altar to sacrifice Isaac. There is also a teaching that claims that this is the same spot upon which Noah built his altar and the same spot where Cain and Abel brought their sacrifices. Having rebuilt the altar, they began to rebuild the Temple: "All the people raised a great shout extolling the ETERNAL because the foundation of House of the ETERNAL had been laid" (Ezra 3:11).

Who responds most strongly to the sight of the Temple being rebuilt? "The old people who had seen the first House, wept loudly at the sight of the founding of this House" (Ezra 3:12).

We can imagine that standing in Jerusalem in their old age alongside their grandchildren, these elders of the community drifted back over time to their youth when they stood next to their parents gazing on the original Temple of Solomon.

Rashi explains,

> These were the many people, [the larger portion of the community], who had not seen the First Temple. They greatly rejoiced and raised their voices in happiness and celebration. Those who heard them could distinguish the shouts of joy from the sound of weeping of the people. The sound of the rejoicing was loud but the sound of the weeping was louder to people listening at a distance. (Rashi on Ezra 3:12)

Why were these elders of the community weeping so loudly? I imagine that these were tears of joy. They had lived long enough to see the return from exile. They had "returned." Over my years as a rabbi, I have heard many older people battling disease set a goal, saying, "I just want to live until my granddaughter's wedding."

The Talmud presents a different way to understand these tears. The sages imagine these older returnees making amends for having committed the sins which led to the destruction of the Temple:

> The sin sacrifices for idolatry presented by the returning exiles were not in fact offered on behalf of the people who had died. Rather, when they sacrificed these sacrifices for the sins of idolatry committed during the reign of Zedekiah, they offered them on behalf of the living survivors who had served idols in the time of Zedekiah and remained alive many years later and had returned to participate in the rebuilding of the Temple. As it is written: "But many of the priests, Levites, and heads of fathers' houses, the old men that had seen the first house standing on its foundation, wept with a loud voice when this house was before their eyes; and many shouted aloud for joy" (Ezra 3:12). (BT Terumah 15b)

The process of any return home is often complicated. From Homer's *Odyssey* onward, stories of return include tales of the hero overcoming obstacles and traps to complete the journey home. And like Odysseus, when we finally arrive home, we discover that things have changed.

A few years ago, I went to Minneapolis for the retirement festivities for one of my rabbi buddies. On a free afternoon I took two of my friends on a tour of my childhood. We parked in front of my childhood home, which my family sold when I was nineteen. At my friends' urging I walked up to the front door and rang the bell. I introduced myself to the homeowner as Rabbi Steven Bob, explaining that I grew up in the house. He said, "I have a question that I think you can answer, Rabbi. Can you explain to me what that is?" pointing at the mezuzah. In gratitude for my explanation, he invited us in the house.

I was prepared to see that many parts of the house had changed in the forty-seven years since 1969. The kitchen had been renewed. All the rooms had been redecorated. I was surprised by one major change. I grew up in a four-bedroom house with a bath and a half. The house had been transformed into a three-bedroom home with two and a half baths. My childhood bedroom had been converted into a large luxurious primary bathroom. I showed my friends my "bedroom," or more accurately, where my bedroom had once been.

Twenty five years ago, our congregation added a large addition to the synagogue. We added classrooms and office space and made several changes to the sanctuary, but the committee cleverly understood the importance of maintaining the front wall of the sanctuary and the ark. When we walked in to the "new" sanctuary, we saw in front of us that old wall and the ark. We felt that we were home.

The Minnesota Twins no longer play their games in Metropolitan Stadium. They no longer play their games in the Humphrey Dome, which replaced Metropolitan Stadium. Since 2010 the Minnesota Twins have called Target Field home. But I know that if I make my way to Target Field, I will hear the old song and see enough reminders of the old days to make me feel at home.

Comedian George Carlin had a bit in which he demonstrated that baseball was superior to football. He concluded by explaining, "In baseball the object is to go home! And to be safe!—I hope I'll be safe at home!"[1]

1. Carlin, *Brain Droppings*, 53.

The returning exiles rebuilt the altar and the Temple on the foundations of that which the Babylonians had destroyed. They knew that they had returned home. They felt confident that once they had rebuilt the altar, they would be safe at home.

Chapter 25

One Temple or Two?

Popular and scholarly sources often speak of the First Temple and the Second Temple. The First Temple was built by King Solomon about 930 BCE and was destroyed by Nebuchadnezzar and the Babylonian army in 586 BCE. About fifty years later the returnees from exile built the Second Temple, which stood until the Romans destroyed it in 70 CE. Religious Jews refer to these two destructions as Churban Bayit Rishon and Churban Bayit Shaini.

But the Hebrew Bible never refers to what we call the Second Temple by that name. The two biblical books which describe the period of return from exile, Ezra and Nehemiah, do not label the rebuilt Temple as "the Second Temple." Ezra and Nehemiah mention the Temple a total of fifty-seven times, but the text never refers to the rebuilt Temple as the Second Temple. The only time the text of the two books uses the phrase "First Temple" is in Ezra 3:12: "Many of the priests and Levites and chiefs of the clans, the old men who had seen the first house, wept loudly at the sight of the founding of this house."

The book of Ezra uses a few terms to refer to the Temple in Jerusalem. In the Hebrew segments, Ezra refers to the Temple a total of twenty-one times. The text uses five different names.

Beit adonia, "House of the Eternal": seven times (Ezra 1:3, 1:5, 1:7, 2:68, 3:8, 3:11, 7:27)

Bet elohim, "House of God": six times (1:4, 2:68, 7:1, 8:36, 10:1, 10:9)

Heichal adonai, "Sanctuary of the ETERNAL": four times (3:6, 3:8, 3:10, 4:1)

Bayit leiloheinu, "House of Our God": three times (4:3, 8:33, 9:9)

Bayit, "House": one time (1:2)

The Aramaic sections of Ezra also refer to the Temple twenty-one times:

Beit elaha, "The House of God": twelve times (4:24, 5:2, 5:14, 5:15, 5:16, 5:17, 6:3, 6:7, 6:8, 6:12, 6:17, 7:24)

Heichla, "The Temple": two times (4:14, 6:5)

Beita, "House": two times (5:3, 6:15)

Beitna, "The House": two times (5:11, 5:12)

Beit elaha raba, "The House of the Great God": one time (5:8)

Beit elohachom, "The House of Your God": one time (7:17)

Beit elahach, "The House of Your God": one time (7:20)

Bet elah sh'maya, "The House of the God (or Heaven)": one time (7:23)

Nehemiah mentions the Temple fifteen times:

Bet haelohim, "The House of God": four times (Neh 6:10, 13:7, 13:9, 13:11)

Heichal, "The Temple": two times (6:10, 6:11)

Beit eloheinu, "The House of Our God": seven times (10:33, 10:34, 10:37, 10:38, 10:39, 10:40, 13:4)

Beit adonai, "House of the ETERNAL": one time (10:36)

Beit elohai, "The House of My God": one time (13:14)

In none of these fifty-seven verses does the text describe the rebuilt Temple as the "Second Temple." The rebuilders did not see their project as the construction of something new. They saw their Temple as a continuation of the original Temple. As I explained in the previous chapter, they very carefully placed the new altar on the foundations of the original altar (Ezra 3:3).

First Maccabees continues this practice of seeing the rebuilt Temple as an extension of the original Temple. It never describes the Temple as the Second Temple. While First Maccabees is not part of the Hebrew

Bible, it does provide a window into the world in which it was written. The original Hebrew text of First Maccabees has not survived. We have the Greek version of the text. First Maccabees is considered part of the Old Testament by the Roman Catholic Church and Greek/Eastern Orthodox Churches. First Maccabees tells the story of the Jewish rebellion against the oppressive rule of Antiochus IV Epiphanes. Most scholars agree that it was written in around 100 BCE, while the Temple still stood in Jerusalem. During the five hundred years that this Temple stood in Jerusalem, Jews saw it simply as the Temple.

After the Romans destroyed the Temple in 70 CE, sources began to distinguish between the two Temples. The Babylonian Talmud, which was compiled five hundred years after the second destruction of the Temple, does differentiate between the First Temple and the Second Temple. A well-known passage explaining the reasons for the destruction of the Temple by the Romans does explicitly refer to it as the Second Temple:

> We know that during the Second Temple period the residents of Jerusalem engaged in Torah study, observance of mitzvot, and acts of loving kindness, and that they did not perform the sinful acts of idol worship that were performed during the First Temple period. So why was the Second Temple destroyed? God brought about the destruction of the Second Temple because of senseless hatred which took place during those years. This comes to teach you that the sin of senseless hatred equals the three most severe transgressions: idolatry, adultery, and murder. (BT Yoma 9b)

The author of this talmudic passage wanted to clearly distinguish between the two destructions. The prophets describe the destruction of the First Temple as a result of the idolatrous and broadly sinful lives of people of Judah. The prophets Hosea, Isaiah, and Jeremiah all warned the people that their misdeeds would bring destruction on Jerusalem. The talmudic sage stresses that the people of Jerusalem in the early Roman period had not acted in the same manner as the generation preceding the first destruction. Other Talmud passages, including Makkot 24b and Taanit 29a, also use the First Temple / Second Temple terms.

Why do the sources from the age of the rebuilt Temple avoid the first/second terminology? They proclaimed the rebuilt Temple as the authentic continuation of original Temple to stress that what that they had was genuine. They did not want to see their Temple as a lesser replacement for the original Temple. Their Temple was the authentic article, not a Temple*.[1]

Today when Jews speak of rebuilding the Temple, we generally do not describe it as the Third Temple but rather as the rebuilt Temple or as the rebuilt Jerusalem. In our aspirations we strive for continuity.

Traditional Jewish daily worship includes prayers urging God to bring about the rebuilding of the Temple. At the conclusion of our Passover Seder, we proclaim, "Next year in Jerusalem."

Everyone who says "next year in Jerusalem" may not understand the intent behind the phrase. It is not an announcement of travel plans. The phrase is meant to express the hope that before next Passover, the messiah will have come, the exiles will be gathered back to the land of Israel, and the Temple will be rebuilt, so that next year in rebuilt Jerusalem we will offer the Paschal lamb.

We seek authentic continuity in our lives. The Ashkenazic custom of naming babies for family members who have died connects the generations. The first great-grandchild born after my mother's death was named for her. It took a bit of creativity, but my niece and nephew named their son, Charlie, for his great-grandmother, Shirley. We cook and bake following recipes we learned from our parents and grandparents. My late mother made mandel bread following the recipe she had learned from her mother. When my sister, Ellen, bakes mandel bread, she follows the authentic Bob/Kaplan/Gitlin recipe.

The Chicago Cubs won the World Series in 2016 after a gap of 108 years since their previous World Series victory in 1908. Many Cubs fans visited cemeteries to share the victory with deceased parents and grandparents.

Many towns and cities in America were named for European locations. The German immigrants who founded New Ulm in Minnesota named it after their previous home in Germany. The town features a 102-foot-high statue of Arminius/Herman who led the Teutonic tribes in their victory over the Romans in Teutoburg Forest. This is a replica of a larger 173-foot statue in Detmold, Germany. The builders of the

1. In 1961 Roger Maris hit sixty-one home runs, breaking Babe Ruth's single-season home run record. Baseball Commissioner Ford Frick, a friend of Babe Ruth, stated that Maris's accomplishment did not actually break Babe Ruth's record because the Babe hit his sixty home runs in the old 154-game season. Maris hit his sixty-one home runs in the newly expanded 162-game season. Sports writer Dick Young suggested that Maris's new record should be listed with an asterisk, 61*.

American statue of Herman saw it expressing the authentic connection of their previous home in Germany to their new home in America.

In 2005 the Montreal Expos moved to Washington and became the Washington Nationals. Some sports franchises moved to new locations but kept their original name, even though the original name was deeply tied to the original home of the franchise. The New Orleans Jazz moved to Salt Lake City but kept their Louisiana name. The Minneapolis Lakers moved to Los Angeles but kept their Minnesota name. Both teams continue to take pride in the accomplishments of the teams in their original homes.

The Nationals chose to change their name to create a new identity. When they built a new stadium, it included a Ring of Honor to pay tribute to stars of the team from the past. They could have chosen to connect with the previous Washington MLB team, the Senators, or they could have chosen to connect with the years that the franchise spent in Montreal as the Expos. They decided to do both and also honor stars of the Negro League team, the Grays, that had played in Washington. So, the Nationals' Ring of Honor includes Andre Dawson and Gary Carter from the Montreal Expos, Joe Cronin and Walter Johnson of the Washington Senators, and Cool Papa Bell and Josh Gibson of the Washington Grays. This display tells the fans that the Nationals are the authentic continuation of all three teams.

As Jews, we see our lives as the authentic continuation of the generations who came before us. We celebrate the same holidays and recite the same prayers as did those who came before us. But we celebrate and pray in our own way. We hold on to the past with one hand and reach out to grasp the future with our other hand. The generation who rebuilt the Temple in Jerusalem saw it as a continuation of the Temple which King Solomon had built on the same spot. They, too, wished to hold on to the past as they reached out to touch the future.

Chapter 26

The Walls of Jerusalem

CHAPTER 3 OF THE book of Nehemiah describes in detail specific families rebuilding and repairing sections of the walls and the gates of the city of Jerusalem. The text mentions each of the gates by name. For example, "The sons of Hassenaah rebuilt the Fish Gate; they roofed it and set up its doors, locks, and bars" (Neh 3:3).

The text repeats the phrase "they roofed it and set up its doors, locks, and bars" in its description of the rebuilding of each of the gates. This repeating refrain emphasizes the completeness of this process of reconstruction. The builders did not throw together temporary or shoddy gates. They built proper sturdy gates with the appropriate "doors, locks, and bars."

Most of the thirty-eight verses of this chapter mention a different individual or family rebuilding their section of Jerusalem's wall. Nehemiah did not hire a team of Persian experts to rebuild the walls and gates of Jerusalem. The Judean people themselves rebuilt the walls and gates of their city. We can imagine that the process of rebuilding strengthened their sense of security and ownership of their old, and now new, land. A song of the Chalutzim (pioneers) of the Second Aliyah of 1905 describes the impact of rebuilding the land: *Anu banu artza livnot uli'heebanot ba*, "We have come to this land to build it and be to personally rebuilt in that process." Nehemiah, and the families listed in these verses, may have felt the same way about their rebuilding the walls and gates of Jerusalem.

The author of Nehemiah seems to assume that the readers will recognize and easily identify the gates described. The list includes the Sheep

Gate, the Fish Gate, the Valley Gate, the Dung Gate, the Water Gate, the Fountain Gate, the Horse Gate, and the Inspection Gate.

Walls still surround the Old City of Jerusalem. The Ottoman Sultan Suleiman the Magnificent built the current walls of the Old City of Jerusalem in the sixteenth century. But the eight gates of today's Old City are not the same as those mentioned in Nehemiah. The contemporary list and that of Nehemiah share only one gate, the Dung Gate.

The Ottomans built their city wall on foundations of earlier walls. The gates in the sixteenth century were built where earlier gates once stood. Archeologists can point out the foundations of the Crusader walls from the Middle Ages. We can even see stones from King Herod's reign, 37–4 BCE. But the outline of city has shifted significantly from the early Second Temple period.

When people say "Second Temple Jerusalem" they generally mean Herodian Jerusalem at the end of the Second Temple era. We call King Herod "Herod the Great" not because he was a wonderful human being. He was not Herod the good. He was actually Herod the awful. He killed relatives and then built memorials to remember them. Then why is he called Herod the Great? He built the grandest structures that ever stood in the premodern land of Israel. And he built them out of the biggest stones. Much of what he built has lasted. Visitors to Israel learn to recognize Herodian construction such as the Western Wall, which features huge cut stones with a depressed margin around their edges.

As I read the book of Nehemiah's description of the walls of Jerusalem, I have a hard time imagining the path. I know the contemporary Old City of Jerusalem quite well. And I am familiar with the model of the Herodian Jerusalem adjacent to the Shrine of the Book near the entrance of the Israel Museum. The model was designed by archaeologist Michael Avi-Yonah based on the writings of Flavius Josephus and other historical sources.

The Jerusalem that Nehemiah helped rebuild, at the beginning of the Second Temple era, was much smaller than the Herodian Jerusalem of the last years of the Second Temple. Jerusalem at the end of the First Temple period provided the foundations for the rebuild which Nehemiah led. Nehemiah restored the walls and gates of Jerusalem. The leaders of each of the waves of returning exiles saw themselves as rebuilding what had been knocked down by the Babylonians. As the leaders of the first wave restored the altar, Nehemiah restored the walls and gates.

While there remain scholarly disputes over some of the details of Nehemiah's Jerusalem, everyone would agree that it certainly included the Temple Mount, the large flat platform that we see today which was constructed by Herod the Great. The wall we call the Kotel, or the Western Wall, was not a wall of the Temple. It was built as a retaining wall as part of Herod's plan to enlarge the Temple Mount for his grander, larger Temple. The Temple Mount platform in Nehemiah's time was smaller.

The area of the contemporary City of David excavations outside the current city walls was certainly part of the early second Temple Jerusalem, as it had been during the First Temple period. This area just south of the Temple Mount is generally called the "lower city." The current Jewish quarter was the ancient "upper city." If you have visited Jerusalem, you will recall descending stairs as you moved from the Jewish quarter to the Western Wall plaza.

The text of Nehemiah mentions specific special sections of the city's walls. We can connect some of these special features with specific spots in contemporary Jerusalem. Nehemiah 3:8 mentions "the Broad Wall." In the Jewish Quarter today one can see a portion of the excavated "Broad Wall" generally dated to the time of Hezekiah, who reigned in Jerusalem towards the end of the First Temple period, 715–686 BCE. This broad wall probably marked the western edge of Jerusalem in Nehemiah's time.

In Neh 3:15 we read, "The wall of the irrigation pool of the King's Garden as far as the steps going down from the City of David." We know that the City of David ran along a ridge running southward and downward from the Temple Mount. Jerusalem's water source sits at the bottom of this ridge, as mentioned in the verse. An extensive archeological project continues to unearth buildings from the City of David.

In verse 26 we read, "The temple servants were living on the Ophel, as far as a point in front of the Water Gate in the east, and the jutting tower." Chapter 8 of Nehemiah mentions the Water Gate as the location of the massive gathering of the entire nation to hear the reading of the Torah. The verse specifically describes the Water Gate as being in the "east." We can imagine that it was located near the southeast corner of the city in the direction of the Gihon Spring, Jerusalem's water source.

Other specific places mentioned in chapter 3 of Nehemiah are more difficult to place.

> After him, Nehemiah son of Azbuk [a different Nehemiah], chief of half the district of Beth-zur, repaired, from in front of

> the graves of David as far as the artificial pool, and as far as the House of the Warriors. (Neh 3:16)

The phrase "graves of David" is curious. Why is *graves* in the plural? David, like all other human beings, was buried in a single grave. I understand the use of the plural form to refer to the graves of the house of David. I believe this phrase describes the burial area for the rulers of Jerusalem. We do not know the actual location of this royal burial ground.

In the early years of the modern State of Israel, tour guides showed visitors a tomb located on Mount Zion, describing it as "King David's Tomb." The ceasefire lines at the conclusion of Israel's War of Independence left the Old City of Jerusalem under the control of Jordan. From 1948 until 1967 Jordanian authorities did not allow Jews to visit the Western Wall and other Jewish sites in the Old City. During those years, the Tomb of David on Mount Zion became an oft-visited "holy spot." Scholars agree that there is no evidence to suggest that this medieval tomb has any connection to King David. After the reunification of Jerusalem in 1967, visits of tourist groups to this spot have diminished as better holy spots became accessible for visitors to Israel.

The Bible reports the death of King David: "Then David slept with his ancestors, and was buried in the city of David" (1 Kgs 2:10). The Bible uses similar language to describe the death of other kings of Judah. For example, "Hezekiah slept with his ancestors, and his son Manasseh succeeded him as king" (2 Kgs 20:21). This phrase "slept with his ancestors" can be taken to be a metaphor describing the king joining those who came before him in death. Or it could be understood to indicate that the king's body was buried in the same location as earlier kings. This leads back to the use of the plural term *graves* in 3:16. I understand the phrase "graves of (the house of) David" and the phrase "slept with his ancestors" to both refer to a specific location where the rulers of the kingdom were buried. The locations of these graves of the kings of Judah remains a topic of scholarly debate.

Nehemiah's rebuilding of the walls and gates of Jerusalem provided the Judeans with security and protection from those who sought to do them harm. In Nehemiah's time walls and gates meant security. In 122 CE the Romans built a wall across the breadth of England to protect the Romans living south of the wall from the "barbarians" living north of the wall. Portions of this seventy-three-mile-long Hadrian's Wall still stand. Walls encircled medieval European cities to protect their inhabitants against enemy armies. As gunpowder weapons grew more powerful, walls became less important as defense against foreign armies.

City walls did continue to provide protection from brigands. The Jewish residents of Jerusalem all lived within the city's wall until 1860. The walls of the city offered protection from marauders and bandits. When philanthropist Sir Moses Montefiore built Mishkenot Sha'anim outside the city walls across the valley from Mount Zion in 1860, he had a difficult time persuading Jews to leave the overcrowded city to enjoy the fresh air of these new homes.

As confidence grew, other new neighborhoods began to spring up in the following decades of the late nineteenth and early twentieth centuries. The modern builders of the roads, apartments, schools, offices, and stores of Jerusalem created "roofs, doors, locks, and bars" to protect themselves as Nehemiah had done for an earlier generation of pioneers. We will look at the security threats that Nehemiah and his generation faced in chapter 41.

Chapter 27

Where Is the Ark?

The last three verses of the first chapter of Ezra list the items which the Persian ruler Cyrus the Great returned to Sheshbazzar from the royal treasury where they had been stored since they were looted from the Temple in Jerusalem by the Babylonian King Nebuchadnezzar in 586 BCE:

> And this is the inventory: 30 gold basins, 1,000 silver basins, 29 knives; 30 gold bowls, 410 silver double bowls and 1,000 other vessels; in all 5,400 gold and silver vessels. Sheshbazzar brought all these back when the exiles came back from Babylon unto Jerusalem. (Ezra 1:9–11)

The text provides this detailed list of all the Temple items which the exiles would be carrying back to Jerusalem. It is an impressive list written to indicate the generous spirit with which Cyrus fulfilled the divine instruction for the rebuilding of the Temple. We should also notice what is missing from this list. The text does not mention the ark of the covenant.

The book of Exodus (25:10–22) describes the construction of the ark at the foot of Mount Sinai, including God's instruction, "And deposit in the Ark the tablets of the covenant which I will give you" (verse 16). The people carried the ark through the wilderness for forty years.

Second Samuel 6:1–11 contains the story of King David bringing the ark of the covenant into the city of Jerusalem. It is a key moment in the process of David making Jerusalem the capital city of the unified nation. First Kings 8:1–9 tells of King Solomon moving the ark of the covenant into its permanent home in the newly completed Temple. The installation of the ark served as the final step in the dedication of the Temple. The ark stood in the holy of holies in the Temple in Jerusalem, representing God's presence in the midst of the people.

So, we would expect that this description in the book of Ezra, of Cyrus providing the treasure of the Temple, would include a mention of the ark. But it does not appear. None of the postexilic texts mention the ark. The holy of holies in the rebuilt Temple remained an empty room. Ezra and Nehemiah do not explain the absence of the ark. This leads us to ask, Why is the ark absent? What happened to the ark? We can consider several possibilities:

1. First Kings 14:25–26 describes an attack on Jerusalem by Pharaoh Shishak of Egypt during the reign of King Rehoboam. The text says that Pharaoh Shishak "carried off the treasures of the House of the ETERNAL." Egyptian sources describe Pharaoh Shoshenq's very similar military campaign in the land of Israel. Scholars agree that Pharaoh Shishak and Pharaoh Shoshenq are the same person. The treasure that Pharaoh Shishak/Shoshenq removed could have included the ark. The authors of the script for the Steven Spielberg movie *Raiders of the Lost Ark* imagined that Pharaoh Shishak/Shoshenq brought the ark back to Egypt and placed it in the Well of Souls in his capital city, Tanis. While extensive archeological projects have explored Tanis, the ark could still be buried somewhere in a yet-to-be-excavated ancient site in Egypt.
2. Second Kings 25 describes the destruction of the Temple by the Babylonians. The description of the Temple treasures which the Babylonians took with them does not include any mention of the ark. This leads some people to believe that the Temple priests hid the ark in a secret tunnel or a cave in the Temple Mount. By the time of the return from exile none of these priests remained alive. Because of the sacred nature of the Temple Mount to Jews and Muslims, little to no archeological investigation has been possible in the area. So, the ark could still be hidden in a long-forgotten cave within the Temple Mount.
3. The Church of Our Lady Mary of Zion in Aksum, Ethiopia, claims to possess the ark in a room that no one is allowed to enter. According to the legend, Menelik, the son the queen of Sheba and King Solomon, brought the ark from Jerusalem back to ancient Sheba,

now known as Ethiopia. Graham Hancock promoted a variation of this theory in his popular book *The Sign and the Seal: The Quest for the Lost Ark of the Covenant*. He argues that the ark was brought to the Jewish Temple in Elephantine Island, Egypt during the reign of King Manasseh (687–642 BCE).[1] Second Kings 21:10 says that this happened because "King Manasseh has done abhorrent things." After a two-hundred-year sojourn there it was brought to Aksum, Ethiopia, where it rests today. Serious scholars have rejected Hancock's creative and fanciful theories.

4. Many people know about Scotland's Rosslyn Chapel from Dan Brown's novel *The Da Vinci Code*. In the novel, and the subsequent film, the hunt for the Holy Grail leads to the Rosslyn Chapel. Some people have suggested that the Knights Templar designed the chapel as a re-creation of Solomon's Temple. There is a story that during the Crusades the Knights Templar discovered the ark and brought it back to Scotland where it remains hidden in Rosslyn Chapel to this very day. While I enjoy stories about knights and valuable artifacts, including a particular statue of a bird, I know that serious scholars do not see even a hint of truth in these stories.
5. A much simpler explanation seems much more likely to me. I believe that the ark was destroyed in the general destruction of the Temple in 586 BCE. The ark is not mentioned in Ezra 1:9–11 because by the time of the return from exile the people all knew that the ark had been destroyed with the Temple.

In any case, the people returning from the exile did not have the ark to place in the holy of holies in the center of the Temple. In the rebuilt Temple the holy of holies was an empty room.

During the First Temple period nobody went into the holy of holies except the high priest on Yom Kippur. The people in general did not ever get to see the ark or the tablets within it. But they knew that this sacred object, which linked the community to God, was in their midst. While the tablets of the covenant rested in the holy ark in the holy of holies of the Temple in Jerusalem, the people felt the presence of God protecting them.

The Bible includes several stories which depict the power of the ark. The ark plays a key role in the entrance into the land and the conquest

1. Hancock, *Sign and the Seal*.

of Jericho. The book of Joshua describes the ark leading the procession of the Israelites as they prepare to enter the land of Israel by crossing the Jordan River. When the priests carrying the ark step into the Jordan, the river stops flowing, allowing the people cross on dry land (Josh 3:3–17). When the Israelites marched around the walls of the city of Jericho, "the Ark of the ETERNAL" led them (Josh 6:6–14).

Later stories express other aspects to the power of the ark. The Israelites, after losing a battle with the Philistines, brazenly try to harness the power of the ark by asking Hophni and Phinehas, the sons of the Eli the high priest, to bring the ark to the battlefield to ensure their victory in the next battle. A disaster ensues. The Philistines rout the Israelites, killing and capturing much of the Israelite army. The Philistines take the ark as war booty. But wherever in their cities the Philistines place the ark, God causes chaos and illness. Eventually the Philistines send the ark back to the Israelites (1 Sam 4:1—7:21).

While King David's procession was bringing the ark to Jerusalem, it began to slide off its cart.

> Uzzah reached out for the Ark of God and grasped it, for the oxen had stumbled. The ETERNAL was incensed at Uzzah. And God struck him down on the spot for his indiscretion and he died there beside the Ark of God. (2 Sam 6:6–7)

The rebuilt Temple did not include the tablets of the covenant resting in the holy ark in the holy of holies. The absence of the ark caused the people to feel more distant from God. What filled this vacuum for the people in the postexilic era? What could replace the ark with its tablets?

We saw in chapter 24 that the people rebuilt the new Temple on the foundations of the previous Temple. They renewed the bringing of sacrifices. But that was not enough. The people needed a deeper connection to God. We read in chapter 7 of the book of Ezra that "Ezra came up from Babylon a scribe expert in the Torah of Moses which the ETERNAL God of Israel had given"(Ezra 7:6).

In chapter 8 of Nehemiah Ezra reads from the Torah and teaches from the Torah. As we saw in chapter 1 of this book, the Torah scroll as a sacred object, and the public reading of the Torah scroll as a ritual, emerges as the new center of the religious life of the people. After the return from exile, the Torah scroll takes the place of the ark of the covenant in the lives of the people.

We renew our covenant with God each time we hear the Torah read and every time we study the text of the Torah. When we rise to take a Torah scroll from the ark in our synagogues, we sing the words of the prophet Isaiah, *Ki mitziyon teitazei torah, udvar adonai miyerushalayim*, "For out of Zion shall come the Torah, the word of the ETERNAL from Jerusalem" (Isa 2:3). Torah began coming forth from Jerusalem in the days of Ezra and Nehemiah.

Chapter 28

The Presence of God

On the last night of winter break during our first year of rabbinic school in Jerusalem, I hosted a party for everyone: students, faculty, and administration. We spoke about the snow that was predicted for the next day. The Dean said, "This is Jerusalem; it will just be flurries." He assured us that the second semester would begin on schedule the next morning. We woke up the next morning to find Jerusalem covered by a foot of snow. The city was closed for several days.

Two of my classmates hiked through the snow from the Rechavia neighborhood to the Kotel in the Old City. The usually bustling Western Wall plaza was deserted. No one else was there.

In the quiet they felt a spiritual presence near the place where the Temple once stood. When Elijah flees to the wilderness, he encounters the Divine speaking in the "still small voice" of God (1 Kgs 19:12). My friends reported that they heard that voice in that place on that day. They felt the words of Hab 2:20: "But the Eternal in the holy Abode—Be silent before [God], all the earth!"

Many people describe experiencing the presence of God in specific places at specific moments. But do we believe that God dwells in a specific place? More specifically, does God live in Jerusalem? One of my congregants delighted in telling the very old joke about a phone call to God from Jerusalem being a local call. The Hebrew Bible and Jewish rabbinic tradition offer more than few thoughts on this topic.

The proclamation of Cyrus in the first chapter of Ezra includes the phrase "and build the house of the Eternal, the God of Israel, He is the

God who is in Jerusalem" (Ezra 1:3). This phrase depends on two important theological points. First that God has specific location. Secondly, that for God, that the special location is Jerusalem. These ideas can be found in many other biblical verses.

During the early months of the forty years in the wilderness, God tells Moses to build the tabernacle in the wilderness: "And let them make Me a sanctuary, that I may dwell among them" (Exod 25:8). Later God assures Moses and Aaron of the abiding presence of the Divine: "And I will make My dwelling place among you, and I will not reject you" (Lev 26:11).

Later God instructs the prophet Nathan to tell King David, "From the day that I brought the people of Israel out of Egypt to this day I have not dwelt in a house, but have moved about in Tent and Tabernacle" (2 Sam 7:6). All three of these verses describe God as being located in a specific place and desiring a building as a home.

This theology is not limited to the biblical period. It led to the creation of the grand cathedrals of Europe. These gigantic buildings, far bigger than any other building of their times, took centuries to build. The buildings inspired awe in the hearts of all who entered them. Worshipers felt the presence of God.

The Jewish people built grand synagogues in the major European cities and in North America in the late nineteenth and early twentieth centuries. The Dohany Street Synagogue in Budapest, completed in 1859, seats over three thousand people. It suffered great damage during World War II and the communist years. It was brought back to grandeur in 1998. It was designed to be awe-inspiring.

The Bible does contain texts that express other ideas about the presence of God. The book of Deuteronomy offers a slightly different image: "But look only to the site that your God the Eternal will choose amidst all your tribes as God's habitation, to establish the divine name there. There you are to go" (Deut 12:5). This is a recurring expression in Deuteronomy. We read the phrase "to establish the divine name there" in multiple verses in Deuteronomy: 12:4, 12:11, 12:13, 12:18, 14:23, 14:24, 15:20, 16:6, 17:8, 26:2, 31:11. It is one of phrases that identifies a biblical verse as being from Deuteronomy.

Nehemiah offers a similar image:

> Be mindful of the promise You gave to Your servant Moses: "If you are unfaithful, I will scatter you among the peoples; but if you turn back to Me, faithfully keep My commandments, even

> if your dispersed are at the ends of the earth, I will gather them from there and bring them to the place where I have chosen to establish My name." (Neh 1:8–9)

What is the difference between God's presence and God's name? "God's name" may be a metaphor for the presence of God. I think that by using this phrase the writer is backing away from the belief that God has an actual, physical presence and requires an actual house.

As King Solomon reflects on the task of building the Temple that he is about to complete, he does not describe it as the "House of God" but rather as the "House of the name of God."

> But the ETERNAL said to my father David, "As regards your intention to build a House for My name, you did right to have that intention. However, you shall not build the House yourself; instead, your son, the issue of your loins, shall build the House for My name." And the ETERNAL has fulfilled the promise that He made: I have risen in place of my father David and have ascended the throne of Israel, as the ETERNAL promised. I have built the House for the name of the ETERNAL, the God of Israel. (1 Kgs 8:18–20)

We can see a third thread in the Bible that suggests God does not live in one place. Some verses in the Bible express the thought that God can be found anywhere in the whole earth, not just Jerusalem. King Solomon the builder of the Temple explicitly says, "But will God really dwell on earth? Even the heavens to their uttermost reaches cannot contain You, how much less this House that I have built!" (1 Kgs 8:27). The fact that the author of 1 Kings quotes the builder of the Temple to explain that it is not actually God's house expresses the strength of that position.

That position is supported by the prophet Isaiah, who shares a vision of God sitting on the divine throne in the holy of holies in the Temple in Jerusalem:

> In the year that King Uzziah died, I beheld my Lord seated on a high and lofty throne; and the skirts of His robe filled the Temple. Seraphs stood in attendance on Him. Each of them had six wings: with two he covered his face, with two he covered his legs, and with two he would fly. And one would call to the other,
> "Holy, holy, holy!
> The ETERNAL of Hosts!
> His presence fills all the earth!"
> (Isa 6:1–3)

Isaiah explains that while we might imagine that God dwells in the Temple, in truth God is present throughout the world.

Modern religious thinkers have more fully developed the argument against thinking of God as dwelling in the Temple. Abraham Joshua Heschel, in his beautifully written book *The Sabbath*, explains that to Jews sacred time is more important than sacred space. He describes the Sabbath as a "palace in time":

> Judaism is a religion of time aiming at the sanctification of time. Unlike the space-minded man to whom time is unvaried, iterative, homogeneous, to whom all hours are alike, quality-less, empty shells, the Bible senses the diversified character of time. There are no two hours alike. Every hour is unique and the only one given at the moment, exclusive and endlessly precious. Judaism teaches us to be attached to holiness in time, to be attached to sacred events, to learn how to consecrate sanctuaries that emerge from the magnificent stream of a year. The Sabbaths are our great cathedrals; and our Holy of Holies is a shrine that neither the Romans nor the Germans were able to burn.[1]

Another path to God is through the study of texts. We do not need a fancy building to study these texts. Poker players say that all they need is a "chip and a chair." Torah scholars only need a "book and a bench." In the traditional community people immerse themselves in Talmud. I am more at home in slowly reading the Bible's text. Looking at each word, I ask, "How is that word used in other places?" As I study the text before me, I hear echoes of other texts. The prophet Jonah's name means "dove," which connects me to the dove in the Noah story. This connection helped me see the two stories in conversation with one another. Noah sends the dove out twice. God sends Jonah out twice. These are the only two stories in the Hebrew Bible in which people travel in a boat. In both stories people have been so wicked that they will be destroyed. In the Jonah story the people of Nineveh avoid destruction because they repent as a result of Jonah's prophecy. In the Noah story no one warns the people. I understand the Jonah story to be a response to the Noah story.

I read the traditional commentaries and Midrash and the essays of modern Bible scholars. I look at how rabbis and ministers use these words in contemporary sermons. Stretching myself, I look at new texts, including the church fathers.

1. Heschel, *Sabbath*, 8.

In Genesis we read the story of Jacob fleeing from his brother, Esau. He stops for the night in a barren place. He uses a rock for a pillow. As he sleeps, he dreams of God talking to him. After the dream,

> Jacob awoke from his sleep and said, "Surely the ETERNAL is present in this place, and I did not know it!" Shaken, he said, "How awesome is this place! This is none other than the house of God, and that is the gateway to heaven." (Gen 28:16–17)

We can read the words "the house of God" in two ways. The rabbinic interpretive tradition suggests that this is the unique spot where God is connected to the world. The rabbis say that this is the spot on which God was connected to the world at creation. This is the spot on which Abel offered his sacrifice. This is the spot on which Abraham built the altar to sacrifice Isaac. This is the spot on which the altar in the Temple, the "House of God," will be built.

The alternative approach is to read the verse to teach that even this spot in the middle of nowhere can be a "house of God" because any spot can be the house of God. God can be found anywhere if only we open our eyes and see. This is how I understand the term "the house of God."

My rabbinic school classmates felt the presence of God in the absolute quiet of the snow-covered Western Wall. Many Jews see the loud and busy Western Wall as a means to feel connected to the Divine. Some Jews visit the graves of prominent rabbis to feel closer to God. I know that many people feel closer to God in certain sacred places. For me, the texts provide the means and the moment. Wherever and whenever I open my books and seek the deeper meaning of the sacred texts, I draw closer to God.

PEOPLE

Chapter 29

Grouping the Community

As a reform rabbi, I belong to the Central Conference of American Rabbis (CCAR). The CCAR's web page includes an online membership directory. The names are listed alphabetically. The web page provides the means to resort the list by geography, by ordination year, or by birth year. The CCAR does not offer the option to sort the rabbis by height or weight. The CCAR does not provide a means to sort which rabbis are right-handed or left-handed.

A list of possible draft choices for a National Football League team could be sorted by weight and height. A baseball manager's list of available pitchers in the bullpen would sort them by left-handed versus right-handed. We often divide people into groups. Most often we use criteria that organically grows out of the project with which we are engaged.

The Bible does not use any of these modern Western criteria for sorting the names of the people who returned to Jerusalem within the first wave. But it does not list the names in a random order. It uses a few methods of grouping appropriate to the time and place.

Chapter 2 of the book of Ezra contains a lengthy list of the people who comprised the first wave of returnees to Jerusalem. A similar list appears in chapter 7 of Nehemiah. These are not famous biblical characters. They appear in the biblical narrative only here in Ezra/Nehemiah. And then they quickly move offstage. But the text does not list them randomly. It uses meaningful groups growing out of the context in which the chapter is set.

- Verses 2–35 group people by family. This portion of the text lists fathers and sons ignoring mothers and daughters.
- Verses 36–40 list priests and Levites, which are both family groups and professional designations.
- Verse 41 begins listing people by profession: singers, gatekeepers, Temple servants, and Solomon's servants.
- Verse 59 lists people from distinct geographic locations.
- Verses 61–63 describe the situation of people whose priestly status is uncertain.

Some of people might have had a choice to gather with their extended family, or with people from their town or their profession.

The Chicago Jewish United Fund/Federation runs fundraising events by professional groups, congregations, country clubs, gender, age groups, and level of giving. Individual givers receive invitations to more than one event. They can choose to donate at the event their congregation holds or at the event their professional cohort holds.

We can ask, How do we list ourselves? What are our key groups? How do people identify me? One of my first retirement projects was to create a family-and-friends fantasy football league. I named the group The Big Fish League after the big fish in the book of Jonah. Most fantasy football leagues involve all ten players kicking in a certain amount of money, which at the end of the season goes to the winner. The amount of money varies from modest sums to very large sums. The participants in the Big Fish League do not compete for money, just for "glory" and the handmade Big Fish trophy. The league includes two of my children, three grandchildren, my brother, my nephew and his wife, and three of my rabbinic school classmates.

I serve as league commissioner. When I wrote my first letter to the members of the league, I had to decide how to sign my name. It turned out not to be a simple question. My rabbinic school classmates call me by my Hebrew name, Simcha. My brother thinks my name is Steve. My children call me Dad. And their children call me Grandpa. So, I sign the letters to the league as Steve/Simcha/Dad/Grandpa.

I have more than just these four names. People who encounter me professionally call me Rabbi Bob. At camp in our Hebrew immersion program, I am Rav Bob. Each of my many names expresses an aspect of my personal identity.

The various groups to which I belong could also be used to identify me:

Age cohort: baby boomers

Professional group: rabbis

Political group: Democrat

Music I listen to: Bob Dylan, The Grateful Dead, Opera, and folk music

The musical instrument I play: banjo

Hobbies: woodworking, chess, and golf

Is group membership fate or choice? Some of these groups I was born into, other groups I chose to join. Circumstances of birth provide a starting point. We are easily aware of many public examples of blessings of birth. Wealth may be the most obvious.

I am a baby boomer because I was born in 1950. I grew up in the suburbs of the Midwest, in St. Louis Park, Minnesota, because of choices my parents made. As I grew closer to entering adulthood life, choices became more my own.

As a youth, my friends and I actively participated in Habonim Labor Zionist Youth, which pointed us to living on a kibbutz in Israel as the ideal life path. As we reached our early twenties, some of my friends made aliyah. As I was approaching college graduation in 1972 I made a decision to not go with my friends to live on a kibbutz in Israel. I chose instead to remain in America. I applied to rabbinic school. The Hebrew Union College accepted me. And in the fall of 1972, I began my first year of rabbinic school, which took place not in Cincinnati but rather in Israel. Having decided not to live in Israel, I went to spend a year in Jerusalem.

I loved that year living in Israel. It was a wonderful and optimistic time in Israel. The national mood was still very influenced by the Six-Day War. In the spring of 1973 Israel celebrated its twenty-fifth year. We went to the large military parade. We even went to the rehearsal for the military parade held in the dark a few days before Yom Hatzmaut. We also attended the national song festival featuring the star singers of the first twenty-five years of the state.

Throughout that year, we could travel everywhere without fear. We went to Bethlehem, Hebron, Nablus, and Gaza without incident. We learned to speak Hebrew confidently. We enjoyed Israeli food that was not yet available in America. The Red Owl grocery stores in Minneapolis in those days did not carry hummus. We learned to feel at home in Israel. We were fully caught up in the romantic Israel narrative.

Many of us spent the week of Passover after the Seder on a camping tour of the Sinai, then under Israeli control. We had two large trucks with benches in the back to carry the group of rabbinic students, Israeli school teachers, and new immigrants from France. We had a great time. We spent the last night of the trip camped on the shore of the Red Sea near Dahab. The tour leader broke out bottles of brandy he had brought along for this conclusion party.

An Israeli army patrol stopped by. We invited them to join the party. They agreed but explained first they had to go for a short ride back to their base to check in. One of the soldiers invited me to come along in their half-track for the ride. We chatted in Hebrew as we drove. After I told him my story, he asked, "Why are you going back to the States? Why don't you stay here?" At that moment under the star-filled Sinai sky, I did not have a good answer for him. It was the closest that I came to making aliyah. But I chose to return to the States and continue my rabbinic education in Cincinnati.

While one might say that fate led to my birth in 1950 in Troy, New York, and my Minnesota childhood, my adult life in Chicago grew out of my choices. I chose to be a rabbi. I chose to marry Tammie. I accepted the job at Temple Beth El that brought us to Chicago, and the job at Congregation Etz Chaim that kept us in the Chicago metropolitan area.

Fate brought the exiles to Babylonia, but they chose to return to Jerusalem or remain in Babylonia. Chapter 2 of Ezra lists the people who chose to return to Jerusalem in the first wave of immigration. Chapter 8 contains a shorter list of people who came up to Jerusalem with Ezra eighty years later. And some people chose not to return at all. Our people remained in Babylonia for centuries, as I explained in chapter 18.

In 1986 I travelled to the Soviet Union with my friend Mike to visit Jewish activists. In Leningrad (today St. Petersburg) we met with Anna. Her husband had been arrested for anti-Soviet slander. The Soviet government sent him to a prison camp on the Kamchatka Peninsula, at the other end of the Soviet Union. Her son Boris was in an army hospital in Archangel. We brought items she could sell on the black market. She shared with us the newest details of her situation so that we could report them to those working on her behalf in the United States.

During our visit, Anna's ten-year-old daughter, Masha, came home from school. Masha asked me where my family came from. I told her that my grandparents left Lithuania before World War I. Masha asked her mother, "Why were his grandparents smarter than mine? Why did mine stay here?" The choices my great-grandparents made to leave Lithuania spared all of their descendants the horrors of the Holocaust and the tyranny of lives in Soviet Union.

The first wave of returnees listed in the second chapter of Ezra chose to journey back to Jerusalem. We can only speculate about what motivated some of the exiles to remain in Babylonia while others made the choice to return. In the next chapter we look at the support those returning to Jerusalem received.

Chapter 30

Help from Others

JEWISH TRADITION TEACHES US that our Passover Seder should conclude before midnight because the departure from Egypt took place in the middle of the night in immediate response to Pharaoh's granting permission for the Israelites to depart. Pharaoh acted in an agitated state, directing the Israelites to leave Egypt in response to the tenth plague, the death of the firstborn. Moses feared that Pharaoh might change his mind if the people waited for the sun to rise.

Here in the Ezra/Nehemiah story, the people do not fear Cyrus the Great changing his mind. Cyrus is acting not out of fear but rather out of awe in response to God's direction.

> In the first year of King Cyrus of Persia, when the word of the ETERNAL spoken by Jeremiah was fulfilled, the ETERNAL roused the spirit of King Cyrus of Persia to issue a proclamation throughout his realm. (Ezra 1:1)

So, this journey back to Jerusalem could take place without haste and in an orderly fashion. In this story the people do not grab "dough that did not have time to rise" (see Exod 12:39). This generation could methodically prepare for their journey back to the land of Israel.

The text tells us,

> So, the chiefs of the clans of the fathers' houses of Judah and Benjamin, and the priests, and the Levites, all whose spirit had been roused by God got ready to go up to build the house of the ETERNAL that is in Jerusalem. (Ezra 1:5)

The tribes of Judah and Benjamin together with the Levites serving in the Temple were the tribes living in the Southern Kingdom of Judah at the time of the Babylonian conquest in 586 BCE. The other ten tribes had lived in the Northern Kingdom. When the Assyrian Empire conquered the Northern Kingdom earlier in 722 BCE the members of those tribes were completely removed from Samaria. The Assyrian authorities dispersed the members of those tribes in other areas of the Assyrian Empire, as I explained in chapter 18. Only Judah, Benjamin, and a portion of Levi remained in existence at time that the book of Ezra begins.

The text of Ezra tells us that the general Babylonian population helped provide for the people for their trip to Jerusalem: "And all their neighbors supported them with silver vessels, with gold, with goods, and with livestock, and with precious objects, besides what had been given as a freewill offering" (Ezra 1:6).

The commentators want to make sure to narrow the scope of the support provided by outsiders. Rashi explains the distinction between what the Jews paid for and what the gifts from the gentile neighbors funded: "All of this was done by the neighbors of the Jews, beyond what they had themselves given to rebuild the Temple" (Rashi on Ezra 1:6).

The Jews themselves would pay for the actual construction of the Temple. The other people provided secondary support to the Jews. Throughout his commentary to Ezra/Nehemiah, Rashi emphasizes the point that the rebuilding of the Temple was funded and actually done by the Jews themselves. He resists any reading of the text to infer that Cyrus, later Persian kings, or the gentile population funded the rebuilding of the Temple.

People resist help. When adults see young children struggling with a task, they may try to help. But often the children resist the help saying, "Let me do it."

Several times in my career as a congregational rabbi I approached people I knew to be facing difficult financial situations with an offer of help. Very often they declined the offers of assistance. Once in response to a flood affecting a community in which some of our members lived, the congregation raised money to help them rebuild. The lay leaders of the congregation asked me to confidentially distribute the money to our families affected by the flood. I spoke privately to the affected families. Every one of these families declined. I knew that some of our families needed the help we were offering, but they would not accept it. I explained to the congregation's leaders that I was not willing to put unmarked bills in plain brown bags and throw them through our members' windows in the middle of the night. Ultimately, we contributed the money we had collected to a general fund in the community for flood relief.

I recall a television commercial from my childhood in the 1960s with the catch phrase, "Mother please, I would rather do it myself." We want to be proudly independent. Our sense of self would be diminished by accepting help from others.

Despite our sense of rugged individualism, we do face times when we accept help—when our life situation grows dire, when we realize that we have little strength and meager resources.

As a people, we often think of Jewish history as a long list of other people doing things to us rather than for us. But we know that individuals, groups, and nations have come to our aid. We honor Righteous Gentiles who risked their own lives to protect Jews during the Holocaust. Some of these Righteous Gentiles have become well-known: Oskar Schindler and Raoul Wallenberg. Others remain nameless, even to the people they saved.

My late father-in-law, Eric Blaustein, grew up in Germany. He started school on the day the Nazis came to power. Throughout the war he hid with the help of many people. Some of the people who helped him were friends of the family. But I am most moved by the stories of the anonymous strangers who played a brief but essential role in his survival. In the fall of 1944 Eric was arrested in a train depot and was taken to the police station. He writes,

> There were only three policemen in the otherwise empty station. The S. D. man told me to stand in front of a file cabinet. Under no circumstances was I to move. He told the policemen to watch me.
>
> Turning to the lieutenant in charge, he said,
>
> "Prepare a report and lock him up."
>
> I thought the lieutenant looked sympathetic.
>
> "Why didn't you guys do that?" he asked.
>
> "We didn't get around to it," said the S. D. man.
>
> The lieutenant argued that he wasn't willing to do paperwork for the S. D., and besides, it was against regulations. The arresting authority had to make the report. The S. D. man grumbled.
>
> "Fine, I'll do it, but I have another assignment. Just watch this guy for ten minutes and I'll be back."
>
> He left, with the two policemen behind him.

> That left me alone with the police lieutenant.
>
> He shouted, "Don't block my way in front of my desk! Move over there!"
>
> He was pointing to the exit door. I moved fast. He sat down with his back toward me, picked up the handgun on his desk and threw it into a drawer. Under his breath he said, "Get out of here, quick."
>
> I bolted into the crowded railroad station hall. Over my shoulder I saw the lieutenant had pushed himself and his chair in front of the door, blocking it. He screamed for help, obviously to cover himself. Yet by blocking the door he prevented anyone from quick pursuit.[1]

We have no idea who this lieutenant was or why he acted to save Eric. Most of us live lives that are less dramatic than Eric's. We have not faced threats to our lives. I have lived a quiet Midwestern suburban life. But like most people, I have received help along the way. I have been helped by friends and relatives. And I have been helped by people I hardly knew, random strangers who offered a helping hand.

The generation that returned from Babylonian exile received help from Cyrus the Great. The generation of our people who escaped slavery in Egypt received help from the Egyptians as they departed Egypt.

> And the Israelites had done Moses' bidding and borrowed from the Egyptians objects of silver, and of gold, and clothing. And the ETERNAL had disposed the Egyptians favorably toward the people and they let them have their request what they asked. And they stripped the Egyptians. (Exod 12:35–36)

As the Jewish people began to return to Palestine in the late nineteenth century, we received support from many sources, including non-Jews. One of Theodor Herzl's key supporters was an Anglican minister, Reverend William Hechler. The son of a British mother and a German father, Reverend Hechler first encountered Zionist ideas in Odessa, Russia, where he met Leon Pinsker, the author of *Auto-Emancipation*, an early description of Zionist principles. Reverend Hechler developed his own ideas about the importance of the Jewish return to the land of Israel; he saw himself as a Restorationist.

While serving as the chaplain to the British Embassy in Vienna, Hechler discovered Herzl's book *The Jewish State*. He quickly sought a

1. From Eric Blaustein's unpublished memoir, 1984.

meeting with Herzl. In his diary Herzl described his first meeting with Rev Hechler:

> A likeable, sensitive man with the long grey beard of a prophet. He waxed enthusiastic over my solution. . . . He wants to place my tract in the hands of some German princes. He used to be a tutor in the household of the Grand Duke of Baden, he knows the German Kaiser and thinks he can get me an audience.[2]

Hechler provided key introductions for Herzl to powerful and important European leaders. His participation in the early stages of organizing the Zionist movement provided an added level of legitimacy to a fledgling endeavor.

Cyrus the Great provided the opportunity and the means for our return from the Babylonian exile. Cyrus the Great is known in Hebrew as *koresh*. If one flips the sequence of the last two letters of his name we get *kosher*, "proper." One might imagine that Kosher King would be the name of a butcher shop or a caterer. But in truth, Cyrus the Great is "the Kosher King." We have explored Cyrus's place in Jewish tradition and Israeli life more fully in chapter 15.

2. Herzl, *Complete Diaries*, 312 (entry for Mar. 10, 1896).

Chapter 31

What Were Their Names?

Do you think you know the Hebrew Bible? Do you think that you can identify the people mentioned in the Bible? I am confident I can stump you. Ready? Who was Eved ben Yonatan? He does appear in the Hebrew Bible. I have informally surveyed several groups of Bible "experts": the students in two Wheaton College Bible classes, the readers of the Reform Rabbis Facebook page, my personal Facebook friends, several Bible professors, and prominent Chicago rabbis. Nobody had ever heard of him. The Bible does mention him, but only once.

Chapter 2 of Ezra contains a detailed list of the people who came with Zerubbabel to Jerusalem in the first wave of returning exiles during the reign of Cyrus the Great. The same list appears again in chapter 7 of Nehemiah. Chapter 8 of Ezra contains a different list of later returning exiles who were led by Ezra during the reign of King Artaxerxes. It is in this later list that we meet Eved ben Yonatan (Ezra 8:6).

Most people would not carefully read these lists of names. Most readers would just lump them together as "names." This one name jumps out because it is an odd Hebrew name. *Yonatan* is a fine, well-known Hebrew name translated into English as Jonathan. But *Eved* creates difficulties. It strikes Hebrew readers as a category rather than a name. The word literally means "slave," which makes it an unexpected name for a person. Rashi says, "Thus was his name" (Rashi on Ezra 8:6). In this brief simple comment Rashi acknowledges that the name is unusual but insists that it was indeed his name.

I am drawn to Eved ben Yonatan because of my own unusual name. Regularly I have the opportunity to respond to people who question the correctness of my last name. Generally, when asked who I am I say, "Steven Bob. Bob, like a man's first name, but it is my last name." People have said to me, "Bob can't be your last name." As if somehow I do not know my own last name. Often people ask me to explain the name. They think that it was shortened at Ellis Island. They imagine that in the old country we were Bobinski, Bobover, or Bobowitz. Truly "clever" people ask if I am from the South. They suggest that Steve Bob might be like Jim Bob or Billy Bob.

I have been willing to play around with my own name. Before our children were born, I did enjoy telling people that we if we had a son, we would name him Dylan. One year for Purim I came to services dressed as SpongeBob SquarePants. I saw him as my cousin Sponge.

Another year, two of my children and I came to Purim as "the Israeli BOBsled team." I shared a whole explanation of how my great-great-grandfather invented this type of sled. So, it was named after him. A few visitors to the congregation, who did not know me well, thought that I was telling a true story.

Joseph Heller's World War II novel, *Catch-22*, includes a character named Major Major Major. Heller explains that this fellow's father chose to give the first name Major and the middle name Major, as a joke. He chose these names over his other ideas: "Drum Major, Minor Major, Sergeant Major, or C Sharp Major." He becomes an actual major in the Army Air Corps because "an IBM machine with a sense of humor almost as keen as his father's" promoted him.[1]

So, what should we make of the name Eved ben Yonatan? Was he an actual slave? We annually encounter the plural form of the Hebrew word *eved* at the Passover Seder. We say, *Avadim hayinu l'pharoah b'mitzrayom*, "We were slaves to Pharaoh in Egypt." While the Hebrew word *eved* is often used to describe a slave, it could also mean "worker." If Eved ben Yonatan had been an actual slave his name would not have been included in the Bible's list of those who accompanied Ezra on the return to Jerusalem. I imagine that he was called Eved because he was a skillful worker. So, let's think of him as a fellow who worked skillfully with his hands.

Ezra describes the rebuilding of the Temple. Nehemiah in greater detail describes the rebuilding of the city's walls and gates. Neither book

1. Heller, *Catch-22*, 347.

tells us what specific role Eved ben Yonatan played in the rebuilding of Jerusalem. Big projects require the efforts of many regular people whose names are not recalled. Every day, large crowds visit the magnificent Hoover Dam. The visitors to the dam hear a vivid description of the strength of the dam. But nowhere in the tour does one see a list of the names of the people who built the Hoover Dam. We can ask, Who built that dam? Or similarly, Who dug the Erie Canal?

If we ask similar question about the State of Israel, I have many answers! I will share one story, the story of Moshe Blaustein, my wife's great-uncle, a founding member of Kibbutz Givat Brenner. At its peak, in 1968, Kibbutz Givat Brenner had 1,520 inhabitants, making it the largest kibbutz in Israel. One of its first members was Uncle Moshe. The official history of Givat Brenner members describes Uncle Moshe:

> Moshe was born on January 30, 1909, to Benjamin and Tzipora Blaustein in Chemnitz, Germany. . . . When Moshe came on aliyah to Givat Brenner in 1929, it was a place of tents with 40 people. He was part of the group that created the first economic project, "Grove Aleph" under the leadership of Avraham Katz.
>
> After that he was part of a group that went down to the Dead Sea. First, they built the factory there and then the road from the Dead Sea to Jericho. Afterward Moshe worked on roads or in groves. . . . For most of the early years he lived in a tent with his friends. For the cabins were filled with families. In 1939 he married Nechama Pergament who arrived on the ship "Tiger Hayaal" the last ship to leave Poland before the Germans invaded. [Nechama became a painter known as "The Grandma Moses of Givat Brenner."]
>
> Moshe continued to work in the grove for many years. He was one of the greatly beloved personalities by all the generations.[2]

None of the standard histories of Israel and Zionism mention Moshe Blaustein. I know his story because I met Moshe when he was an old man enjoying retirement at Givat Brenner. Moshe built roads and then worked in the citrus orchards of his kibbutz for decades. Writers describe many famous people as "builders of the State of Israel." Most of those famous people did very little actual building. Moshe Blaustein built the State of Israel with his own hands. So, who is Eved ben Yonatan? He is like Moshe Blaustein, who built the State of Israel with his own hands. I imagine that Eved ben Yonatan built the walls of Jerusalem with his own hands.

2. Sipurei Givat Brenner, "Moshe Blaustein"; author's translation.

The regular, everyday people shape and build every community—in the Bible, in modern Israel, in the communities in which we live. Frank Capra's movie *It's a Wonderful Life* illustrates this point. I know, many people think of *It's a Wonderful Life* as a Christmas movie. To me it is a Yom Kippur movie. On Yom Kippur we act as if we are no longer alive. We engage in none of the basic human activities for a whole day: no eating, drinking, working, or sex. Traditional Jews wear a white kittel, like a burial shroud. After a day in the kingdom of death we reemerge back into the kingdom of the living. We get another chance to live. In *It's a Wonderful Life* George Bailey, played by Jimmy Stewart, has the opportunity to see what the world would be like if he had never lived. At the conclusion of the film, he reemerges with renewed energy and purpose to continue to live his life. Earlier in the movie George Bailey explains the importance of regular people to the banker, Mr. Potter, played by Lionel Barrymore:

> You, you said that they . . . had to wait and save their money before they even thought of a decent home. Wait? Wait for what?! Until their children grow up and leave them? Until they're so old and broken down that—you know how long it takes a working man to save five thousand dollars? Just remember this, Mr. Potter, that this rabble you're talking about, they do most of the working and paying and living and dying in this community. Well, is it too much to have them work and pay and live and die in a couple of decent rooms and a bath?[3]

We do not know the names of all the people who rebuilt Jerusalem, the people who did "most of the working and paying and living and dying" in Jerusalem. But we can honor those people who, like Eved ben Yonatan, built the walls of Jerusalem with their own hands.

3. Capra, *It's a Wonderful Life*, 40:40.

Chapter 32

Ahasuerus and Ahasuerus

After the first wave of returnees arrived in Jerusalem, they rebuilt the altar and began to rebuild the Temple. As I will explain in chapter 36, that process was interrupted by enemies. In the description of the halt in chapter 4 of Ezra we read, "And during the reign of Ahasuerus [Achashveirosh in Hebrew] at the beginning of his reign they wrote a calumny against the inhabitants of Judah and Jerusalem" (Ezra 4:6). While the name *Ahasuerus* is familiar to us from the Purim story, its appearance here does raise a question. Is this king, mentioned here in Ezra 4:6, the same Ahasuerus found in the book of Esther?

Rashi confidently places Ahasuerus of Ezra 4:6 in historical context by identifying him as the Ahasuerus we know from the book of Esther. Rashi explains that this is the king "who ruled after Cyrus. This is Ahasuerus who took Esther to be his wife" (Rashi on Ezra 4:6).

Other traditional sources, Targum Esther, Seder Olam, Masechet Megillah in the Babylonian Talmud, and Yalkut Shimoni, connect the events described in Ezra 4 with characters from the book of Esther. The Talmud clearly identifies the Ahasuerus in Ezra as being the same Ahasuerus in Esther. The Talmud presents ways to understand the meaning of Achashveirosh's name. One approach sees in the name *Achashveirosh* three Hebrew words, *achi shel rosh*, "brother of the head." The Talmud identifies "the head" to be Nebuchadnezzar. The sages of the Talmud do not argue that Achashveirosh was literally Nebuchadnezzar's brother but rather that he pursued the same path as Nebuchadnezzar.

Nebuchadnezzar destroyed the Temple. His "brother," Achashveirosh, interrupts the rebuilding of the Temple.

Masechet Megillah connects another verse of Ezra to the Purim story. Chapter 9 of Ezra includes a prayer that Ezra recites: "For we are bondmen; yet our God has not forsaken us in our bondage, but has extended mercy unto us in the sight of the kings of Persia" (Ezra 9:9).

The Talmud seeks to connect this poetic image to a specific time and place: "When did this occur? In the time of Haman." This page of the Talmud continues with arguments from four different sages, each presenting their own way to connect this Ezra verse to Esther. Each of the sages begins with a verse in the wisdom literature: Psalms, Proverbs, or Ecclesiastes. They then each artfully wind their way to Ezra.

Seder Olam presents Haman and his ten sons playing a direct role in the stoppage of work on the rebuilding of the Temple described in chapter 4 of Ezra. The rabbis tell of them journeying from Shushan, the Persian capital, to Jerusalem to prevent the Jews from rebuilding the Temple (Seder Olam Rabbah 29).

The text of Ezra reports, "And in the reign of Ahasuerus, at the start of his reign, they drew up an accusation against the inhabitants of Judah and Jerusalem" (Ezra 4:6). The Ezra text does not clearly identify to whom the word *they* refers. The appearance of the name Ahasuerus in the verse prompts the author of Seder Olam to suggest that the *they* were actually the sons of Haman.

As a result of lighthearted Purim celebrations, many Jews view the book of Esther as a heroine/hero story in which Esther and Mordecai bravely save the Jewish people from destruction at the hands of the wicked Haman. I learned from Professor Elsie Stern that the book of Esther is actually a story written in the land of Israel to point out to diaspora Jews the dangers of remaining in exile.[1] In the Esther story the powerless Jews of Persia face the threat of complete destruction at the hands of Haman. The author of the book of Esther was urging the Jews of Persia to return to the land of Israel where they would be safer. It is possible that the book of Esther was written during the Hasmonean period. In the first hundred years after the events we celebrate at Hanukkah, the family of Judah the Maccabee, the Hasmoneans, ruled an independent Jewish state in the land of Israel. The author of the book of Esther was encouraging the Jews remaining in exile to come home where they would be safe.

1. Stern, "Megillat Esther."

The common mention of Ahasuerus is not the only connection between Ezra/Nehemiah and Esther. Esther and Ezra/Nehemiah present supportive arguments concerning the path that Jews should follow. Ezra and Nehemiah describe the importance of returning to Jerusalem from exile, while Esther describes the danger of them remaining in exile.

Now we can ask, What is the connection between Ahasuerus in Ezra 4:6 and Ahasuerus in the book of Esther? Many scholars agree that the events described in Esther and retold during Purim celebrations have no basis in history. The author of the book of Esther was not a historian carefully reconstructing the past. This author had a message to convey. The tale was an engaging means to present his concerns. He was trying to persuade the diaspora Jews of his own time to realize the fragility of their situation and return to the land of Israel. In constructing his cautionary tale set in the Persian court, he gleaned the name *Ahasuerus* for his Persian king from the book of Ezra 4:6. Because we are so much more familiar with book of Esther than with the book of Ezra, we asked if the Ahasuerus in Ezra is the same Ahasuerus we know from Esther. My analysis is that the flow of information was in the other direction. The mention of Ahasuerus in Ezra was the source that the author of the book of Esther used for choosing a name of the king in his story.

When I first heard the song "Memphis" it was Johnny Rivers's 1964 version. In 1964 I was fourteen years old. I had only recently begun listening to rock music. I thought that Johnny Rivers had created the song "Memphis." I was not yet familiar with the concept of a "cover" song. When Johnny Rivers followed the success of "Memphis" by recording "Maybelline," I thought that was his original song as well. It was only later that I learned about Chuck Berry. Johnny Rivers's 1964 version of "Memphis" climbed the charts to the number 2 spot. The 1959 original record by Chuck Berry only made it to number 87 in 1959. I am sure that I was not the only young teenager in 1964 who thought of these songs as Johnny Rivers songs.

The Beach Boys introduced me to other Chuck Berry melodies. Their "Surfin' USA" is Chuck Berry's "Sweet Little Sixteen" with new lyrics. Carl Wilson's guitar introduction to "Fun, Fun, Fun" is pure Chuck Berry. It sounds just like Chuck Berry's guitar riff at the beginning of "Johnny B. Goode." Eventually the Beach Boys gave appropriate credit and financial compensation to Chuck Berry. I came to be a big fan of Chuck Berry's songs, but I first learned about him from the records of Johnny Rivers and The Beach Boys.

Sometimes in popular music a cover version of a song becomes much more popular than the original. People think of the 1967 song "Respect" as an Aretha Franklin song. Many people see it as her signature song. But she did not write it. Nor was she the first person to record it. Otis Redding wrote and recorded "Respect." Otis Redding's 1965 recording reached number 35 on the Billboard charts. His live version at the Monterey Pop Festival shows him at his finest. But Aretha took the song to a new level. She rearranged it and gave it new meaning. Aretha's record became an anthem for women demanding respect. The background singers, Aretha's sisters Carolyn and Erma, urge her on, singing, "Re, Re, Re, Re," the name by which Aretha was known in the Franklin family. Aretha's recording in 1967 reached number 1 on the Billboard. Even Otis Redding acknowledged that it had become her song.[2]

Ahasuerus's first appearance in biblical literature was this mention in the book of Ezra. A century or two later when the author of the book of Esther was crafting the now famous story of Esther, Mordecai, and Haman, he gave his book a historical foundation by borrowing a name for his king from this mention of Ahasuerus in Ezra. The reading of the book of Esther is the centerpiece of celebrating the joyous holiday of Purim. Because of the popularity of Purim, that mention of King Ahasuerus is well-known. In contrast the book of Ezra is not part of any annual moment in the life of synagogue-attending Jews. As a result, one might think that the original source of the name Ahasuerus was the book of Esther. But we now know that this name was used first by the book of Ezra.

2. Hickey, "Respect."

Chapter 33

How Do You Say Ahasuerus in Persian?

In the previous chapter we explored the connection of the uses of the name *Ahasuerus* in the book of Esther and here in the book of Ezra. We can now take the next step and ask, Which of the Persian kings is the biblical Ahasuerus?

In America we know the names of many foreign countries and major world cities by names that are different from the names that actual residents of those countries and cities use. Sometimes the differences are small. Paris is spelled the same way in English and French. But when Americans pronounce the capital of France they say *Paris*, while its resident say they live in *Paree*. Americans call the country east of France, *Germany*. But the people who live there call it *Deutschland*. The country that we call *Switzerland* is called *Schweiz* by most of the people who live there. Swiss email addresses conclude with *CH*, from the Latin name of the country, *Confoedetario Helvetica*. I do not remember much from the Latin classes that I took in high school. But we did spend a lot of time memorizing Julius Caesar's *Gallic Wars*. As a result, I know that *Helvetica* was the Latin name for the area we now call *Switzerland*.

If I were to ask you to list the kings of Persia, you would not respond by using the names these kings actually used. The names we know for the Persian kings are not the rulers' genuine Persian names. The earliest Western historians were Greeks, including Herodotus, Xenophon, and Thucydides. They used Greek names when writing about the Persian kings. Western sources have continued to use these rulers' Greek names. So, we know them under these names:

Cyrus the Great (559–529 BCE)

Cambyses II (529–521 BCE)

Darius I (521–485 BCE)

Xerxes I (485–464 BCE)

Artaxerxes I (464–424 BCE)

Xerxes II (423 BCE)

Darius II (423–404 BCE)

Artaxerxes II (404–358 BCE)

We see that this list of Persian kings by their Greek names does not include an *Ahasuerus*. So, which of these Persian kings is the Ahasuerus from the book of Esther and Ezra? Some sources have connected Ahasuerus/Achashveirosh with Artaxerxes I. These sources saw the similarity between the Hebrew *Achashveirosh* and the Greek *Artaxerxes*. These sources, like us, probably did not know the Persian names of the Persian kings. Modern scholars who have studied this matter more fully explain that the Hebrew name *Achashveirosh* comes from the Persian *Khshayarasha* with an *aleph* added to the beginning. Khshayarasha is known in Greek as Xerxes.

Xerxes is well-known as a strong leader of the Persian Empire's invasion of Greece. The 2006 film *300* brought new popular attention to the story of the battle of Thermopylae, in which Leonidas led the Spartan forces in their confrontation with the much larger Persian forces led by Xerxes. I knew of Xerxes from an early age because in the south Minneapolis neighborhood of my childhood, the streets were alphabetical. We lived on France Avenue in the second alphabet. The X street in the first alphabet is Xerxes. In the second alphabet the X street was Xenwood, and in the third alphabet it was Xylon.

The very first verse of the book of Esther describes Ahasuerus as ruling over a vast kingdom "from Ethiopia until India." The historical Xerxes ruled over a kingdom even larger than that. Under his leadership the Persian Empire extended into Europe. He led the Persian efforts to conquer Greece. The geographic high-water moment of the Persian Empire occurred during the reign of Xerxes.

The image of Xerxes that we know from history presents a powerful leader. Ahasuerus in the book of Esther seems most interested in "wine, women, and song" rather than conquering the known world. The author of the book of Esther is not interested in teaching history. That author has a cautionary tale to tell. The author of Ezra seems more interested in relating actual historic events.

Is the Ahasuerus mentioned in Ezra 4:6 Xerxes? The identification of the Ahasuerus mentioned in Ezra 4:6 as Xerxes creates timeline problems. The first wave of return took place during the reign of Cyrus the Great in 539 BCE. Ezra describes the rebuilding of the Temple to have resumed and to have been completed during the reign of Darius in 516 BCE. Xerxes came to the throne in 485 BCE after the death of his father, Darius. The king who ruled Persia between Cyrus and Darius was Cambyses. He was probably the king at the time of the halt in the reconstruction of the Temple.

The classic scholars, Gerson B. Levi, Kaufman Kohler, and George A. Barton, in the *Jewish Encyclopedia* write, "In like manner the reference to Ahasuerus in Ezra, iv. 6 occurs where Cambyses or Darius is to be expected, if the statement is historical, and is no doubt the result of the ignorance of a late writer."[1] These scholars conclude that the author of this chapter of Ezra did not have a clear understanding of the sequence of Persian rulers. Subsequent scholars have offered a variety of theories to untangle this "sequence of rulers" challenge. Lisbeth Fried suggests that this Ezra verse does not refer to events during the building of the Temple but rather to the rebuilding of the walls of Jerusalem in the time of Nehemiah during the reign of Artaxerxes.[2]

I agree with Levi, Kohler, and Barton that the one hundred or more years between the occurrence of the events described in Ezra 4:6 and the composition of the book of Ezra created a lack of precision in the reporting of the correct names of the kings. Often the passage of time clouds the way in which events are recalled.

On November 19, 1863, a group of dignitaries and a crowd of local residents gathered at the site of the battle of Gettysburg, which had taken place earlier that year in the first week of July. They came together to dedicate the cemetery as the Soldiers' National Cemetery. Abraham Lincoln was not the main speaker that day. The "oration" was delivered by Edward Everett. It contained 13,607 words and lasted two hours. Contemporary reports mention that Everett's speech was well-received. After a musical interlude, President Lincoln was called upon to share "dedicatory remarks." Lincoln spoke 271 words. Nobody reads Everett's long oration today. But Lincoln's short speech became known as the Gettysburg

1. Levi et al., "Ahasuerus," 285.
2. Fried, *Ezra*, 209.

Address. Lincoln artfully positions the ongoing Civil War in the context of American history. He defines the purpose of the war and the destiny of our country. The organizers of the event thought that Everett's long oration would be the Gettysburg Address. But when that day is now recalled, people do not mention Edward Everett. In his own time, Edward Everett was a very well-known speaker. Very few twenty-first-century Americans know his name. It is as if he was not there.[3]

The events described in Ezra 4:6 probably took place during the reign of King Cambyses. But in selecting a name for the king to mention in Ezra 4:6, the author of the book of Ezra chose Xerxes. Xerxes was a major Persian king. He was the son of Darius, and through his mother he was the grandson of Cyrus the Great. He ruled for twenty-one years. Under his leadership important events took place. He led the Persian invasion of Europe, doing battle in Greece, and he was seen as a major builder, completing projects in Persepolis begun during his father's reign.

In contrast Cambyses was a transitional figure who reigned for only eight years between Cyrus the Great and Darius I. It seems likely that the author of the book of Ezra knew the name of Xerxes and did not know of Cambyses. People in the author's time did not tell stories of Cambyses's great victories. The author had not seen or heard of any grand buildings constructed by Cambyses. Just as people today no longer remember that Edward Everett spoke at the dedication of the Gettysburg Cemetery, the author of Ezra no longer recalled that Cambyses had been the king after Cyrus the Great.

Many Americans can speak confidently about the most prominent presidents of our country. They could discuss the accomplishments of Lincoln, Washington, and FDR. My fellow baby boomers can recall the years that Eisenhower, Kennedy, and Nixon led our country. But they might get a bit confused sorting out the accomplishments of James Monroe and James Madison. Now if I asked most Americans to tell me about the presidency of Franklin Pierce, they would be stumped. President Pierce is usually not included in telling the story of American history.

I am suggesting that Cambyses was the Franklin Pierce of Persian history. The author of the book of Ezra probably did not know the name of King Cambyses. So he used the name of an important Persian king that he did know, Xerxes, known in Persian as Khshayarasha and in Hebrew as Ahasuerus.

3. Wills, *Lincoln at Gettysburg*, 19–40.

Chapter 34

He Was Wearing a Hat

As a child I enjoyed wearing a cowboy hat like the ones my heroes, Hopalong Cassidy and Roy Rogers, wore. When I attended a rabbis' convention in San Antonio in the 1980s I saw it as an opportunity to buy a quality cowboy hat. I was seeking a store where the locals bought their hats. As soon as we entered Paris Hatters, I felt we were in the right store. It is "the oldest surviving retail business in downtown San Antonio."[1] Then, I saw a photograph of the proprietor placing a Stetson on the head of Pope John Paul II. I knew it was exactly the right place for a rabbi to buy a Stetson. For many years that Stetson was my signature hat at summer camp.

In a famous photograph of Butch Cassidy, the Sundance Kid, and the rest of their gang, Butch is wearing a bowler, not a cowboy hat. When I first saw the bowler, I was surprised. In movies and TV shows, cowboys wear cowboy hats. The large brim of the cowboy hat provided more shade during hours in the saddle guiding the herd. Present-day cowboys continue to wear cowboy hats. These classic American hats remain popular in the West today, even when the wearer is not actually riding a horse.

At the end of the nineteenth century the bowler was the new modern hat. We might think of a bowler as a British hat worn by "city gents." In America it became known as a derby. As a youth I associated it with Laurel and Hardy. As an adult I connect it with René Magritte's paintings.

1. As stated on their website home page: https://parishatters.com/.

So why was Butch Cassidy wearing a bowler in this famous photograph? Was he imitating "big-city" types as a joke? The answer is more practical. Historians explain that some bandits and law officers preferred a bowler because at a high-speed gallop a bowler was less likely to fly off one's head than a wide-brimmed Stetson.[2]

In my favorite movies, *The Maltese Falcon* and *Casablanca*, Humphrey Bogart wears a fedora. In the TV series *The Untouchables*, Elliot Ness and his team of government agents wear gray fedoras. The gangsters often wore fancier hats with a curved brim, a homburg.

Hats often tells us a great deal about the wearer's identity. As part of the process of exploring the world of Ezra and Nehemiah, we can ask, What kind of head covering did the Jews of the second commonwealth wear? Certainly not a bowler, a homburg, a fedora, or a Stetson. What can we learn about the garments of these Jews from Ezra/Nehemiah? The text does not offer much information. We do know that the men of Nehemiah wore swords.

> From that day on, half my servants did work and half held lances and shields, bows and armor. And the officers stood behind the whole house of Judah who were rebuilding the wall. The basket-carriers were burdened, doing work with one hand while the other held a weapon. As for the builders, each had his sword girded at his side as he was building. The trumpeter stood beside me. (Neh 4:10–12)

So, we know that some of the men wore swords, but what did Ezra and Nehemiah put on their heads? While the Bible does not provide much information on how people dressed, we do have visual images from reliefs carved into buildings and monuments from the Achaemenid (Persian) Empire of this period. We also have written Greek sources describing the Persians that the Greeks encountered. From the decorative relief in the palace of Xerxes in Persepolis and from the words of Herodotus we learn that prominent Persians wore cylindrical "fluted hats most commonly associated with 'Persian' dignitaries."[3]

We know from the first chapter of Nehemiah that he was the king's cup bearer before he came to Jerusalem to serve as governor. As a member of the Persian court and then as that court's official representative in

2. Donahue, "Old West Cowboys."

3. Shahbazi, "Clothing."

Jerusalem, we can imagine that Nehemiah dressed in the manner of the court and wore a Persian hat.

So, what kind of headgear did Ezra wear? The biblical text describes Ezra as a priest. The Torah describes the headgear to be worn by priests: "And for Aaron's sons also you shall make tunics, and make sashes for them, and make turbans for them, for dignity and adornment" (Exod 28:40).

The Hebrew term, translated here by JPS as "turbans," is *migba'ot*. The first step in determining the meaning of a word in the Hebrew Bible is to look at the other times it is used. This word occurs only four times in the Hebrew Bible. In each occurrence the text uses it to describe the priest's headgear. So, we cannot learn much from that step. The next step is to look at other words which come from the same three-letter root. This word's three-letter root is *gimel-bet-ayin*, which is the root for the well-known Hebrew word for "hill," *geva*. We can see that a turban resembles a hill. So I imagine that Nehemiah wore a cylindrical Persian hat, while Ezra wore the priestly turban.

I see a contemporary expression of these two head coverings in a twentieth-century family artifact. I am very familiar with a 1930 photo of the leading Jews of Mosul, Iraq. I saw it on the wall of Zadok and Shoshana Nagola's home in Nehariya. They are the parents of my son-in-law Assaf. Both Zadok and Shoshana have relatives in the photograph. In this formal 1930 photograph of the leading Jewish men of Mosul, some of the men are wearing a cylindrical fez while others are wearing a turban, which the community called a sudra. As it happens, Zadok's relative is wearing a fez while Shoshana's is wearing a turban. My wife's brother Oded and his wife, Ziva, have the same photo in their home in Jerusalem. Ziva's ancestor in the photo is wearing a turban.

The turban has been popular headgear with the general population in the Middle East for thousands of years, from before the biblical period to the twenty-first century. Jews in those areas followed the local fashion. While the fez was created in North Africa, it was embraced by the Ottoman leader Mahmoud II in the early nineteenth century. His navy brought the fez back from North Africa. He made it the official headgear of the army and later of all Ottoman government employees. It became a symbol of modernity and of Ottoman authority.

The Republic of Turkey emerged from the collapse of the Ottoman Empire following World War I. As one of the steps Mustafa Kemal Ataturk took to create a modern secular republic, he banned the wearing of a fez, which he saw as holdover from the Ottoman era. Ataturk's fez ban only covered the Republic of Turkey. In countries like Iraq, created from the land once governed by the Ottoman Empire, some men continued to wear a fez. In Mosul in 1930 a fez may have expressed a commitment to modernity or membership in the urban upper class, and a turban may have expressed an allegiance to tradition or connection to the rural way of life.

Jews of my generation who attended midcentury Hebrew schools are familiar with turban-wearing Jews from the illustration on the cover of our classroom notebook, our *machberet*. The front cover of the machberet featured a drawing of Moses Maimonides, also known as the Rambam, wearing a turban. As a Minnesotan ten-year-old I may not have appreciated the meaning of Rambam's turban. As an adult I have seen the statue of the Rambam in his birth place, Cordoba, Spain. There he is also portrayed wearing a turban in keeping with the custom of his time and place.

Today hats often indicate one's group affiliation. A knowledgeable person can determine much about an Orthodox Jewish man based on what he is wearing on his head. Is he wearing a kippah or a hat? What type of kippah or what type of hat? Does he wear it on the back of his head or on the top of his head? The answers to these questions will indicate where he studies and what type of synagogue he attends.

In rabbinic school in Cincinnati in the mid-1970s many students taught Bar/Bat Mitzvah students for the local congregations. I taught at a Reform congregation with a long, distinguished history. At that congregation, it was the custom that the tutor / rabbinic student was invited to be on the bima with their student at their Bar/Bat Mitzvah. My supervisor, the congregation's assistant rabbi, told me that I would not be allowed to wear my kippah on the bima of the temple. Being "hatless" was part of the congregation's identity. I could not imagine going into a synagogue without a kippah, so I declined the honor.

We express our identity and affiliation with our hats. In Chicago in the summer some people wear the blue cap of the Chicago Cubs, and others wear the black cap of the Chicago White Sox.

In the old song "The Streets of Laredo," Marty Robbins sang about identifying a man as a cowboy by his clothing. In many places and in many ages, we announce our identity by what we place on our heads. When Nehemiah placed the cylindrical fluted hat on his head, everyone was reminded that he represented the Persian Empire. When Ezra wore his special turban, everyone was reminded that he was a priest. Their hats identified their roles in the community.

Chapter 35

Foreign Wives

Ezra and Nehemiah each contain a story of Judean men taking foreign wives. The traditional commentators imagine that these texts tell of two separate incidents. As I will explain, we should actually read these texts as two reports of the same event. Paired stories in the biblical text are not unique to Ezra/Nehemiah.

In several places the Hebrew Bible contains two conflicting versions of the same story. For example, the Hebrew Bible contains two complete versions of the water from the rock story. In the book of Exod 17:2–7, we find a version from the E source, while in Num 20:2–13 we find a version of the same story from the P source.

The E version of the story depicts Moses acting alone. The P version of the story adds in priestly elements. Aaron the high priest, unmentioned in the other version of the story, becomes a leading figure in the P version. The E version of the story does not specify the location of the conversation between Moses and God. In the P version God speaks to Moses and Aaron at the entrance of the tent of meeting where the priests bring offerings. The P version of this story reflects the author of the P document's general approach, which elevates the status of Aaron and the priesthood.

In the first version of the story about Israelite men marrying foreign women, found in Ezra/Nehemiah, Ezra hears a description of a troubling pattern:

> Now when these things were done, the princes drew near unto me, saying: "The people of Israel, and the priests and the Levites, have not separated themselves from the peoples of the lands, doing according to their abominations, even of the Canaanites, the Hittites, the Perizzites, the Jebusites, the Ammonites, the Moabites, the Egyptians, and the Amorites. For they have taken of their daughters for themselves and for their sons; so that the holy seed have mingled themselves with the peoples of the lands; yea, the hand of the princes and rulers hath been first in this faithlessness." (Ezra 9:1–2)

Then Ezra speaks to the people strongly denouncing these marriages:

> And Ezra the priest stood up, and said unto them: "You have broken faith, and have married foreign women, to increase the guilt of Israel. Now therefore make confession unto the ETERNAL, the God of your fathers, and do His pleasure; and separate yourselves from the peoples of the land, and from the foreign women." (Ezra 10:10–11)

Finally, the text reports the people responding to Ezra in an unprecedented manner: "Then all the congregation answered and said with a loud voice: As you have said, so it is for us to do" (Ezra 10:12).

This entire thread should be read as hyperbole. It is filled with over-the-top exaggerations. The first indication of this pattern is in the list of nations. It is not composed of the names of the actual other peoples living in and around the land of Israel at the time of Ezra. Rather it features the list of the nations who had been living in the land at the time of the conquest led by Joshua. This list of the nations—"the Canaanites, the Hittites, the Perizzites, the Jebusites, the Ammonites, . . . and the Amorites"—occurs four times in the book of Exodus, twice in Deuteronomy, and three times in Joshua. The conquest led by Joshua took place about eight hundred years before the time of Ezra. The author of Ezra adds in the ancient enemy of Israel, the Egyptians. The only groups mentioned in this list which remained a part of the lives of the people at the time of Ezra were the Moabites and Ammonites.

The response of the people to Ezra's exhortation to leave their foreign wives is completely unbelievable. We should not imagine that Ezra spoke and the entire people quickly did exactly what he directed them to do. Nowhere else in the entire Hebrew Bible does any group of Israelites respond to any exhortation in such a manner. The Bible contains hundreds of verses from the prophets of God demanding that the people change their ways. The universal response of the people of Israel and Judah to all the prophets was to ignore them. The Bible does not contain any reports of the people of Israel or Judah changing their behavior in response to any of the prophets. The people do not listen to the exhortations of Isaiah, Jeremiah, Hosea, or Amos.

The single unique example of a group of people in the Bible responding positively to such a strongly worded condemnation is the reaction of the people of Nineveh, the capital of the Assyrian Empire, to the words of Jonah:

> Jonah started out and made his way into the city the distance of one day's walk, and proclaimed: "Forty days more, and Nineveh shall be overthrown!" The people of Nineveh believed God. They proclaimed a fast, and great and small alike put on sackcloth. . . . "Let everyone turn back from his evil ways and from the injustice of which he is guilty." (Jon 3:4–5, 8)

We should not read the book of Jonah as a story depicting actual events. It is a tall tale meant to convey important truths. Exaggerations fill the book. The people of Nineveh are the most evil. The storm is bigger than any other storm. A large fish swallows Jonah; he survives and is able to calmly pray. Everybody else in the Bible ignores the repeated messages of prophets to change their ways, but the people of Nineveh hear one short phrase from Jonah, and they turn their lives upside down.

Just in case the readers are missing the point, as part of the description of the repentance in chapter 3, we are told that the large domestic animals of Nineveh follow the example of their owners by putting on sack cloth and fasting. I spend three weeks in Wisconsin every summer. I have never seen a contrite cow.

This account of the foreign wives from Ezra should also be seen as exaggerated telling of the events, not to be taken literally. The use of other peoples from a previous age and the report of the complete repentance of the people are not meant to be read as literal accounts of what actually happened in the real world.

The second version of the "foreign wives" story in the twenty-third chapter of the book of Nehemiah contains a more realistic description of a very similar incident. Nehemiah says,

> In those days I saw the Jews that had married women of Ashdod, of Ammon, and of Moab; and their children spoke half in the speech of Ashdod, and could not speak in the Jews' language,

> but according to the language of each people. And I contended with them, and cursed them, and smote certain of them, and plucked off their hair, and made them swear by God: "Ye shall not give your daughters unto their sons, nor take their daughters for your sons, or for yourselves. Did not Solomon, king of Israel sin by these things? Yet among many nations was there no king like him, and he was beloved of his God, and God made him king over all Israel; nevertheless, even him did the foreign women cause to sin. Shall we then hearken unto you to do all this great evil, to break faith with our God in marrying foreign women?" (Neh 13:23–28)

We notice right away that Nehemiah does not include the Canaanites, the Hittites, the Perizzites, the Jebusites, and the Egyptians in his list of the nations. Rather than harking back to the legendary "other nations" of the Moses/Joshua texts, he only mentions the nations that actually bordered Judah is his time.

The other significant difference is that this version of the story, from the very conclusion of the book of Nehemiah, does not describe the entire nation embracing the call to discard foreign wives. It limits the scope of Nehemiah's efforts to the priests and the Levites. Nehemiah claims credit for persuading the priests and the Levites who serve in the rebuilt Temple to send away their idol-worshiping wives:

> Remember to their discredit, O my God, how they polluted the priesthood, the covenant of the priests and Levites. I purged them of every foreign element, and arranged for the priests and the Levites to work each at his task by shifts, and for the wood offering [to be brought] at fixed times and for the first fruits. O my God, remember it to my credit! (Neh 13:29–31)

In both of these two versions of the story, the problem with the foreign wives is not their foreignness but rather their commitment to idolatry. Neither of these two versions of the story contemplates the possibility of a foreign wife who denounces idolatry.

The book of Ruth introduces just such a person. Ruth, a Moabite woman, renounces idolatry.

> And Ruth said [to Naomi, the mother of her late husband]: "Entreat me not to leave you, and to return from following after you; for where ever you go, I will go; and where ever you lodge, I will lodge; your people shall be my people, and your God shall be my God." (Ruth 1:16–17)

Many leading scholars believe that the book of Ruth was written as a response to the foreign wives stories in Ezra/Nehemiah. The text praises Ruth's eventual marriage to Boaz. King David, the central human figure in the Hebrew Bible, results from this relationship.

> So Boaz took Ruth, and she became his wife; and he went in unto her, and the Eternal gave her conception, and she bore a son. . . . And they called his name Obed; he is the father of Jesse, the father of David. (Ruth 4:13, 17)

The book of Ruth clearly argues that we do not need to concern ourselves with a person's origin once they say, "Your people shall be my people, and your God shall be my God." Ruth, and all who have followed in her footsteps, should be seen as full Jews. I have often said to people who have completed the process of conversion, "I believe that I am Jewish, but I know that you are Jewish."

Chapter 36

The Davidic Line

WHEN I WAS FOURTEEN years old, we took a family trip to Washington. A highlight of that 1964 visit to the capital was seeing senators in person. We went to the office of Minnesota's Senator Eugene McCarthy to pick up passes to the Senate gallery and for our White House tour. Senator McCarthy invited us into his inner office. In the hallway of the Senate office building, we saw Senator Leverett Saltonstall of Massachusetts. His distinguished physical appearance matched his upper-crust name. Our parents explained to us that he was the latest political leader from this important family who could trace themselves back to the *Mayflower*.

Senator Saltonstall was one of many American politicians of that era who had followed the family path of national leadership. Henry Cabot Lodge served in the Senate in the mid-twentieth century. His grandfather of the same name had served in the Senate in the early decades of the twentieth century. The Democratic nominee for president in 1952 and 1956 was Illinois Governor Adlai Stevenson II. His grandfather, Adlai Stevenson, served as vice president, 1893–1897. His son, Adlai Stevenson III, later served as senator from Illinois, 1970–1981. As scions of prominent political families, these individuals entered the public arena with name recognition and preexisting cohorts of supporters.

The Hebrew Bible describes many national leaders of Judah as descendants of a specific prominent family. The twenty-one men who ruled Judah after the death of King David—from Solomon, who built the Temple, to Zedekiah, who ruled at the time of its destruction—were all direct descendants of David. These Davidic kings could point to God's promise as spoken to David by the prophet Nathan: "Your house and your kingship shall ever be secure before you; your throne shall be established forever" (2 Sam 7:16). The "forever" in Nathan's promise turned out to be an exaggeration. Often when people say "forever" they mean a very long time, not literally forever. The Davidic line did indeed reign in Jerusalem for a very long time, about five hundred years.

The book of Ezra introduces Zerubbabel and Sheshbazzar as the leaders of the first wave of the return from exile. In describing the treasures of the First Temple, which King Cyrus had returned to the people so that they might carry them up to Jerusalem, the first chapter of Ezra reports, "These King Cyrus of Persia released through the office of Mithredath the treasurer who gave an inventory of them to Sheshbazzar the prince of Judah" (Ezra 1:8). Later we read, "Then Jeshua son of Jozadak and his brother priests and Zerubbabel son of Shealtiel and his brothers set out to and built the altar of the God of Israel" (Ezra 3:2). We might have expected the Bible to tell us that Zerubbabel and Sheshbazzar were a continuation of the Davidic line. But that is not the case. If they are not of the Davidic line, who are they?

Even to the casual reader, these two names do not sound like Hebrew names. *Sheshbazzar* shares sounds with *Nebuchadnezzar*, suggesting that it is a Babylonian name. The last portion of the two names likely originates in *nezzar*, meaning "guard" or "protect." Zerubbabel actually contains the word *babel*, the Hebrew expression for Babylonia. The first part of his name, *Zeru-*, is probably connected to the Hebrew word *zera*, meaning "seed." So, his name could be understood as "Seed of Babylon." Both Sheshbazzar and Zerubbabel have very Babylonian names.

The book of Ezra does not identify either of them as part of the Davidic line. If the authors of Ezra and Nehemiah had perceived either of these men to be a descendant of King David, they certainly would have mentioned it. Such a connection would have provided either of these leaders with significant instant status. Later sources make significant efforts to ascribe this Davidic status to Zerubbabel and Sheshbazzar.

The author of Chronicles portrays Zerubbabel as a direct descendant of King David. Chronicles focuses much attention on King David and the Davidic line. In chapter 3 the Chronicler lays out in detail the descendants of King David. There we read that Zerubbabel was the son of Pedaiah, the nephew of Shealtiel, and the grandson of Jeconiah (also known as Jehoiachin). Before we evaluate this grand claim of the Chronicler let us understand who Jeconiah was.

The story of the final kings of Judah is complex and not well-known. The last major king of Judah was Josiah, who reigned for thirty-one years. He died in a battle at Megiddo in 608 BCE. Three of Josiah's sons and one of his grandsons ruled in Jerusalem during the final three decades of the First Temple period. Jeconiah was the king of Judah when Nebuchadnezzar conquered Jerusalem. Nebuchadnezzar brought Jeconiah to Babylonia and imprisoned him for thirty-seven years. Second Kings concludes with the story of Evil-merodach succeeding Nebuchadnezzar as king of Babylonia. He released Jeconiah from prison and gave him a proper position together with the other exiled kings of territories conquered by the Babylonian Empire.

The author of Chronicles claims that Zerubbabel is the grandson of Jeconiah to supply proof that Zerubbabel continues the Davidic line. Can we accept the Chronicler's claim that Zerubbabel is the grandson of Jeconiah? There are a few problems.

1. Second Kings does not include any mention of Jeconiah having children.
2. The prophet Jeremiah cursed Jeconiah, proclaiming explicitly that none of his descendants would ever sit on the throne of Israel:

> Thus says the ETERNAL:
> Record this man as childless,
> One who shall never be found acceptable;
> For none of his offspring shall be accepted,
> To sit on the throne of David,
> And to rule again in Judah.
> (Jer 22:30)

3. Ezra (3:2, 8; 5:2), Nehemiah (12:1), and Haggai (1:1, 12, 14) all identify Zerubbabel's father as a person named Shealtiel, not Pedaiah as claimed by Chronicles.
4. Zerubbabel quickly disappears from story in Ezra. If he was truly of the Davidic line, we would have expected him and/or his children to continue to lead the people.

What is going on? The author of Chronicles singularly focused on King David and the Davidic line. In Chronicles we read a great deal about David and all of his positive accomplishments. While Chronicles repeats most of the stories about David found in 1 Samuel, it leaves out the

Bathsheba story that portrays David in a negative manner. Also Chronicles adds in additional new material, not found in 1 Samuel, to bolster the importance of David, the original King David, and the imagined future king, a descendant of David.

Chronicles was written many years after Ezra/Nehemiah. Ezra and Nehemiah reflect the political reality of the Persian period. The oppressive Babylonian Empire had been replaced by the more sympathetic Persian Empire. The leadership had returned to Jerusalem and the Temple had been rebuilt. But there was no political independence. Judea remained a province in the Persian Empire.

Chapter 8 of Nehemiah describes a grand rededication ceremony. The ceremony in Neh 8 does not mention David or the Davidic line. It does not include a recollection of King David or his descendants who ruled in Jerusalem during the First Temple period. Nor does it express the hope that one day a future descendant of King David will again rule in Jerusalem. Perhaps this is because no descendant of King David survived to see the return from exile. Or perhaps it reflects the acceptance of the political reality that Judah is part of the large and powerful Persian Empire and not an independent kingdom

By the time of the composition of Chronicles the international world situation had changed. Persian power had diminished. Egypt had become an independent power. The strength and influence of the Greek city-states was rising. The possibility of the return of a Davidic king to the throne of an independent Judea may have seemed more of a possibility than it had been years earlier during the height of Persian power at the time of Ezra/Nehemiah. The author of Chronicles constructs a connection between King David and Zerubbabel to encourage the reestablishment of an independent kingdom of Judea.

Later Christian sources, for much different reasons, also promote the claim of Zerubbabel's Davidic connections. The Gospels of both Luke and Matthew include a genealogy connecting Jesus to David. According to Matthew, "after the deportation to Babylon: Jeconi'ah was the father of She-al'ti-el and She-al'ti-el the father of Zerub'babel" (Matt 1:12). So Matthew makes Zerubbabel a grandson of Jeconiah as opposed to a son, as Chronicles does.

Both Chronicles and Matthew try to jump across narrative chasms of time and space to bind stories together which in truth are separate. The author of Chronicles stressed the importance of the Davidic line to promote the reestablishment of the Davidic monarchy in the Second

Temple period. The author of Matthew shared his genealogy to support his presentation of Jesus as a literal descendant of King David in fulfillment of prophecies.

The traditional medieval commentators were not drawn to the "Davidic line" position. But they promote the status of Zerubbabel and Sheshbazzar by connecting their names to other biblical personages.

Rashi in his comment on Ezra 1:8 says Sheshbazzar is Daniel. According to Rashi, Sheshbazzar's name is a mash-up of two Hebrew words: *sheish tzarot*, "six difficulties." Midrash Pesiqta Rabbati describes Daniel's six trials.

The Talmud (Sanhedrin 38a) speculates that Zerubbabel was Nehemiah, born in Babylonia. Rambam disagrees. He notes in his introduction to Mishneh Torah that he sees them as two different people. It is impossible to believe that Nehemiah was part of the first wave of returnees during the reign of Cyrus the Great because the book of Nehemiah begins with Nehemiah serving in the court of King Artaxerxes in Babylonia eighty years after the first wave of return.

So, who were Zerubbabel and Sheshbazzar? Many of the most successful national leaders rose to position despite a lack of prominent family connections: American Presidents Abraham Lincoln and Harry Truman came from modest backgrounds. Former German Chancellor Angela Merkel did not come from a connected family; her father was a Lutheran minister, and her mother a schoolteacher. Golda Meir and Naftali Bennett rose to positions of leadership in Israel without family connections. Similarly, Zerubbabel and Sheshbazzar were two men who rose to positions of leadership on their own, without any connections to the house of David.

SELF-RELIANCE

Chapter 37

The Adversaries

When I was in high school, I wanted part of the "in" crowd. I wanted to be one of the cool kids. People want to be confident that their group is the right group. Many of us recall being warned by our parents to stay away from "those dangerous people." The author of the book of Ezra also expresses a concern about those dangerous people.

Chapter 3 of Ezra describes the first wave of returnees quickly beginning to rebuild the altar out of fear of the local population. Zerubbabel and his contemporaries saw the other *am haaretz*, "people of the land," as hostile. Chapter 4 of Ezra describes the reaction of the local population to the progress of the rebuilding of the Temple:

> When the adversaries of Judah and Benjamin heard that the returned exiles were building a temple to the Eternal God of Israel, they approached Zerubbabel and the chiefs of the clans and said to them, "Let us build with you, since we too worship your God having offered sacrifices to Him since the time of King Esarhaddon of Assyria who brought us here." (Ezra 4:1–2)

The text of Ezra does not speak of these neighbors in positive or even neutral terms. It calls them *tzarei*, "adversaries." The Hebrew word appears here in the construct form as *tzade-resh-yod*: "adversaries of." This form derives from the root *tzade-resh-resh*. Deuteronomy 32:41 uses the exact form which appears in our Ezra verse. Various published translations of Deut 32:41 render it as "adversaries" or as "enemies." The

Ezra text presents these peoples as a group that seeks to oppose and undermine the efforts of the returning exiles.

Zerubbabel rejects this offer of assistance. Rashi explains,

> They were idolaters who [the Assyrian king], Sennacherib, settled in the Land of Israel. As it says in 2 Kings 17:24, "The king brought [people] from Babylon, Cuthah, Avva, Hamath and Sepharim and he settled them in the towns of Samaria in place of the Israelites." (Rashi on Ezra 4:1)

Rashi describes these people as "idolaters," but they describe themselves as worshipers of the God of Israel. In which category do they actually belong? Both of these descriptions are accurate. To fully understand the religious identity of these people we need to look at more of the 2 Kings text:

> They took over Samaria and lived in its towns. When they first lived there, they did not worship the ETERNAL; so, He sent lions among them and they killed some of the people. It was reported to the king of Assyria: "The people you deported and resettled in the towns of Samaria do not know what the god of that country requires. He has sent lions among them, which are killing them off, because the people do not know what he requires."
>
> Then the king of Assyria gave this order: "Have one of the priests you took captive from Samaria go back to live there and teach the people what the god of the land requires." So one of the priests who had been exiled from Samaria came to live in Bethel and taught them how to worship the ETERNAL. . . . Nevertheless, each national group made its own gods in the several towns. They worshiped the ETERNAL, but they also served their own gods in accordance with the customs of the nations from which they had been brought. (2 Kgs 17:25–34)

So, while these transplanted people began to worship the ETERNAL, they did not become monotheists. They worshiped the God of Israel and also their own gods. Josephus, in the first century CE, saw the word *Samaritans* as a geographic term, connecting the people in Ezra with the group of that name living during his time in Samaria.[1]

Rabbinic tradition refers to them as Cutim, growing out of their place of origin, Cuthah. The Talmud in Sanhedrin 85b, and other places, uses the term Cuti/Cutim, without explanation, to refer to these other

1. See, e.g., Josephus, *Antiquities* 11.341.

people. The editors of the Talmud assume that their readers will be familiar with the term.

If we combine the Hebrew singular, *Cuti*, and a plural English ending, we have the word *cooties*. Midcentury modern American children used the term *cooties* to describe a condition you could acquire by touching the wrong people in a game. Language scholars explain the term *cooties* as coming from a term in Asian languages for a type of bug. I am intrigued by possibility that this twentieth-century term actually came from the talmudic term *Cuti*.

Christian Scripture written at the end of the first century and the beginning of the second century mentions the Samaritans twice. Luke contains the story of the good Samaritan. And in chapter 4 of John, Jesus has a long conversation with a Samaritan woman at a well. The conversation begins with Jesus asking the Samaritan woman for a drink of water: "The Samaritan woman said to him, 'How is it that you, a Jew, ask a drink of me, a woman of Samar'ia?' For Jews had no dealings with Samaritans" (John 4:9).

The Gospels use the Greek term *Samararitis* (Σαμαριτις) to describe this group. The eighth-century Christian scholar the Venerable Bede, in his commentary on our Ezra verse, writes,

> This story is well known. By the enemies of Judah and Benjamin he means the Samaritans whom the king of the Assyrians, when the ten tribes had been captured, transported from various peoples of the Gentiles into their cities and lands; they accepted God's law and observed it to a degree and yet continued to be slaves to the same idols as before.[2]

Bede confidently identifies these "adversaries" in Ezra as the same Samaritans mentioned in Luke and John. Bede joins Josephus in connecting these "adversaries" of the book of Ezra with the Samaritans of the first century BCE. Neither Ezra nor Nehemiah uses the term *Samaritans*.

Did these "adversaries" think of themselves as adversaries of the returnees? They present themselves as appropriate partners to participate in the rebuilding of the Temple. Zerubbabel refuses their help because he sees them as not being part of the people. He sees them as "other."

Throughout the rabbinic period the Samaritans/Cutim appear as the "other." Determining who are our friends and who are our "adversaries" has been an ongoing human project. We struggle to clearly

2. Bede the Venerable, *On Ezra and Nehemiah*, Ezra 4:1–2 (DeGregorio, 67).

understand who truly wants to help us and who draws us close in order to do us harm.

Some people truly are our "adversaries." Members of the German Army shot at my father during World War II. Members of the Egyptian Army shot at my father-in-law during Israel's War of Independence. My father and my father-in-law saw these armies as enemy forces. In 2006, a Hezbollah rocket destroyed part of my son-in-law's family's home in Nahariya. I know that some people actually do wish me harm because I am a Jew or because I am an American.

But too often, people quickly label those with whom they disagree as "adversaries." How do we determine who is part of our group and who is not? Who is "us" and who is "them"? How much do we have to share with a person to accept that person as one of "us"?

In today's world, we can use various tools to sort people into categories. We have in Chicago two separate groups: Cubs fans versus White Sox fans. As one moves southwest from Chicago to Springfield in Central Illinois one begins to encounter fans of the St. Louis Cardinals. I could think of the fans of the White Sox and the Cardinals as the foreign, threatening "other." But I prefer to think of them as sharing my deep devotion to baseball.

I could divide the people who teach Bible at Wheaton College into two groups by religion. I would be in the Jewish group, and everybody else would be in the Christian group. But if the criterion was deep concern for meaning of the words of the Hebrew Bible, I can place myself in the same category as my faculty friends. I disagree with them on profound questions of theology, but they are certainly not my adversaries. We may not worship together, but we can learn and teach together.

If the criterion for group formation is how God has been involved with the world, I will be in a group with other Jews, while Christians and Muslims will each have their own groups. But if the criterion is how to provide opportunities and support to the most vulnerable members of our society, I can work together with people of many religious groups.

When I feel under attack, I naturally make common cause with those who share my vulnerability. But I feel supported by those who are not themselves under attack but do feel my pain and offer support. I can offer support to other communities when they are attacked. When our synagogue was vandalized, the leaders and members of the churches and mosque in the community came to our support. When vandals attacked the nearby mosque I literally and metaphorically stood with the Imam.

We do not need to imagine that all people who are different are our adversaries. Often, they are simply people we have not yet met. The Torah teaches us to love our neighbors as ourselves. The first step to loving our neighbors is to know our neighbors.

Chapter 38

The Samaritans

SHORTLY AFTER THEY ARRIVED in Jerusalem, the first wave of returnees undertook the reconstruction of the altar. The text tells us that "they set up the altar on its site because they were in fear of the peoples of the land" (Ezra 3:3).

The people had returned to the land from which they had been exiled but they feared their neighbors. Rashi explains,

> For they were frightened that the peoples of the land would interfere with them and slander them to the king. So, they built the altar to offer upon it offerings so that the people would hear and understand that they, the Israelites, were acting according to the word of the king. And refrain from interfering as they [the Israelites] rebuilt the Temple. (Rashi on Ezra 3:3)

Here the text does not identify these "peoples." We generally refer to them as Samaritans because they dwell in the part of the land of Israel known as Samaria. Also Christian Gospels use the Greek term *Samaritis* (Σαμαριτις) to describe this group. The actions of the good Samaritan in Luke are a surprise because nobody in first-century Jerusalem expected a Samaritan to act in a positive manner. The Jews of the rabbinic period understood the Samaritans as heretics who sought to undermine mainstream Jewish religious life. The Mishnah provides an example:

> Initially, after the court [in Jerusalem] sanctified the new month they would light torches on the mountaintops, from one peak to another, to signal to the community in Babylonia that the

> month had been sanctified. After the Samaritans corrupted and ruined this method by lighting torches at the wrong times to confuse the Jews, the Sages instituted that messengers should go out to the Diaspora and inform them of the start of the month. (Mishnah Rosh Hashanah 2:2)

There remains a small community of Samaritans in Nabulus. Our cohort of first-year HUC rabbinic students visited their temple in 1972. The Samaritan priest showed us their Torah scroll and explained their beliefs. They describe themselves as the authentic descendants of the ancient Israelites and see conventional Jews as a confused breakaway sect.

Contemporary Samaritans call themselves *shamerim*, "guardians." Modern Hebrew speakers use a geographic term, *shomronim*, "people of Samaria." From the time of Ezra until today, the Samaritans have remained the "other" in the eyes of Jews.

The three waves of returning exiles did not come home to an empty land. The first wave led by Zerubbabel, the second wave led by Ezra, and the third wave led by Nehemiah all encountered "people of the land" who objected to their presence in Jerusalem. No matter where you go, someone else was always there before you.

A thread of Zionist mythology imagined that the modern returnees from exile in the nineteenth and twentieth centuries would be coming home to an empty land. The phrase "A people without a land and a land without a people" is often associated with Zionist writer Israel Zangwell, but in truth it originated with nineteenth-century Christian British Restorationists.

The phrase "a country without a nation" in need of "a nation without a country" appears in a letter that Anthony Ashley-Cooper, an earl and a leader of the British Restorationist movement, sent to Lord Aberdeen the prime minister. Ashley-Cooper continues, "Is there such a thing? To be sure there is, the ancient and rightful lords of the soil, the Jews!"[1]

William Eugene Blackstone, an American Christian Restorationist, after an 1891 visit to Palestine wrote,

> And now, this very day, we stand face to face with the awful dilemma, that these millions cannot remain where they are, and yet have no other place to go. . . . This phase of the question

1. As quoted in Wikipedia, "Anthony Ashley-Cooper."

> presents an astonishing anomaly—a land without a people, and a people without a land.[2]

It was not until 1901 that Israel Zangwill wrote in the *New Liberal Review* that "Palestine is a country without a people; the Jews are a people without a country."[3]

This was never true. It was not true in 1881 or in 1948. The Zionist pioneers encountered Palestinians living on the land. It was not true, as we have seen above, at the time of Ezra and Nehemiah. It was not true at the time of Moses and Joshua. In describing the land God speaks of the people living on it:

> And I am come down to deliver them out of the hand of the Egyptians, and to bring them up out of that land unto a good land and a large, unto a land flowing with milk and honey; unto the place of the Canaanite, and the Hittite, and the Amorite, and the Perizzite, and the Hivite, and the Jebusite. (Exod 3:8)

The book of Joshua describes the bloody conquest of the promised land. And it was not true at the time of Abraham. The Torah describes Abram and Sarai arriving in the new land: "And Abram passed through the land unto the place of Shechem, unto the terebinth of Moreh. And the Canaanites were then in the land" (Gen 12:6).

I do not mean to diminish the claim of the Jewish people to the land of Israel. It has been our home for a very, very long time, at least three thousand years. But at the same time, we should be aware that we have always had neighbors. Even at the height of the unified kingdom in the time of King David, other people lived in and around us. When David becomes involved with Bathsheba the Bible tell us that she was the wife of Uriah the Hittite: "Is not this Bath-sheba, the daughter of Eliam, the wife of Uriah the Hittite?" (2 Sam 11:3).

The author of the biblical text is not bothered by the fact that Bathsheba is married to a Hittite. Uriah is not the first Hittite mentioned in the Torah. When Abraham sought to purchase the cave of Machpelah as a burial location for Sarah in Hebron, he negotiated with "Ephron the Hittite"(Gen 23:10). That chapter of Genesis suggests that Hittites were the group of people living in Hebron at the time. The fact that several hundreds of years later, in the time of King David, Hittites continue to

2. Blackstone, *Palestine for the Jews*, 16, 17.
3. Zangwill, "Return to Palestine," 615.

dwell in the land should help us understand that the land of Israel has always been home to "others."

Rarely in recorded human history has a group of people come to a completely uninhabited area. When the first Vikings arrived in Iceland in the 870s CE nobody else was living there. But if we explore the history of just about any other place on earth, we will learn that another people or peoples lived in the area before the current local population arrived. Human history is the story of peoples moving from place to place.

In what is today the country of Turkey, nobody spoke Turkish before the eleventh century. Anatolia was part of the Greek-speaking Christian Byzantine Empire. The name *Anatolia* is derived from a Greek term for the East. It is used in the Gospel of Matthew: "Behold wise men have come from the east [*anatolon*, ανατολων]" (Matt 2:1). Greeks saw Anatolia as the eastern portion of Greece. The Seljuk Turks originated in Central Asia and slowly moved west. At the Battle of Manzikert in 1071 the Turkish army defeated the forces of the Byzantine Empire, completing the Turkish conquest of Anatolia. Turkish replaced Greek as the local language, and Islam replaced Christianity. Anatolia became Turkey.

In the thirteenth century, ethnic Germans began moving into the areas of Bohemia adjacent to German principalities. After World War I, Bohemia became part of the new country, Czechoslovakia. In 1938 Adolph Hitler demanded that the German portions of Czechoslovakia, by that time referred to as Sudetenland, be turned over to Germany. After the defeat of Germany in World War II, Czechoslovakia expelled the German population of Sudetenland.

Many cities and towns in Eastern Europe have been parts of several different countries over the past 150 years. The change in sovereignty among Austrian, Lithuanian, Poland, German, Russian, and Ukrainian governments caused many shifts in population, religions, and languages. My late mother-in-law grew up in Czernowitz in Romania that is now Czernivsti in Ukraine. Her first language was not Romanian, Ukrainian, or Yiddish. The educated Jews of Czernowitz spoke German. From 1775 to 1918 Czernowitz was part of the Austro-Hungarian Empire. Despite the collapse of the Austro-Hungarian Empire, Czernowitz remained an outpost of Viennese culture.

When nations choose to go to war and then lose, they suffer negative consequences, including shifts of national borders and movement of populations. The Persian conquest of the Babylonians triggered the events described in Ezra/Nehemiah.

Every definition of "us" seems to include a definition of "them." Part of knowing who we are, includes being certain about who we are not. Zerubbabel knew that the Samaritans were "them" not "us." As I explained in the previous chapter, the returning people worshiped the one God of Israel, while the Samaritans worshiped the God of Israel and a host of other gods. The monotheist Judeans saw the polytheist Samaritans as "them" not "us."

Chapter 39

The Letters

THE RESIDENTS OF SAMARIA who opposed the effort to rebuild the Temple wrote to the Persian court to persuade the authorities of the empire to halt the construction. By that time Cyrus the Great, who had issued the order supporting the return from exile and the rebuilding of the Temple, no longer ruled the Persian Empire. Samaritan leaders, Rehum the commissioner and Shimshai the scribe, wrote to the new king. As I explained in chapter 33, the text refers to the Persian king as Artaxerxes, but the king who actually ruled during this period was Cambyses.

> To King Artaxerxes [Cambyses] from your servants, men of the province Beyond the River. And now be it known to the king that the Jews who came up from you to us have reached Jerusalem and are rebuilding that rebellious and wicked city; they are completing the walls and repairing the foundation. Now be it known to the king that if this city is rebuilt and the walls completed, they will not pay tribute, poll-tax, or land-tax, and in the end it will harm the kingdom. Now since we eat the salt of the palace, and it is not right that we should see the king dishonored, we have written to advise the king [of this] so that you may search the records of your fathers and find in the records and know that this city is a rebellious city, harmful to kings and states. Sedition has been rife in it from early times; on that account this city was destroyed. We advise the king that if this city is rebuilt and its walls are completed, you will no longer have any portion in the province Beyond the River. (Ezra 4:12–16)

One might, from a land of Israel point of view, assume the river mentioned in the phrase "the province Beyond the River" is the Jordan River. Many scholars believe that in this context it actually refers to the Euphrates River. From the Babylonian/Persian point of view the land west of the Euphrates River was the "wild west" and thought of as "beyond the river."

This letter is one of a series of letters in this section of the book of Ezra which appear in the Hebrew Bible in Aramaic. I avoid using the term *the Old Testament*. In a Jewish setting I say *Tanakh*. But in a Christian setting I often use the phrase *the Hebrew Bible*, which is generally accurate but not 100 percent true. This letter and the other letters in Ezra appear in Aramaic. They were included in the Bible in Aramaic to suggest that the texts of the letters in Ezra are the authentic documents. Are they actually authentic?

We can prepare to respond to this specific scholarly question of determining when and where a document was written by exploring a parallel question in popular culture. We will consider the song "Bad to Me" by the band Billy J. Kramer and the Dakotas. When and where was it written? From their name one might imagine that Billy J. Kramer and the Dakotas come from North Dakota or South Dakota. Perhaps they were a late nineteenth-century Wild West show like Buffalo Bill's.

This is not be correct. Let's take a different path. Thinking about other groups with similar names that mention a leader and a backing band, I could come up with Gerry and the Pacemakers, Freddie and the Dreamers, and Rory Storm and the Hurricanes. All three of these groups were part of the "English Invasion" of the midsixties. Two of them were from Liverpool. So, Billy J. Kramer and the Dakotas might be a British band from the midsixties. A next step could be to ask who composed the song "Bad to Me." The answer is that John Lennon and Paul McCartney wrote this song. Then, if we actually listen to "Bad to Me," we would hear Billy J. Kramer's distinct English accent. Billy J. Kramer and the Dakotas were an English group managed by Brian Epstein of Beatles fame.

So, what methods do we use to determine the authenticity of these letters? Professor Aubrey Buster writes, "The arguments both for and against their authenticity can be grouped into three debated areas: epistolary form (Persian or Hellenistic), linguistic character (Imperial or later

Middle Aramaic); and ideology (whether the contents of the letter are historically probable)."[1]

Scholars continue to debate all three of these topics. What is at stake in these debates? If the letters are Persian in form, written in Imperial Aramaic, and make sense in a Persian context, then one can argue that the letters are authentic and that the book of Ezra was written close to the events it describes. If the letters are Hellenistic in form, written in later Middle Aramaic, and make sense in the post–Greek conquest period, then one could argue that the letters are inauthentic and that the book of Ezra was written long after the events it describes.

The events described in the book of Ezra begin with Cyrus the Great's proclamation in 538 BCE and describes the ongoing events of Ezra's arrival in Jerusalem in 458 BCE and his subsequent years. Alexander the Great's army arrived in the land of Israel in 331 BCE. So, if one holds to early authorship one is speaking about approximately 400 BCE. If one holds to late authorship one is speaking about 300 BCE or thereafter. I am with the first group. I see Ezra and Nehemiah as reflecting the realities of the Persian Empire. As I pointed out in chapter 8 these books include Persian loan words. We find no Greek loan words in either book. As I explained in chapter 35 on the Davidic line, 1 and 2 Chronicles, which emphasize the Davidic line, were written after Ezra and Nehemiah and express the perspective of the Hellenistic period. Ezra and Nehemiah express the political and cultural reality of the Persian period.

The letter I quoted above is one of a series of Aramaic letters. Following this first letter we read a response from Persian court:

> "To Rehum the commissioner and Shimshai the scribe, and the rest of their colleagues, who dwell in Samaria and in the rest of the province of Beyond the River, greetings. Now the letter that you wrote me has been read to me in translation [from Aramaic to Persian]. At my order a search has been made, and it has been found that this city has from earliest times risen against kings, and that rebellion and sedition have been rife in it. Powerful kings have ruled over Jerusalem and exercised authority over the whole province of Beyond the River, and tribute, poll-tax, and land-tax were paid to them. Now issue an order to stop these men; this city is not to be rebuilt until I so order. Take care not to be lax in this matter or there will be much damage and harm to the kingdom." When the text of the letter of King

1. Buster, "Ezra-Nehemiah," 221.

> Artaxerxes was read before Rehum and Shimshai the scribe and their colleagues, they hurried to Jerusalem, to the Jews, and stopped them by main force. At that time, work on the House of God in Jerusalem stopped and remained in abeyance until the second year of the reign of King Darius of Persia. (Ezra 4:17–24)

The protests of Rehum and Shimshai brought the rebuilding of the Temple in a halt. Nothing happened during the rest of the reign of Cambyses, 529–521 BCE. After his death Darius I came to the throne. Early in the reign of Darius I, pressure built in Jerusalem for the rebuilding to resume. The book of Ezra reports,

> Then the prophets, Haggai the prophet and Zechariah son of Iddo, prophesied to the Jews in Judah and Jerusalem, in the name of the God of Israel upon them. Thereupon Zerubbabel son of Shealtiel and Jeshua son of Jozadak began rebuilding the House of God in Jerusalem, with the full support of the prophets of God. (Ezra 5:1–2)

Time had passed since the halt of the building. The opponents of the construction mentioned in chapter 4, Rehum and Shimshai, have left their positions. The opposition to the rebuilding of the Temple is now led by Tattenai, identified as the "governor of the province of Beyond the River" (verse 3). He protests the resumption of the rebuilding, "but God watched over the elders of the Jews and they were not stopped" (Ezra 5:5). Since he is not able to put a halt to the construction on his own authority, Tattenai writes to the new ruler of the Persian Empire, Darius I. First, he describes the construction project. Then he recounts the events that led to the destruction of the original Temple. Finally, he asks if there is any actual record of Cyrus the Great issuing any order for the rebuilding of the Temple:

> And now, if it please the king, let the royal archives there in Babylon be searched to see whether indeed an order had been issued by King Cyrus to rebuild this House of God in Jerusalem. May the king convey to us his pleasure in this matter. (Ezra 5:17)

The book of Ezra reports that Darius orders a search of the archives which turns up Cyrus's original proclamation. Darius writes a very stern letter back to Tattenai instructing him to stop obstructing the Jews in their efforts of rebuilding. Darius tells Tattenai to provide financial support to the rebuilding effort and to provide animals for the sacrifices. Darius concludes his letter with a warning:

> I also issue an order that whoever alters this decree shall have a beam removed from his house, and he shall be impaled on it and his house confiscated. And may the God who established His name there cause the downfall of any king or nation that undertakes to alter or damage that House of God in Jerusalem. I, Darius, have issued the decree; let it be carried out with dispatch. (Ezra 6:11–12)

The fact that all of these letters appear in the book of Ezra in Aramaic can lead us to conclude that in the period in which Ezra was written the general Jewish population spoke Aramaic. Bible scholars writing for an academic readership will uses phrases in Hebrew, Greek, and German without translating them. They assume their audience will understand those languages. I am strong in Hebrew, adequate in Greek, and I have close relatives who speak German. Writing for a more general audience I translate all but the most well-known Hebrew words. I assume that my readers will understand the Hebrew word *Torah*. The author of the book of Ezra assumed that his readers would understand the Aramaic of these letters, and that reading them in Aramaic would persuade the readers that these letters were the genuine documents. While we cannot know for sure if the letters are genuine, it is possible that they are—or at least that they contain elements of the original letters.

Chapter 40

Defending Ourselves

In the previous three chapters we explored the problems that the local population created for Zerubbabel and the first waves of returnees. A hundred years later when Nehemiah began to rebuild the walls and gates of Jerusalem, he also faced difficulties from the local population. Nehemiah had come to Jerusalem because while serving in the Persian court he heard a report of the dire situation facing the Judeans in Jerusalem.

> Hanani, one of my brothers, together with some men of Judah, arrived, and I asked them about the Jews, the remnant who had survived the captivity, and about Jerusalem. They replied, "The survivors who have survived the captivity there in the province are in dire trouble and disgrace; Jerusalem's wall is full of breaches, and its gates have been destroyed by fire." (Neh 1:2–3)

Nehemiah received permission from the Persian king to journey to Jerusalem to organize efforts to rebuild the walls and gates of Jerusalem. Once the rebuilding got underway the enemies of the Judeans took notice. The text reports the response of local leaders to Nehemiah's construction project: "When Sanballat the Horonite and Tobiah the Ammonite servant heard it displeased them greatly that someone had come, intent on improving the condition of the Israelites" (Neh 10:10).

As Nehemiah made progress on the effort to rebuild the walls of Jerusalem, these local leaders begin to conspire to stop him.

> When Sanballat and Tobiah and the Arabs, the Ammonites and the Ashdodites heard that healing had come to the walls of

> Jerusalem, that the breached parts and had begun to be filled, it angered them very much, and they all conspired together to come and fight against Jerusalem and to throw it into confusion. (Neh 4:1–2)

Rashi's commentary to verse 1 explains, "And the people of the city who had been until now exposed will now be protected as a result of the rebuilt wall." Once completed the walls of the city would provide security for the Judeans, but in the meantime, they faced imminent danger.

In previous chapters we explored "the threatening, foreign other." Nehemiah did not see the threats as mere hostile words. He understood that the Judeans needed to protect themselves from a possible attack. He moved quickly to oversee the major project of rebuilding the walls and gates of the city of Jerusalem. As they built, the people of Jerusalem remained ready to defend themselves. Nehemiah describes the steps they took:

> When our enemies learned that it had become known to us, since God had thus frustrated their plan, we could all return to the wall, each to his work. From that day on, half my servants did work and half held lances and shields, bows and armor. And officers stood behind the whole house of Judah who were rebuilding the wall. The basket-carriers were burdened doing work with one hand while the other held a weapon. As for the builders, each had his sword girded to his side as he was building. (Neh 4:9–12)

Nehemiah was an agent of the king of Persia, but he did not have military support from the Persian army to defend Jerusalem. He had to depend on the people who had returned from exile to defend themselves. Self-defense has continued to be a concern for Jews over the centuries.

During the modern return from exile, the First Aliyah (1881–1903), communities hired local Palestinians to provide security for their new Jewish towns and farms. For centuries, Jews' experience of weapons was what the anti-Semites pointed at us. No European country allowed Jews to own weapons. In 1907 a small group of Palestinian Jews came together to form Bar Giora as a Jewish self-defense group, named after a leader of the Bar Kokhba rebellion. In 1909 the group expanded and changed its name; it became Hashomer, "The Guard." Its members learned how to fire guns and ride horses.

Josef Trumpeldor served in the Russian Army during the Russo-Japanese war in 1905. He lost his left arm as a result of battle injuries.

After the war he became involved in Zionist activities. Trumpeldor made aliyah in 1911. Despite his lack of an arm, he applied his military knowledge and experience to the defense of Jewish settlements. During World War I, he helped organize Jews to fight in the British Army. The first unit was called the Zion Mule Corps, which served in the Gallipoli campaign. The corps grew into a larger unit called the Jewish Legion. The veterans of the Jewish Legion became the foundation of the Haganah created in 1920. The Haganah served as the primary defense force of the Yishuv until it grew into the Israeli Army.

The Haganah's elite strike force was called the Palmach. This name grew out of the Hebrew words for "strike forces," *plugot machatz*. I learned about the Palmach during my years in Habonim Labor Zionist Youth. I knew the Palmach song with its proud refrain *Anu, anu hapalmach*, "We, we are the Palmach." I heard stories about the Palmach's heroic deeds during Israel's War of Independence in a Midwestern summer camp in the sixties. I thought of the Palmachnicks as legendary, strong Israeli heroes.

I first started dating my wife, Tammie, in the mid-1970s in Cincinnati. One day she wore a sweater that she casually told me was her father's Palmach sweater. He had served in Palmach's Negev brigade in the War of Independence. His unit captured Beer Sheva from the Egyptian army and then moved south to establish an Israeli presence on the Red Sea where the city of Eilat was later built.

The Palmachnicks did not have an actual Israeli flag to raise over the newly acquired Israeli presence on the coast of this branch of the Red Sea, so they created one out of a sheet. They drew the blue stripes with ink. The famous photograph of an Israeli soldier climbing the flag pole, having affixed this flag, was thought of as the Israeli version of the American Marines raising the Stars and Stripes over Iwo Jima during World War II. For years members of our family believed that the photo included my father-in-law. Actual historical research has proven that while he was present at the event, he is not in the photograph. We are proud of his contribution to the establishment of the State of Israel. He continued to proudly wear his Palmach pin until his death in 2025.

When I read the Nehemiah verses I quoted at the beginning of this chapter, I think of my father-in-law, and thousands of other Israeli soldiers who I do not know, who fought to establish the modern State of Israel. My father-in-law lived a long life. Many others gave their lives so that the State could be established. The State of Israel was able to declare and maintain its independence because, like Nehemiah's builders, the builders of the state of Israel had a "sword girded to their side."

I have been to the Israeli national military cemetery on Mount Herzl many, many times. The simple headstones record the day the person was born, the day they arrived in Israel, and the day they fell in battle. Each time I visit the cemetery, reading the headstones moves me to tears.

In the nineteenth century and earlier, old Jews came to the land of Israel to spend their last days. They said, *Tov lamoot b'artzeinu*, "It is good to die in our land." Josef Trumpeldor died defending the small Jewish village of Tel Chai in northern Galilee in 1920. According to legend his last words were a twist on that old phrase. He was reported to have said, *Tov lamoot* ba'ad *artzeinu*, "It is good to die *for* our land." Clearly it would be much better if nobody had to die for the land. We look forward to the day when the words of Isaiah will be fulfilled: "And they shall beat their swords into plowshares and their spears into pruning hooks: Nation shall not take up sword against nation; They shall never again know war" (Isa 2:4). But that day has not yet come.

> Upon the completion of the walls Nehemiah's efforts were again opposed. When the word reached Sanballat, Tobiah, Geshem the Arab and the rest of our enemies that I had rebuilt the wall . . . Sanballat and Geshem sent a message to me. . . . They planned to do me harm. (Neh 6:1–2)

Sadly, in the twenty-first century various groups and individuals continue to plan to do harm to Jews around the world and to the State of Israel. While others continue to plan to do us harm, we will continue to need to defend ourselves.

Chapter 41

Nehemiah's Enemies

In the last chapter we looked at Nehemiah's response to threats described in chapter 4 of the book of Nehemiah. In chapter 6 of Nehemiah his enemies try again. Tobiah and Sanballat hire an agent, Shemaiah, to entrap Nehemiah. Shemaiah presents himself as a prophet. But Nehemiah is not deceived.

> Then I realized that it was not God who sent him, but that he uttered that prophecy about me—Tobiah and Sanballat having hired him—because he was a hireling, that I might be intimidated and act thus and commit a sin, and so provide them a scandal with which to reproach me. (Neh 6:12–13)

Nehemiah was able to see through the ruse and avoid the trap that his enemies had set for him. In the next verse, Nehemiah turns to God in prayer: "Remember Tobiah and Sanballat, O my God, according to these things that they did, and also the prophetess Noadiah and the rest of the prophets who wanted to make me afraid" (Neh 6:14).

This prayer introduces a new character to the narrative, "the prophetess Noadiah." This is the only time that the Hebrew Bible mentions Noadiah. We may want to know more about her, but the text does not provide any details. Scholars and speculative interpreters have suggested creative ideas about who Noadiah might have been. If we stick to the facts provided in this verse, we can conclude that she was making common cause with Nehemiah's enemies, Tobiah and Sanballat. Nehemiah views her as one of the people who claim to be prophets but do not actually speak for God. If these prophets truly spoke for God, they would not be resisting the rebuilding of the walls and gates of Jerusalem.

In Deuteronomy God warns Moses that future generations will have to distinguish between actual prophets of God and false prophets who deliver messages contrary to what God has told Moses. One method of distinguishing genuine prophets from false prophets is to ask, Does their message confirm and support the teachings contained in the Torah?

Nehemiah understood that Tobiah, Sanballat, and Noadiah were looking for God in all the wrong places. Nehemiah knew that including Tobiah, Sanballat, and Noadiah in the life of the community would lead the people backwards to an old pattern of the spiritual corruption of worshiping multiple gods. Nehemiah and the rebuilders of Jerusalem saw themselves as living in a new era that would be better than the old, corrupt, idolatrous First Temple era. They wanted to remain pure and focused on building a new, less corrupt, and more pure world.

We can see similar aspirations in the hopes of other creators of national new beginnings. During World War II, the Resistance in France wanted to do more than just free their country from the Nazis. They wanted to build a new and better France. Albert Camus and his colleagues on the staff of the underground resistance newspaper, *Combat*, wrote of the new France that would emerge after liberation. They did not want to fall back into the problems that plagued France before the war. They were neither Stalinist nor fascist. They saw themselves as progressives dedicated to more than personal self-interest. Their new France would be a better France.

John E. Ferling, in his recent book *Winning Independence: The Decisive Years of the Revolutionary War, 1778–1781*, describes the motivation of the partisan fighters who followed Francis Marion. He explains that people who joined the "Swamp Fox" did not only share a dislike for British rule. They wanted to build a "new" South Carolina on the foundation of their values. They were Scottish Presbyterian farmers from the back country, rather than British Anglican merchants from the coastal cities. They saw themselves as creating a new society in the new world of America.[1]

My favorite movie, *The Maltese Falcon*, depicts Sam Spade, the hard-boiled detective, as also dedicated to something higher than personal self-interest. As he says, "Don't be too sure I'm as crooked as I'm

1. Ferling, *Winning Independence*.

supposed to be."[2] The film tells the story of the quest to acquire the jewel-encrusted, gold Maltese Falcon statue. Near the end of the film a statue arrives, but it turns out to be a fake. Kaspar Gutman and Joel Cairo quickly depart to continue their eighteen-year pursuit of this treasure. Brigid O'Shaughnessy wants Sam to join her in continuing the treasure hunt. But Sam is not bought off by love or the search for gold. He chooses duty over desire, love, and the quest for wealth.

In the final scene of the movie, Sam explains to Brigid that he is going to turn her in to the police for murdering his partner, despite the fact that he may love her.

> Yes, angel, I'm gonna send you over. You'll never understand me, but I'll try once and then give it up. When a man's partner is killed, he's supposed to do something. It makes no difference what you thought of him. He was your partner, and you're supposed to do something about it, and it happens we're in the detective business. Well, when one of your organization gets killed, it's bad business to let the killer get away with it, bad all around, bad for every detective everywhere. Maybe I do [love you]. I'll have some rotten nights after I've sent you over, but that'll pass.[3]

The first wave of returning Judean rebuilders of the Temple sent the Samaritans over. Those rebuilders could have completed their huge task more easily and more quickly if they had accepted the help of the Samaritans. But working with the Samaritans would completely compromise the entire purpose of their mission. Here Nehemiah and the rebuilders of the walls and gates of Jerusalem send Tobiah, Sanballat, and Noadiah over. Nehemiah identifies them as enemies, not friends.

In navigating community leadership, distinguishing between enemies and friends has continued to be a challenge. In 1944 Hubert Humphrey was a young local leader of the Democratic Party of Minnesota who helped negotiate its merger with the progressive Farmer–Labor Party of Minnesota. In Minnesota, the combined party is still called the Democratic–Farmer–Labor Party, often shortened to DFL. One of the challenges facing Humphrey was the presence in the merged party of Communists. He worked to banish these avowed Communists from the DFL. Later, on the national stage, Humphrey was a founder of Americans for Democratic Action, a faction in the Democratic Party committed to

2. Huston, *Maltese Falcon*, 1:38:52.
3. Huston, *Maltese Falcon*, 1:36:52.

continuing the New Deal approach of Franklin Delano Roosevelt while opposing Communism.

When we think of anti-Communism of the post–World War II period, we recall the Red Scare tactics of House Un-American Activities Committee and Senator Joe McCarthy in the 1950s, falsely accusing innocent writers, actors, musicians, and civil servants of disloyalty. In 1945, following the victory of the Allies over Germany and Japan, some on the American political left viewed Josef Stalin and the Soviet Union positively. Later, as the true nature of Stalin's tyrannical regime became known, support for Communism in America dissolved. It was during the immediate post-war years that Humphrey worked hard to push Communists out of the Democratic Party.

Humphrey was a leader of the left wing of the Democratic Party. He rose to a position of national prominence as a result of a speech that he gave at the Democratic National Convention in the summer of 1948 denouncing segregation. His message on July 14, 1948, was a response to those who dressed their advocacy of continuing segregation in claims for the rights of the southern states to set local policies. Hubert Humphrey, the mayor of Minneapolis, told the assembled Democratic delegates, "The time has arrived for the Democratic Party to get out of the shade of state's rights and walk forthrightly into the bright sunshine of human rights."[4]

Humphrey was a progressive, but he knew that these Communist members of the DFL had an agenda that was categorically different from his. Nehemiah knew that Tobiah, Sanballat, Noadiah, and their co-conspirators had a different agenda from his. To stay true to his mission, Nehemiah had to stay away from Tobiah, Sanballat, Noadiah, and everybody else who wanted to prevent him from rebuilding the walls and gates of Jerusalem.

4. Friedman, *Into the Bright Sunshine*, 370.

THE END OF PROPHECY

Chapter 42

Haggai and Zechariah

THE PROPHETS HAGGAI AND Zechariah appear briefly, speaking as a pair in the book of Ezra. They also each have a book of their own as part of the Twelve Minor Prophets.

Fifteen books of the Hebrew Bible containing stories and prophecies are named for prophets: Isaiah, Jeremiah, Ezekiel, and the Twelve Minor Prophets. We call them the Twelve Minor Prophets, not because they are less important but because their books are brief. In 1 and 2 Kings we meet other prophets who do not have their own books: Nathan, Elijah, and Elisha. The prophet Samuel is a unique transition figure between the era of the judges and era of the kings and prophets.

All of the prophets of the Hebrew Bible brought messages appropriate for their time and place. During the First Temple period, the prophets challenged the community and the kings. They reminded the people that sacrifices alone are not what God wants. God wants the people to lead just lives (Isa 1:11–17 and Amos 5:21–24). The prophets also called upon the people to turn away from idols and worship the one God of Israel (1 Kgs 18:20–40).

During the exile the people no longer needed to hear this criticism. They no longer need to be told that unless they straighten out God will punish them. "Sitting by the waters of Babylon," they were fully experiencing the consequences of their misdeeds. They needed a new message, a message that matched the new realities of their lives. They required a message of comfort. They needed to hear that even though they were in exile, God had not forsaken them.

The prophets of the exile brought that supportive message. The prophet we refer to as Second Isaiah begins with the words, *Nachamu, nachamu*, "Be comforted, be comforted" (Isa 40:1). Second Isaiah describes Israel as God's servant who has suffered (41:8–10; 44:1, 21). Second Isaiah reassures the people by telling them that in the future Israel will prosper (52:13). Because Israel's future is so bright, Israel will be a light unto the nations (49:6). The other prophet of the exile, Ezekiel, delivers a similar message, most famously in his vision of the "dry bones" (Ezek 37:1–14).

The message of the first generation of prophets after the return from the exile is to support and celebrate the rebuilding of the Temple in Jerusalem. We see this in Haggai and Zechariah, as they appear in the book of Ezra and in their own books.

Chapter 4 of the book of Ezra describes a delay in the rebuilding of the Temple caused by the protest of local people to the Persian king. At the beginning of chapter 5 we read,

> Then the prophets Haggai the prophet and Zechariah son of Iddo prophesied to the Jews in Judah and Jerusalem inspired by the God of Israel. Thereupon Zerubbabel son of Shealtiel and Jeshua son of Jozadak began rebuilding the House of God in Jerusalem with full support of the prophets of God. (Ezra 5:1–2)

Later, after an exchange of letters between Persian authorities, the Persian King Darius granted permission for the rebuilding to resume. As we read in the chapter 6 of the book of Ezra,

> So the elders of the Jews progressed in the building, urged on by the prophesying of Haggai the prophet and Zechariah son of Iddo, and they brought the building to completion under the aegis of the God of Israel and by the order of Cyrus and Darius and King Artaxerxes of Persia. (Ezra 6:14)

The books named for these two prophets are quite different from each other. The book of Haggai is brief; it has only two chapters containing a total of thirty-seven verses. It mostly focuses on encouraging Zerubbabel to complete the rebuilding of the Temple. The final few verses convey a grand personal future for Zerubbabel.

The book of Zechariah is fourteen chapters long. The first eight chapters contain mystical visions of God's messages of a rebuilt Temple. It reminds many people of the mystical visions one reads in Ezekiel.

Chapters 9–14 of Zechariah contain redemptive end-of-days visions, which I will address in the next chapter.

Haggai praises Zerubbabel for leading the rebuilding of the Temple:

> On that day—declares the ETERNAL of Hosts—I will take you, O My servant Zerubbabel son of Shealtiel—declares the ETERNAL—and make you as a signet; for I have chosen you—declares the ETERNAL of Hosts. (Hag 2:23)

Zechariah uses mystical images to describe the importance of Zerubbabel's efforts:

> The hands of Zerubbabel have laid the foundation of this house; his hands shall also complete it. . . . The seven are the eyes of the ETERNAL, which range through the whole earth. . . . The two olive trees . . . are the two sons of oil [anointed ones] who stand by the Lord of the whole earth. (Zech 4:9–14)

The most well-known section of the book of Zechariah is the three chapters that comprise the haftarah for the first Shabbat during Hanukkah. Composer Debbie Friedman brought additional attention to one of the verses by taking a phrase from that haftarah as the title song of her second album, "Not by Might, Not by Power."

> This is the word of the ETERNAL to Zerubbabel: "Not by might nor by power, but by My Spirit," says the ETERNAL of Hosts. "Who are you, O great mountain? Before Zerubbabel you shall become a plain! And he shall bring forth the capstone with shouts of 'Grace, grace to it!'" (Zech 4:6–7)

This is not the only case of books of the Bible overlapping with other biblical books. In some cases, we find the same words in two different biblical books. In 2 Sam 22 we read King David reciting poetic words praising God. Psalm 18 contains exactly the same words, with one very small change. Second Samuel 22:51 begins with the word *migdol.* Psalm 18:51 begins with *magdil.* In other cases, we find individuals from one book appearing as characters in another book. We can read the story of King Hezekiah in 2 Kgs 16:20—20:21. And then King Hezekiah also appears in a narrative section of Isaiah (38:4–8, 21), which tells of a specific event that fits into the larger narrative contained in 2 Kings.

Sir John Falstaff is a friend of Prince Hal's in Shakespeare's history plays: *Henry IV Part 1*, and *Henry IV Part 2*. In *Henry V* Prince Hal has become King Henry. Falstaff does not appear onstage, but the play includes a eulogy for Falstaff, who spends most of his time drinking at the Boar's Head Inn. Moving away from Falstaff is part of Prince Hal's taking steps toward a more responsible adult life as King Henry.

In Shakespeare's history dramas, Falstaff is a secondary character, but in his comedy *The Merry Wives of Windsor*, Falstaff stands at the center of the narrative. This play is a broad comic tale of the impoverished Falstaff attempting to improve his position in the world through relationships with wealthy married women. Falstaff's name became the title of Giuseppe Verdi's last opera, which grew directly out of Shakespeare's *The Merry Wives of Windsor*.

In a similar manner, Haggai and Zechariah are secondary supportive characters in the book of Ezra but the central focus of their individual books. In the book of Ezra, they act as catalysts aiding the process of rebuilding the Temple. The text describes Haggai and Zechariah prophesying, but it does not contain the actual words of their prophecies. In their own books, we read the poetic words of God which Haggai and Zechariah brought to the people of Jerusalem.

A detailed exploration of the books of Haggai and Zechariah lies beyond the scope of this project. But we can ask about the relationship of those two books and the book of Ezra. With confidence, I can say that because of vocabulary and style of writing, the book of Ezra was not written by the author of the book of Haggai or by author of the book of Zechariah. Haggai and Zechariah each have their own poetic style. On one hand, Haggai follows the style of the mainstream Hebrew prophets. On the other hand, Zechariah favors the mystical style of Ezekiel and Daniel. In contrast to both Haggai and Zechariah, Ezra does not use any poetic images or the parallel structure of biblical poetry.

We can also ask which came first: the book of Ezra or the books of Haggai and Zechariah? In general, the books of the prophets are collections of their spoken prophecies. It is likely that the core of the words of prophecy in Haggai and Zechariah were spoken by the prophets in a public setting and then written down by scribes. We know that these two prophets were active during the first wave of the return to Jerusalem. While scholars debate exactly when Ezra was written (see chapter 5), it certainly could not have been written until after the events it describes. Ezra arrived in Jerusalem eighty years after the first wave. So, we could conclude that the books of Haggai and Zechariah, or at least the core elements of them, were written before the book of Ezra was written.

An opposing position would be to say that the fact that the author of Ezra does not quote directly from either of these two prophetic books proves that he wrote Ezra before Haggai and Zechariah were written. Support for this position comes from the method that scholars of Christian Scripture use to explain the relationship between Paul's Epistles and the four Gospels. They argue that even though the Gospels describe events that took place before Paul's conversion on the road to Damascus in about 33 CE, the reason that Paul does not quote from any of the four Gospels in his epistles is that he wrote all of his epistles before the first Gospel was written in 72 CE.

Supporters of the "Haggai and Zechariah first" position could respond in either of two way:

1. Even though the books of Haggai and Zechariah were written prior to the composition of Ezra, the author of the book of Ezra was not familiar with them.
2. The author of the book of Ezra did have access to these two prophetic books, but he chose not to quote from them.

We will leave this question unresolved. Unresolved debates over an item in the Talmud sometimes conclude with the word *Teiku*, which is an acronym for *Tishbi yitratz kushiyot uba'ayot*. Meaning that right before the dawn of the messianic age, the prophet Elijah (who never died) will return and solve difficult questions and problems. We can add this question to Elijah's to-do list.

Chapter 43

Already but Not Yet

PASSOVER EXPRESSES OUR SENSE of "already but not yet." At our Passover Seder we celebrate the exodus from Egypt as redemption from slavery. We proudly proclaim that God took us out of Egypt with "a mighty hand and an outstretched arm." But the first night of Passover is also a "night of watching." We look forward to the final redemption. We open the door for Elijah to see if that redemption is taking place. If redemption has not taken place, we conclude the Seder by proclaiming, "Next year in Jerusalem," to express our hope that redemption will take place before we reassemble for the Seder next year. As we celebrate Passover, we look back at the redemption from slavery and forward to the final redemption yet to come.

The return from exile as described in Ezra/Nehemiah is also "already but not yet." These two books celebrate the return from exile and the rebuilding of the Temple. But the returnees remained part of the Persian Empire. They could not recreate an independent nation ruled by a Davidic king.

The English word *messiah* comes from the Hebrew word *hamashiach*, meaning "the anointed one." During the First Temple period the rulers of the united kingdom and later of the divided kingdoms of Judah and Israel were anointed by a representative of God. The Bible describes King David's selection by God to be the king after Saul:

> And the ETERNAL said to Samuel, "How long will you grieve over Saul, since I have rejected him as king over Israel? Fill your

> horn with oil and set out; I am sending you to Jesse the Bethlehemite, for I have decided on one of his sons to be king." (1 Sam 16:1)

After Samuel arrives in Bethlehem the story continues:

> Thus, Jesse presented seven of his sons before Samuel, and Samuel said to Jesse, "The ETERNAL has not chosen any of these." Then Samuel asked Jesse, "Are these all the boys you have?" He replied, "There is still the youngest; he is tending the flock." And Samuel said to Jesse, "Send someone to bring him, for we will not sit down to eat until he gets here." So they sent and brought him. He was ruddy-cheeked, bright-eyed, and handsome. And the ETERNAL said, "Rise and anoint him, for this is the one." Samuel took the horn of oil and anointed him in the presence of his brothers; and the spirit of the ETERNAL gripped David from that day on. Samuel then set out for Ramah. (1 Sam 16:10–13)

The prophet Samuel, following God's detailed instructions, anointed David with oil to publicly indicate God's choice of David to be the next king. David is *hamashiach*, "the anointed one." Those who followed him on the thrones of Judah and Israel were also anointed. Even the evil King Jehu of Israel was anointed. In his instruction to an unnamed prophet sent to carry out this mission, Elisha includes a warning of the danger involved:

> The prophet Elisha summoned a man from the company of the prophets and said to him, "Tuck your cloak into your belt, take this flask of olive oil with you and go to Ramoth Gilead. When you get there, look for Jehu son of Jehoshaphat, the son of Nimshi. Go to him, get him away from his companions and take him into an inner room. Then take the flask and pour the oil on his head and declare, 'This is what the ETERNAL says: I anoint you king over Israel.' Then open the door and run; don't delay!" (2 Kgs 9:1–3)

During the First Temple period the term *hamashiach* had no supernatural connotation. It simply indicated that the flesh-and-blood king had been properly anointed.

During the Second Temple period and the early rabbinic period, we find two threads of messianic thought. Some sources still hoped for a flesh-and-blood messiah who would resemble King David. When Rabbi Akiva in the early second century CE declared Bar Kokhba to be the messiah, he imagined that as the original messiah, King David, defeated the

Philistines, so the new messiah would defeat the Romans. Tragically the Romans crushed the Bar Kokhba rebellion leading to great Jewish suffering. This thread of messianic hope faded after the defeat of Bar Kokhba.

The beginning of the other thread of Jewish messianic expectation can be found in writings of the later prophets. Some of the prophets shift from a near-term flesh-and-blood messiah, a new King David, to a more distant future "anointed one," signaling the end of the world as we know it and the beginning of a new age. Isaiah proclaimed,

> But a shoot shall grow out of the stump of Jesse,
> A twig shall sprout from his stock.
> The spirit of the ETERNAL shall alight upon him:
> A spirit of wisdom and insight,
> A spirit of counsel and valor,
> A spirit of devotion and reverence for the ETERNAL.
> He shall sense the truth by his reverence for the ETERNAL:
> He shall not judge by what his eyes behold,
> Nor decide by what his ears perceive.
> Thus he shall judge the poor with equity
> And decide with justice for the lowly of the land.
> He shall strike down a land with the rod of his mouth
> And slay the wicked with the breath of his lips.
> Justice shall be the girdle of his loins,
> And faithfulness the girdle of his waist.
>
> The wolf shall dwell with the lamb,
> The leopard lie down with the kid;
> The calf, the beast of prey, and the fatling together,
> With a little boy to herd them.
> The cow and the bear shall graze,
> Their young shall lie down together;
> And the lion, like the ox, shall eat straw.
> A babe shall play
> Over a viper's hole,
> And an infant shall pass his hand
> Over an adder's den.
> In all of My sacred mount
> Nothing evil or vile shall be done;
> For the land shall be filled with devotion to the ETERNAL
> As water covers the sea.
>
> In that day,
> The stock of Jesse that has remained standing

Shall become a standard to peoples—
Nations shall seek his counsel
And his abode shall be honored.
(Isa 11:1–10)

In Isaiah's words we see images of the final redemption.

As I explained in the previous chapter, scholars agree that the book of Isaiah contains three types of prophecy from three time periods:

1. Harsh messages criticizing the corrupt behavior of the people of Judah during the latter years of the First Temple period
2. Messages of comfort and hope during years of Babylonian exile
3. Hopeful messages of the end of days delivered during the Second Temple period

We presume that the prophet who spoke during the First Temple period was actually named Isaiah. We do not know the names of the prophets who spoke during the exile and during the years following the return from exile. Scholars refer to these prophets as First Isaiah, Second Isaiah, and Third Isaiah. The "sprout of David" prophecy in Third Isaiah's vision does not resemble the warrior-king who we read about in 1 Samuel. Third Isaiah does not focus on immediate political challenges facing the returnees. The words of Third Isaiah express the image of a future in which all the challenges of our lives will be resolved:

In the days to come,
The Mount of the ETERNAL's House
Shall stand firm above the mountains
And tower above the hills;
And all the nations
Shall gaze on it with joy.
And the many peoples shall go and say:
"Come, Let us go up to the Mount of the ETERNAL,
To the House of the God of Jacob;
That He may instruct us in His ways,
And that we may walk in His paths."
For instruction shall come forth from Zion.

The word of the ETERNAL from Jerusalem.
Thus He will judge among the nations
And arbitrate for the many peoples,
And they shall beat their swords into plowshares

> And their spears into pruning hooks:
> Nation shall not take up
> Sword against nation;
> They shall never again know war.
> (Isa 2:1–4)

These words, which also appear in Mic 1:1–4, express what has become the iconic image of the messianic age.

In the previous chapter we saw that the book of Haggai and first chapters of the book of Zechariah contain messages encouraging the people to complete the rebuilding of the Temple. The later chapters of Zechariah contain descriptions of the end of days. Chapter 14 of Zechariah describes a final battle in the end of days which will result in God ruling the world. While most of the chapter might not be well-known, anybody who participates in Jewish worship will recognize the words of Zech 14:9 as the conclusion of the Aleinu:

> And the ETERNAL shall be ruler over all the earth; on that day the ETERNAL shall be one and his name shall be one.

These words of Zechariah express the new thread in the "already but not yet" dynamic that emerges during the Second Temple period. The hope for an end of days "anointed one" and the hope for a new flesh-and-blood warrior-king as the "anointed one" competed during the Second Temple period. Following the defeat of the Bar Kokhba rebellion in 136 CE, the end of days "anointed one" becomes the dominant messianic idea for the Jewish people.

Chapter 44

A Mighty Hand, and an Outstretched Arm

EACH FALL THE EIGHTH-GRADE teacher at my synagogue invites me to speak with the students about God and the Holocaust. The students want to know why God didn't intervene in history to save the Jews of Europe. One year a student said, "You always talk about God's mighty hand. Where was God's mighty hand during the Holocaust?"

For many years at Passover, I have enjoyed reciting the famous phrase that describes God rescuing us from Egyptian slavery "with a mighty hand, and with an outstretched arm" (Deut 26:8). I learned from my father-in-law to make a fist and raise my arm as I say these words at our family Seder. I added an exaggerated lengthening of "ouuuuuuuuuuut-streached" combined with the volume of my natural enthusiasm to create a "catchphrase." The members of my family and the students in the Etz Chaim religious school have enthusiastically joined me in proclaiming this phrase with triumphant confidence.

The book of Deuteronomy and the early prophets (Deuteronomic History) express a belief in God's close involvement in the history of the Jewish people. Chapter 28 of Deuteronomy lays out a system of national rewards and punishments. It describes all of the positive outcomes that will take place if the people follow God's commandments. The rewards include the following:

> Blessed shall be your issue from the womb, your produce from the soil, and the offspring of your cattle, the calving of your herd

> and the lambing of your flock. Blessed shall be your basket and your kneading bowl. Blessed shall you be in your comings and blessed shall you be in your goings. The ETERNAL will put to rout before [your army] the enemies who attack you; they will march out against you by a single road, but flee from you by many roads. (Deut 28:4–7)

After detailing the consequences of following God's commandments, the text explains what will happen to the nation of Israel if they turn away from God:

> Cursed shall you be in the city and cursed shall you be in the country. Cursed shall be your basket and your kneading bowl. Cursed shall be your issue from the womb and your produce from the soil, the calving of your herd and the lambing of your flock. Cursed shall you be in your comings and cursed shall you be in your goings. The ETERNAL will let loose against you calamity, panic, and frustration in all the enterprises you undertake, so that you shall soon be utterly wiped out because of your evildoing in forsaking Me. (Deut 28:16–20)

The book of Judges provides a series of illustrations of this dynamic of rewards and punishments. Each story begins, "And the Israelites did what was offensive to the ETERNAL." In each story God punishes the Israelites for turning to idol worship. When the people repent God sends a "judge" to save them. The people fall into this pattern again and again.

After the death of King Solomon, the united kingdom divided into the Northern Kingdom of Israel and the Southern Kingdom of Judah. During that period the people turned again to idolatry. The Bible finds faults with many of the leaders of the nations of Judah and Israel.

First and Second Kings speak positively about none of the kings of Israel and only two of the kings of Judah: Hezekiah and Josiah. All the other rulers of the both the Northern Kingdom and the Southern Kingdom are harshly criticized for their misdeeds of idolatry and misrule.

Second Kings glorifies Josiah, describing him living as Deuteronomy calls upon all Israelites to live: "There was no king like him before who turned back to the ETERNAL with all his heart, with all his soul and with all his might, in full accord with the Torah of Moses; nor did any like him arise after him" (2 Kgs 23:25).

Then Josiah takes the army of Judah north to Megiddo to confront the Egyptian army. Pharaoh Neco had brought his army north to support the Assyrians in their struggle with the Babylonians. Josiah sides with the Babylonians in opposition to Judah's longtime enemy, the Assyrians. One might expect that Josiah's efforts would lead to success, but tragically there was no divine intervention at Megiddo. The Egyptians defeated the army of Judah, killing Josiah.

After Josiah's death, the kingdom of Judah began the descent that led to the destruction of the Temple and the exile of the people. Over the next twenty-two years, three of Josiah's sons and one of his grandsons ruled for brief periods of time as vassals of the Egyptians or Babylonians. The prophet Jeremiah, who had been a strong supporter of Josiah, found serious fault with all of these final four kings of Judah.

According to the system described in Deuteronomy, Josiah should not have died in defeat. The Davidic monarchy should not have come apart. In 2 Sam 7 we read that the Davidic line will rule forever. One might ask, Where was God's mighty hand during the battle at Megiddo?

The Bible presents several examples of God's willingness and ability to interrupt nature to save the Israelites. In addition to the ten plagues and the dividing of the sea in the exodus story, God intervenes in history to assist Joshua. The Jordan River stops flowing to allow the Israelites to cross into the promised land (Josh 3:14–17). Later during the battle with the Gibeonites God causes the sun to stop in the sky to provide Joshua with enough time to fully defeat the enemy (Josh 10:12–15). In calling Gideon, God does private miracles to prove the divine nature of the summons (Judg 6:11–24).

As time passes God's use of wonders and signs diminish. One of the last public displays of God's might reported by the Bible is the confrontation between Elijah and prophets of Baal on Mount Carmel. Fire comes from heaven to ignite and consumes the sacrifice which Elijah has presented to the One God of Israel (1 Kgs 18:16–45).

In the next chapter God speaks to the prophet Elijah in a "still small voice," foreshadowing the nature of God's future involvement in the lives of people:

> And He said: "Go forth, and stand upon the mount before the ETERNAL." And, behold, the ETERNAL passed by, and a great and strong wind rent the mountains, and broke in pieces the rocks before the ETERNAL; but the ETERNAL was not in the wind; and after the wind an earthquake; but the ETERNAL was not in the earthquake; and after the earthquake a fire; but the ETERNAL was not in the fire; and after the fire a still small voice. (1 Kgs 19:11–12)

In this exchange Elijah experienced God's presence in the still small voice, not in the big special effects. The Bible tells future generations that the big public spectacles are coming to an end.

In the first verse of the first chapter of Ezra we read that "the ETERNAL roused the spirit of King Cyrus of Persia to issue a proclamation" that God had charged him with the rebuilding of the Temple in Jerusalem. The departure from Babylonia does not include any of the supernatural events like the ones that played a central role in the exodus from Egypt. This departure does not include any experiences parallel to the ten plagues or the dividing of the sea. We can describe God's role in the events of Ezra/Nehemiah not so much as a "mighty hand" but rather as a "still small voice."

We see God's diminished role in history expressed in another postexilic book of the Hebrew Bible. The book of Esther does not explicitly mention God's role guiding the events. Certainly, we do not read of God's mighty hand upsetting Haman's plans.

Often people think that it is a modern question to ask about the absence of the "mighty hand," but we are not the first generation to ask where was God when we needed saving. Tragically too many times our people have suffered loss and devastation: in 70 CE, when the Romans destroyed the Temple; in 135 CE, during the Bar Kokhba rebellion; and in 1096, during the First Crusade. Since the defeat of King Josiah at Megiddo, people have asked time and time again how God could allow such a thing a thing to happen.

When I was a child, I believed that the Union prevailed in the Civil War because they were "right" and the Confederates were "wrong." I had a similarly unsophisticated view of World War II. The Allies won because they were clearly "right," and the Axis powers lost because they were clearly "wrong." As a child, I knew that God's power and the moral balance of the universe would continue to maintain history along its proper path. As I entered my teenage years I began to think more critically about the world. With this deeper and more serious perspective I gave up my childish view of the inevitable triumph of righteousness. As a rabbi I have had the opportunity to respond to teens as they have entered their own years of critical thinking.

Each fall I explain to the eighth graders that the Holocaust was a massive failure of humanity to heed God's calls. God commands us "to love our neighbors as ourselves" (Lev 19:18). But God gives us free will to choose how we lead our individual lives. We can decide to heed God's call or to reject God's call. The Nazis, their supporters, and their collaborators ignored God. They chose Hitler's vision of racial triumph over God's vision of loving our neighbors.

At the beginning of the book of Ezra, God, through Cyrus the Great, called the people to return to Jerusalem. God did not carry the people back to Jerusalem on eagles' wings. The people had to choose to act. Those who returned to Jerusalem did so as God's agents. They rebuilt the Temple, the walls of Jerusalem, and its gates in response to God's call.

In our time God still calls us to love our neighbors as ourselves. When we do God's will we become agents of God. When we feed the hungry and give housing to the homeless, our hands become God's hands. When we reach out to those in need, our hands become mighty hands and our arms become outstretched arms.

Chapter 45

Ezra and Nehemiah in Rabbinic Literature

THROUGHOUT THIS BOOK I have demonstrated the important role that Ezra played in the creation of Judaism. The rabbis imagined that Ezra played an even larger role. Ezra appears many times in rabbinic literature. Many of these sources present Ezra as the link between the age of prophecy and the sages. They see him as the first rabbi. The rabbis distinguish between laws that are explicitly found in the Torah and those that depend on rabbinic interpretation of the Torah text. They call the first group *d'oraita*, "from the Torah," and the second group *d'rabbanan*, "from the rabbis." The rabbis depict Ezra as playing a large and important part in the creation of these *halachot d'rabbanan*, rabbinic laws.

Midrash Shir Hashirim Rabbah draws on a Bible verse to portray the return from exile as a springtime renewal of the Jewish people, and Ezra as one of the "flowers that appear on the earth" (Song 2:12). Poetically, the Talmud sees Ezra as a second Moses (Sanhedrin 21b). The Talmud traces many halachic standards back to Ezra.

Masechet Baba Kamma presents Ezra as the source of ten specific halachot:

> The Sages taught that Ezra the Scribe proclaimed ten laws: he stated that communities should read the Torah on Shabbat in the afternoon; and they also read the Torah on every Monday and Thursday; since the courts gather every Monday and Thursday; and one does laundry on Thursday; and one eats garlic on

> Shabbat eve. And Ezra also proclaimed that a woman should rise early to bake bread on those days when she wants to bake; and that a woman should don a proper garment; and that a woman should first prepare her hair and only then immerse in a mikva so that she can remedy her condition of having been ritually impure; and that traders of cosmetics and perfumes should travel around from town to town. And Ezra further proclaimed the requirement of immersion for those men who experienced a seminal emission. (BT Baba Kamma 82a)

The rabbis see Ezra as playing an important role in the development of halachah. They see him as a key member of the important body, the Men of the Great Assembly. The rabbis describe a chain of tradition linking themselves back to Moses. The rabbis speak of the Torah that was passed from generation to generation. For the rabbis the term *Torah* includes the written Torah text and the oral explanation of that text. The opening verses of Pirkei Avot explain how Moses is linked to the Men of the Great Assembly:

> Moses received the Torah at Sinai and passed it to Joshua, from Joshua to the elders, and from the elders to the prophets, and from the prophets to the Men of the Great Assembly. The Men of the Great Assembly said three things: be patient in the application of justice, teach many students, and build a fence round the Torah. (Mishnah Pirkei Avot 1:1)

Rabbinic sources also identify Nehemiah as a member of Men of the Great Assembly. Midrash Ruth Rabbah sees the phrase "we make this pledge and put it in writing" (Neh 10:1) as an expression of the Great Assembly in action. In Midrash Exodus Rabbah, Samuel ben Marta, a pupil of Rav, calls attention to Nehemiah's interest in the details of halachah: "We have offended You by not keeping the commandments, the laws, and the rules that You gave to Your servant Moses" (Neh 1:7). Nehemiah chose to use three words to describe halachah when he could have used just one word. The rabbis argue that in saying "commandments, the laws, and the rules," Nehemiah demonstrates his deep interest in halachah and his membership in the Great Assembly.

According to rabbinic tradition, the Men of the Great Assembly were the first rabbis. Rambam, in the introduction to his Mishneh Torah, explains that the Great Assembly was a rabbinic court established by Ezra. Rambam draws on a variety of earlier rabbinic sources including Genesis Rabbah 71:3 and Esther Rabbah 3:7 to establish Ezra's lofty position.

The first chapter of Pirkei Avot traces the leadership of the sages from "Shimon the Righteous, one of the last of the men of the great assembly" to Rabban Gamliel and the first generation of the sages to use the title "rabbi." These verses in Pirkei Avot establish a clear line of transmission of the Torah from Moses at Mount Sinai to the rabbis of the first and second centuries CE. For those early rabbis Ezra stands at an important link on this unbroken chain of tradition.

I appreciate the desire of the rabbis of the first century CE to see themselves as part of a chain of tradition reaching all the way back to Moses at Mount Sinai. As a twenty-first-century rabbi, I certainly see myself as part of that ongoing process of learning and teaching Torah that is the chain of tradition. I often describe my teaching of Jewish children as "forging new links on the chain of tradition." But modern scholars raise serious questions about the Great Assembly. They see the rabbinic imagination at work to directly connect their time with Ezra and Nehemiah.

Establishing origins is often a difficult process. While it may seem reasonable to ask who was the first Impressionist painter, this is not a simple question to answer. Many people consider Claude Monet to be the first major Impressionist artist. But elements of Impressionism can be seen in artists who came before him. If we ask a historian when the Renaissance began, the answer would be an entire article rather than a single sentence.

Some attempts at telling the origin stories get it completely wrong. One of my favorite trips of all time was the visit my brother, Ken, and I took to the National Baseball Hall of Fame in Cooperstown, New York. Cooperstown is an idyllic town on the shores of Otsego Lake. It was the home of prominent nineteenth-century American author James Fenimore Cooper. It has the beautiful opera house of the Glimmerglass Opera. But why is the Baseball Hall of Fame in Cooperstown?

In 1905, baseball's National League appointed a committee chaired by Colonel A. G. Mills to establish the origins of the game of baseball.[1] The Mills committee reported "the first scheme for playing baseball, according to the best evidence obtainable to date, was devised by Abner Doubleday at Cooperstown, N.Y., in 1839."[2] The Hall of Fame opened in Cooperstown 1939 as part of a commemoration of baseball's first one hundred years.

1. Thorn, "Debate over Baseball's Origins."
2. Pecise, "Baseball History Unpacked."

Later research has proved that the Mills committee greatly exaggerated Abner Doubleday's role in the creation of baseball. Everybody agrees that Doubleday was a Civil War general who distributed bats and balls to his soldiers. He played a role in the promotion of the "New York Rules" for baseball, but he did not invent the game. Today scholars believe that baseball emerged in and around New York City in the 1830s. In creating an origin myth for baseball, the need to create a good story got in the way of historic accuracy.

Andrew Hickey has created a wonderful podcast, *A History of Rock Music in 500 Songs.* Andrew tells a good story and he also does careful research in order to maintain historic accuracy. One of the challenges Andrew faced was where to begin. What was the first rock song? Andrew rejects simple answers that would identify "Rocket 88" by Jackie Brenston and the Delta Cats from 1951 or Wynonie Harris's "Good Rockin' Tonight" from 1947 as the first rock song. Andrew understands that one should avoid identifying "firsts." He takes a more careful and serious approach. He points to the emergence of the elements that make a song a rock song. In the second episode of the podcast Andrew explains the "back beat" in "Roll 'Em Pete" by Big Joe Turner and Pete Johnson from 1938. Andrew began his podcast by introducing Charlie Christian's electric guitar solo on the Benny Goodman Sextet's song "Flying Home" from 1939.[3]

Andrew does not claim that "Roll 'Em Pete" and "Flying Home" are rock songs. Benny Goodman was the "King of Swing." Pete Johnson was a boogie-woogie pianist. And Big Joe Turner was a blues shouter. But Andrew points out that one can see the elements that became rock emerging from their songs.

Ezra was not the first of the rabbis, but he played a key role in creating important elements of the text-centered Judaism. Nehemiah does include the revelation at Mount Sinai in his retelling of Jewish history. But Nehemiah was not an early halachic authority.

In telling the story of their origins the ancient rabbis may have embellished the rabbinic nature of Ezra's life to strengthen its connection to their own. They wanted to portray him as the first of the rabbis to provide their endeavors with a longer history. I agree with the scholars who explain that he did not establish halachot as depicted in the Talmud. I do not mean to diminish the status of Ezra by saying he was not the first rabbi. He did create the foundation on which all text-based religions

3. Hickey, "Roll 'Em Pete."

stand. The Bible identifies him as a scribe. As I explained in chapter 3, we should see Ezra as "the Scribe"! I believe that he established the Torah text as we have it today. Chapter 8 of Nehemiah describes the first public reading of the Torah text. As Ezra stood before the people in Jerusalem and read the words of Torah to them, Judaism began.

Chapter 46

Lidrosh

THE FIRST SIX CHAPTERS of the book of Ezra describe the first waves of return to Jerusalem from exile in Babylonia. In those chapters we read of Zerubbabel and Jeshua leading the returnees. Ezra "comes on stage" in the seventh chapter of the book of Ezra. The first ten verses of that chapter introduce Ezra. That section concludes by describing Ezra in terms of his expertise in Torah: "For Ezra had dedicated himself [*lidrosh*] the Torah of the ETERNAL so as to observe it and to teach laws and rules to Israel" (Ezra 7:10).

The Hebrew term *lidrosh* appears 164 times in the Hebrew Bible. In the earlier books of the Tanakh, it describes a person seeking an answer from God. The struggle of the twins within her womb upsets Rebekah, and she goes to "inquire [*tidrosh*] of the ETERNAL" (Gen 25:22) Rebecca's suffering during her pregnancy confused her. She wanted God to explain to her what was going on in her life. So, she "inquired" of God to help her understand the purpose of her suffering

Moses used the word in a similar way in explaining to Jethro the heavy burden of leading the nation: "And Moses said unto his father-in-law: 'Because the people come unto me to inquire [*lidrosh*], of God'" (Exod 18:15). The people wanted direction from God to help them overcome the problems they faced. They wanted God to resolve the conflicts that they had with other people, so they came to Moses to "inquire" of God.

We can also see this use of this word in Hosea's prophetic call for the people to return to God:

> Sow for yourselves righteousness
> Reap the fruits of steadfast love
> Break up your fallow ground;
> For it is time to seek [*lidrosh*] the ETERNAL
> Till He comes and causes righteousness to rain upon you.
> (Hos 10:12)

Hosea summons the people to once again turn to God, to "inquire" of God for direction.

Other religious traditions feature stories of people seeking knowledge of God's plans for them. Ancient Greek stories include episodes of people travelling to Delphi to seek answers from the priestess of Apollo. The pronouncements of the oracle were taken to be the divine word about the future. In the Oedipus story, the pronouncement of the oracle that Oedipus will kill his father and then marry his mother sets the action of the story in motion. As the story develops, we learn that no matter what people do, they cannot escape from their fate as described by the oracle.

Lidrosh is the infinitive form for the Hebrew verb *doraish*. As we have seen, this word occurs in many books of the Hebrew Bible. Generally, the text uses the term to describe a person seeking a response from God. The examples I quoted above are a representative sample. The first sign of the beginning in a shift in the meaning of the word can be seen in the book of Isaiah. The prophet Isaiah used the term to refer to the Torah: "Inquire, and read it in the scroll of the ETERNAL: None of these will be absent, not one will miss its fellow. For it is His mouth that has spoken, and it is His Spirit that has assembled" (Isa 34:16). This chapter of the book of Isaiah describes the coming destruction of the nations. The prophet explains that one can understand these events by "inquiring" of the Torah scroll.

This word takes on a new meaning in rabbinic literature. Rabbinic texts use *doraish* to speak of the sages expounding the meaning of a biblical text. Today the Hebrew noun *drash* is used to describe words a rabbi shares with the congregation in explaining the Torah portion of the week.

When did the meaning of this term change? Ezra 7:10 is the shift point. The author of Ezra uses the term in a brand-new way. During the postexilic period, our method of experiencing God changed. We moved from seeking prophecy to turning to the texts. We continued to inquire of God, but instead of listening to words spoken by God's prophets, we turn to the texts to inquire of God.

The Torah did not become an oracular device. We do treat a Torah scroll with great respect. We stand when the ark is opened. We use a yad when reading so that we can avoid touching the letters with our hands. We dress the Torah scroll in garments like those worn by the priests. But the Torah scroll is not an oracular device or magical icon. We do not come to "inquire" of the Torah scroll. We "inquire" of the words contained in the Torah. We unfold the meaning of the words, as my Midrash professor explained, "to probe the text for its subtleties and nuances."

Ezra 7:10 begins, "For Ezra had dedicated himself [*lidrosh*] the Torah of the ETERNAL." Rashi's commentary on this verse explains the meaning of these words: "And since he wished to proceed and succeed in his path, Ezra 'dedicated himself . . .' [to Torah]. This provided purpose to his words."

Chapter 8 of Nehemiah begins with a description of the rededication ceremony on the first day of the seventh month: Rosh Hashanah. Outside the Water Gate the entire people assembled to hear Ezra read from the Torah. The next day the leaders of the community returned to Ezra to learn more about what the scrolls said: "On the second day of the month, the heads of all the clans of all the people, and the priests and the Levites, gathered to Ezra the scribe to study the words of the Torah" (Neh 8:13).

Since the time of Ezra, we have sought God through the text. When religious Jews want to know what God wants them to do, they do not say, "I will pray on that." We do not expect private personal guidance directly from God. We look to the texts or to a rabbi to explain the text. In discussing our verse, prominent scholar Michael Fishbane explains, "Scripture has become the vehicle of new revelations and exegesis [interpretation] the means of new access to the divine will."[1]

Malbim understands the phrase in our verse "*lidrosh et hatorah*" to mean that Ezra devoted himself to a "deep and intense study of Torah amassing great knowledge and mastering its profoundest meanings" (Malbim on Ezra 7:10). Since the completion of the Torah, generation after generation of Jews have been following Ezra's example.

As I explained in chapter 3, Ezra completed the writing of the Torah. When he began to read the Torah to the people, they asked questions. Thus, the age of interpretation began.

As soon as a work of art is completed and shared with the public, interpretation begins. Readers, appreciators, and critics begin to respond.

1. Fishbane, *Biblical Interpretation*, 266.

They interpret or reinterpret the meaning of the song, painting, sculpture, or book. The meaning of any work of art or religious teaching constantly shifts, never remaining static.

Bob Dylan recorded the song "All Along the Watchtower" for his *John Wesley Harding* album released in December of 1967. Jimi Hendrix began playing that song during his live shows in January 1968. Hendrix worked on a recording for months—changing, adjusting, rerecording sections. Jimi's version of "All Along the Watchtower" was released in October of 1968 on his *Electric Ladyland* album.

Dylan described his reaction to hearing Hendrix's version:

> It overwhelmed me, really. He had such talent—he could find things inside a song and vigorously develop them. He found things that other people wouldn't think of finding in there. He probably improved upon it by the spaces he was using. I took license with the song from his version, actually, and continue to do it to this day.[2]

In the booklet accompanying his *Biograph* album, Dylan said, "I liked Jimi Hendrix's record of this and ever since he died, I've been doing it that way. . . . Strange how when I sing it, I always feel it's a tribute to him in some kind of way.[3]

A central element of our religious lives is to immerse ourselves in studying the texts. As Jews, we draw closer to God through prayer, study, and doing deeds of loving-kindness. By studying the texts, Jews have continued to "inquire" of God. We keep unfolding the text, discovering new meanings that have been hidden within those folds. I feel that I walk in the path created by Ezra. I have dedicated my life to bringing Torah to the people, and the people to Torah. The verse with which I began this chapter describes what it means to me to be a rabbi:

> For Ezra had dedicated himself to interpreting the Torah of the ETERNAL so as to observe it and to teach laws and rules to Israel. (Ezra 7:10)

2. *Sun Sentinel*, "Midnight Chat with Dylan."

3. Dylan, *Biograph*, liner notes.

For Further Reading

For readers interested in pursuing a more scholarly understanding of Ezra/Nehemiah, I would strongly recommend *In an Age of Prose: A Literary Approach to Ezra-Nehemiah* by Tamara C. Eskenazi. Professor Eskenazi is the leading contemporary scholar on these books of the Bible. Professor Eskenazi is also the author of the new Anchor Bible volume on Ezra. In this important new book Professor Eskenazi provides a scholarly commentary on each verse. The Nehemiah volume is forthcoming.

I offer the following suggestions for additional resources on each of the chapters.

CHAPTER 1: SACRED HISTORY

Hoffman, *Beyond the Text*. In chapters 4 and 5 of his insightful book Hoffman provides a wonderful introduction into understanding "Sacred History."

For a deeper explanation of these Torah and history sections of Ezra/Nehemiah, see Duggan, *Covenant Revival.*

CHAPTER 2: TORAH RITUALS

To read more about the Letter of Aristeas, see Lim, *Formation of the Jewish Canon*, ch. 5.

To learn more about the early history of Torah reading, see Graves, "Public Reading of Scripture."

CHAPTER 3: REDACTION

While I do not agree with all of Dr. Friedman's conclusions, he does provide a very readable introduction into the Documentary Hypothesis. See Friedman, *Who Wrote the Bible?*

For a newer perspective on the Documentary Hypothesis, see Schniedewind, *How the Bible Became a Book.*

CHAPTER 4: WHO WROTE EZRA/NEHEMIAH?

For a more scholarly explanation, see Japhet, "Composition and Chronology."

CHAPTER 5: WHEN WERE EZRA/NEHEMIAH WRITTEN?

Schniedewind, *How the Bible Became a Book*, 183–87.

CHAPTER 6: THE SHIFT TO WRITING HEBREW IN ARAMAIC LETTERS

For an introduction into the evolution of Hebrew, see Hoffman, *Short History*, and Schniedewind, *How the Bible Became a Book*, 174–81.

CHAPTER 7: ARAMAIC, HEBREW, AND JUDEO-AMERICAN

For an engaging telling of the development of the Hebrew language, see Oz and Oz-Salzberger, *Jews and Words.*

CHAPTER 8: PERSIAN LOAN WORDS

For a scholarly explanation of how foreign words enter Hebrew, see Noonan, *Non-Semitic Loanwords.*

For more on these specific Persian words, see Fried, *Ezra*, 310.

CHAPTER 9: HOW DO YOU SPELL DAVID?

The Laughing Cow story can be read in English here: Wikipedia, "Laughing Cow."

To learn more about pubs, see Jack, *Old Dog and Duck.*

CHAPTER 10: OUR STORY IN THE MUCH LARGER WORLD

For a full explanation of the historic context of the Bible, see Cline, *1177 BC.*

For a deeper explanation of the emergence of books based on secondary characters in classic literature, see Rosen, *Minor Characters Have Their Day.*

CHAPTER 11: PLACING EZRA AND NEHEMIAH IN THEIR HISTORIC CONTEXT

For a full exploration of the history from the ultra-orthodox position based on Seder Olam, see the ArtScroll Tanach Series editions of *The Book of Ezra* and *The Book of Nehemiah.*

For the accepted standard approach to dating, see Williamson, *Ezra–Nehemiah.*

CHAPTER 12: NATIONAL NARRATIVE

To learn more about Theodor Herzl, see Avineri, *Herzl.*

CHAPTER 13: TAKING POSSESSION OF THE LAND

The story of the Ingalls' family homestead is from Wilder, *By the Shores of Silver Lake.*

For more on early to mid-twentieth-century Zionist activities, see Segev, *One Palestine, Complete.*

CHAPTER 14: PRACTICAL ZIONISM: THE FIRST ALIYAH

For more on the first wave of return from Babylonia, see Fried, *Ezra*, 61.

For more on the modern First Aliyah from a progressive Israeli point of view, see Morris, *Righteous Victims*.

For a dual narrative approach, see Adwarn et al., *Side by Side*.

CHAPTER 15: CYRUS THE GREAT

For more on the creation of the State of Israel, see Kurzman, *Genesis 1948*.

For a greater understanding of Harry Truman's role, see Radosh and Radosh, *Safe Haven*.

To learn more about the experience of Jews under Ottoman rule, see Hacker, "Jews in the Ottoman Empire."

For a more general introduction to the Ottoman Empire, see Goffman, *Ottoman Empire*, and Qataert, *Ottoman Empire*.

CHAPTER 16: POLITICAL ZIONISM

The introduction to Hertzberg, *Zionist Idea*, is actually a concise history of Zionism.

For selected primary texts, see Troy, *Zionist Ideas*, 3–33.

CHAPTER 17: JEREMIAH'S PROMISE

For a brief but interesting conversation about this text between two leading scholars, listen to Wheaton College, "I Have Plans for You," where Dr. David Capes interviews Dr. Michael Graves.

For an introduction to prophets mentioned in this chapter, see Bullock, *Old Testament Prophetic Books*. For Jeremiah see pages 185–214. For Ezekiel see pages 227–53.

CHAPTER 18: BABYLONIAN JEWS

For an explanation of how the experience of the Jews in Babylonia fits into the larger Jewish narrative, see Johnson, *History of the Jews*.

For a full understanding of this key Civil War battle, see Sears, *Chancellorsville*.

CHAPTER 19: THE FIRST JEW

For a brief scholarly introduction to Esther, see Koller, *Esther in Ancient Jewish Thought*, 45–53.

CHAPTER 20: UNDERSTANDING THE SUKKAH

The two scholarly books that I quote from in this chapter are Williamson, *Ezra-Nehemiah*, and Blenkinsopp, *Ezra-Nehemiah*.

To read Professor Milgrom's explanation of the key Sukkah verse, see Milgrom, *Leviticus 23–27*. This is the third book of a three-volume set. The pages are numbered continuously across all three books. On page 2037 Professor Milgrom expresses support for the idea that the sukkah was an "exilic custom."

For a more comprehensive exploration of the origins of this holiday, see Rubenstein, *History of Sukkot*.

Other rabbinic commentaries mentioned but not quoted in the text of the chapter:

Ralbag accepts the Nehemiah text to be speaking about dwelling in the sukkah. But he reads it as metaphoric rather literal. He explains,

> Early generations did dwell in Sukkot but that the generation of Ezra and Nehemiah drew closer to God through their observance of this Mitzvah than the early generations so it "as if" no other generation had dwelled in Sukkot. (Ralbag on Neh 8:17)

Metzudat David sees the Nehemiah text as describing a new manner of dwelling in the sukkah:

> In the time of Ezra and Nehemiah people made the Sukkah their primary dwelling place throughout the festival. In previous generations people had slept in their regular homes and only visited the Sukkah. (Metzudat David on Neh 8:17)

Malbim follows a similar strategy in making sense of the Nehemiah verse but with a different thread of logic:

> Before Ezra, sukkot were only built on privately owned land. The time of Ezra marks the beginning of constructing a Sukkah on publicly owned land. (Malbim on Neh 8:17)

CHAPTER 21: RELIGIOUS LIFE DURING THE EXILE IN BABYLONIA

For an explanation of Jewish worship on this island in the Nile River, see Rosenberg, "Jewish Temple at Elephantine," 4–13.

For a deeper presentation of the specific artifact, see Porten, *Elephantine Papyri in English.*

CHAPTER 22: REDEFINING TIME

The book of baseball essays I mention is Boswell, *Why Time Begins on Opening Day.*

For an explanation of the Jewish calendar, see Kertzer and Hoffman, *What Is a Jew?*

For an explanation of the acquisition of the new month names from a traditional point of view, see Gurkow, "Hebrew Months."

CHAPTER 23: THE RIGHT SONG

To learn more about Jewish worship, see Hoffman, *Way into Jewish Prayer,* and Bradshaw and Hoffman, *Making of Jewish and Christian Worship.*

For an introduction to the lives of these two key American songwriters, see Klein, *Woody Guthrie,* and Kaplan, *Irving Berlin.*

CHAPTER 24: REBUILDING THE TEMPLE

George Carlin regularly compared baseball to football in his stage performances. His 1984 HBO special includes an early version of this bit. The YouTube recording of his 1990 performance has a fully developed version. *The Baseball Almanac* has the full text.

CHAPTER 25: ONE TEMPLE OR TWO

To learn more about the texts composed after the return from the exile, see Simkovich, *Discovering Second Temple Literature.*

The classic resource on this time period is Bickerman, *Ezra.*

CHAPTER 26: THE WALLS OF JERUSALEM

To learn more about Jerusalem following the destruction, see Faust, *Judah*.

Fried, *Nehemiah*, 3–6 provides a comprehensive summary of the scholarly debates about the walls of Jerusalem in Nehemiah's time.

CHAPTER 27: WHERE IS THE ARK?

For a thorough critique of Graham Hancock, see Porten, "Did the Ark Stop."

To learn more of the refutation of the Rosslyn Chapel story, see Nisbet, "Ancient Code."

CHAPTER 28: THE PRESENCE OF GOD

For a moving description of experiencing the presence of God, see Heschel, *Sabbath*.

For an introduction to synagogues, see Krinsky, *Synagogues of Europe*.

CHAPTER 29: GROUPING THE COMMUNITY

To understand Israel in the period following the Six-Day War, I would suggest Elon, *Israelis*.

To learn more about the Soviet Jewry movement from the inside, see Sharankshy, *Fear No Evil*.

CHAPTER 30: HELP FROM OTHERS

To learn more about rescuers during the Holocaust, see Tec, *When Light Pierced the Darkness*.

My father-in-law, Eric Blaustein, wrote a memoir of his Holocaust experiences. While it has not been published, I would be happy to send it to you.

To learn more about Theodor Herzl, see Elon, *Herzl*.

For an introduction to the importance of Zionist ideas to many British leaders and thinkers, see Tuchman, *Bible and Sword*.

CHAPTER 31: WHAT WERE THEIR NAMES?

To learn more about the specific kibbutz I mentioned, see Ziv, *Kibbutz.*

For selected primary sources on the early Zionist pioneers, see Troy, *Zionist Ideas*, 35–61.

Major Major Major Major is a character in Heller, *Catch-22.*

CHAPTER 32: AHASUERUS AND AHASUERUS

The scholarly article on this subject is Stern, "Esther and the Politics of Diaspora."

Professor Stern explained her central arguments for the more general readers in an article on TheTorah.com. See Stern, "Megillat Esther."

CHAPTER 33: HOW DO YOU SAY AHASUERUS IN PERSIAN?

The Ahasuerus article in the *Jewish Encyclopedia* can be found freely online. See Levi et al., "Ahasuerus."

For a deep and insightful analysis of Lincoln's 272 words, see Wills, *Lincoln at Gettysburg.*

CHAPTER 34: HE WAS WEARING A HAT

One can see examples of the fluted Persian hats in the reliefs on the walls of the ruins of Persepolis. See Scalf, "Persepolis."

To learn more about the turban, see Filstrup and Merrill, *Turban.*

CHAPTER 35: FOREIGN WIVES

For a deeper exploration of these two biblical texts, see Fried, *Ezra*, 391–405, and Fried, *Nehemiah*, 386–93.

CHAPTER 36: THE DAVIDIC LINE

Many contemporary Bible scholars have explored the difficulties in the genealogy in Matthew. One helpful source is Borg and Crossan, *First Christmas*, 95.

To learn more about Daniel's trials as described in the Midrash, see Braude, *Pesikta Rabbati*.

For an introduction to Chronicles, see Kalimi, *Ancient Israelite Historian*.

CHAPTER 37: THE ADVERSARIES

Modern scholars offer a wide range of opinions on the origins and history of the Samaritans. For a middle of the road approach, see Cline, *From Eden to Exile*.

The Venerable Bede's commentary has been translated into English. See Venerable Bede, *On Ezra and Nehemiah*.

CHAPTER 38: THE SAMARITANS

There exist reasonable online resources to learn a bit more about the Samaritans. If you want a fuller explanation, see Plumer, *Samaritans*.

To learn more about the history of the Zionist pioneers and the Palestinians, see Morris, *Righteous Victims*.

To learn more about the history of this famous phrase about the land and the people, see Garfinkle, "Origin, Meaning, Use and Abuse."

CHAPTER 39: THE LETTERS

Professor Buster's analysis comes from an article: Buster, "Ezra-Nehemiah and Esther."

For a fuller scholarly explanation of these letters, see Fensham, *Ezra and Nehemiah*, 65–93.

To learn more about Billy J. Kramer and the Dakotas, see Kramer and Shipton, *Do You Want to Know a Secret?*

CHAPTER 40: DEFENDING OURSELVES

To learn more about the Persian province called "Beyond the River," see Rainey, "Satrapy 'Beyond the River.'"

To learn more about the Palmach, see Alon, *Shield of David.*

Eric Blaustein's description of his experiences in the Palmach are described in his yet-to-be-published memoirs.

CHAPTER 41: NEHEMIAH'S ENEMIES

To learn more about Noadiah, see Mariottini, *Those Amazing Women*, ch. 12 ("Noadiah the Prophetess").

For an innovative exploration of the women's prophetic voices, see Lee, *Hannevi'ah and Hannah.*

For a fuller explanation of the importance of Frances Marion, "The Swamp Fox," see Ferling, *Winning Independence.*

For more about the context of Hubert Humphrey's speech to the 1948 Democratic Convention, see Freedman, *Into the Bright Sunshine.*

CHAPTER 42: HAGGAI AND ZECHARIAH

For a summary of the scholarship on these two prophets, see Bullock, *Old Testament Prophetic Books*, 301–23.

For a more scholarly exploration of the importance of these two prophets, see two essays in Eskenazi and Richards's *Temple and Community in the Persian Period*: Marinkovic, "What Does Zechariah 1–8 Tell Us" (for Zechariah), and Clines, "Haggai's Temple" (for Haggai).

For more on Falstaff, see Bloom, *Falstaff.*

CHAPTER 43: ALREADY BUT NOT YET

For a clear and deep analysis of Christian Scripture from a Jewish point of view, see Levine and Brettler, *Bible With and Without Jesus.*

For an explanation of messianic expectation in a Second Temple prophet, see Meyers, "Vision of 6th Century Chanukah."

CHAPTER 44: A MIGHTY HAND, AND OUTSTRETCHED ARM

For a comprehensive selection of Jewish theological responses to the Holocaust, see Cohn-Sherbok, *Holocaust Theology*.

For a deeper understanding of the thinking of one major post-Holocaust Jewish thinker, see Fackenheim, *Jewish Return into History*.

For an understanding of the role of King Josiah in the development of the Bible, see Friedman, *Who Wrote the Bible?*

For the insight of archeology on understanding King Josiah, see Dever, *What Did the Biblical Writers Know*.

CHAPTER 45: EZRA AND NEHEMIAH IN RABBINIC LITERATURE

For an introduction to the process of rabbinic interpretation of the Bible, see Fishbane, *Garments of Torah*.

To learn more about early rock songs, see Hickey, *From Savoy Stompers to Clock Rockers*.

To learn more about the origins of baseball, see Burns, "First Inning."

CHAPTER 46: LIDROSH

For a survey of Jewish scriptural interpretation, see Fishbane, *Midrashic Imagination*.

For an example of Torah interpretation, see Eisen, *Taking Hold of Torah*.

For an example of Talmud interpretation, see Wimpfheimer, *Narrating the Law*.

In addition to all of the specific sources that I listed above, I also consulted the following general commentaries to Ezra/Nehemiah:

Slotki, *Daniel, Ezra and Nehemiah*.

Myers, *Ezra-Nehemiah*.

Throntveit, *Ezra-Nehemiah*.

Angel, *Haggai, Zechariah, and Malachi*.

Rosenberg, *Books of Daniel, Ezra, Nehemiah*.

Bibliography

Adwan, Sami, et al., eds. *Side by Side: Parallel Histories of Israel-Palestine*. New York: New, 2012.

Albeck, Hanoch, ed. *Shisha Sidrei Mishna*. 6 vols. Jerusalem: Bialik Institute; Tel Aviv: Dvir, 1988.

Alon, Yigal. *Shield of David: The Story of Israel's Armed Forces*. New York: Random House, 1970.

Angel, Hayyim. *Haggai, Zechariah, and Malachi: Prophecy in an Age of Uncertainty*. New Milford, CT: Maggid, 2016.

Aristeas. *The Letter of Aristeas*. Translated by R. H. Charles. Oxford: Clarendon, 1913.

Avineri, Shlomo. *Herzl: Theodor Herzl and the Foundation of the Jewish State*. Raymond, WA: Orion, 2013.

Balfour, Arthur James. "Balfour Declaration 1917." Avalon Project, Yale Law School. https://avalon.law.yale.edu/20th_century/balfour.asp.

Bede the Venerable. *Bede: On Ezra and Nehemiah*. Translated by Scott DeGregorio. Translated Texts for Historians. Liverpool: Liverpool University Press, 2006.

Beehner, Lionel. "Pronunciation Protocol." *Los Angeles Times*, May 7, 2008. https://www.latimes.com/archives/la-xpm-2008-may-07-oe-beehner7-story.html.

Bickerman, Elias. *From Ezra to the Last of the Maccabees*. New York: Schocken, 1947.

Blackstone, William. *Palestine for the Jews*. N.p., 1891. https://www.nli.org.il/en/books/NNL_ALEPH990012469030205171/NLI.

Blenkinsopp, Joseph. *Ezra-Nehemiah: A Commentary*. Old Testament Library. Louisville: Westminster John Knox, 1988.

Bloom, Harold. *Falstaff: Give Me Life*. New York: Scribner, 2017.

The Book of Ezra. ArtScroll Tanach Series. Rahway, NJ: Mesorah, 1984.

The Book of Nehemiah. ArtScroll Tanach Series. Rahway, NJ: Mesorah, 1990.

Borg, Marcus J., and John Dominic Crossan. *The First Christmas*. New York: HarperCollins, 2009.

Boswell, Thomas. *Why Time Begins on Opening Day*. New York: Viking, 1985.

Bradshaw, Paul F., and Lawrence A. Hoffman, eds. *The Making of Jewish and Christian Worship (Two Liturgical Traditions)*. Notre Dame: University of Norte Dame Press, 1991.

Braude, William G., trans. *Pesikta Rabbati: Homiletical Discourses for Festal Days and Special Sabbaths*. 2 vols. The Yale Judaica Series 18. New Haven: Yale University Press, 1968.

Bruno, Leonard C. "Mr. Watson, Come Here." Library of Congress. https://www.loc.gov/loc/lcib/9904/bell.html.

Bullock, C. Hassel. *An Introduction to Old Testament Prophetic Books*. Chicago: Moody, 1986.

Burns, Ken. "The First Inning." Episode 1 of *Baseball: A Film by Ken Burns*. Arlington, VA: PBS, 1994.

Buster, Aubrey E. "Ezra-Nehemiah and Esther." In *The State of Old Testament Studies: A Survey of Recent Research*, edited by H. H. Hardy II and M. Danny Carroll, 217–30. Grand Rapids: Baker Academic, 2024.

Capra, Frank, dir. *It's a Wonderful Life*. Hollywood, CA: RKO, 1946.

Carlin, George. *Brain Droppings*. New York: Hachette, 1998.

Cline, Eric. *1177 BC: The Year Civilization Collapsed*. Princeton: Princeton University Press, 2015.

———. *From Eden to Exile: Unraveling Mysteries of the Bible*. Washington, DC: National Geographic, 2008.

Clines, David J. A. "Haggai's Temple Constructed, Deconstructed and Reconstructed." In *Temple and Community in the Persian Period*, edited by Tamara C. Eskenazi and Kent H. Richards, 60–87. Vol. 2 of *Second Temple Studies*. Sheffield: JSOT, 1994.

Cohn-Sherbok, Dan, ed. *Holocaust Theology: A Reader*. New York: New York University Press, 2002.

Danon, Abraham. "Bajazet II." In *The Jewish Encyclopedia*, edited by Isidore Singer, 2:460. 12 vols. New York: Funk & Wagnalls, 1901–1906. https://archive.org/details/the-jewish-encyclopedia-vol.-2/page/459/mode/2up.

Dever, William G. *What Did the Biblical Writers Know and When Did They Know It? What Archeology Can Tell Us About the Reality of Ancient Israel*. Grand Rapids: Eerdmans, 2001.

Donahue, Anne T. "Old West Cowboys and Outlaws Preferred Bowler Hats." HistoryFacts, Nov. 8, 2023. https://historyfacts.com/us-history/fact/a-giant-wave-of-molasses-once-flooded-the-streets-of-boston/.

Duggan, Michael W. *The Covenant Revival in Ezra-Nehemiah (Neh 7:72b–10:40) An Exegetical, Literary, and Theological Study*. Atlanta: Society of Biblical Literature, 2001.

Dylan, Bob. *Biograph*. Recorded 1961–1981. New York: Columbia, 1985.

Eisen, Arnold. *Taking Hold of Torah: Jewish Commitment and Community in America*. Bloomington: Indiana University Press, 1997.

Elephant and Castle. "The Story of Elephant and Castle." https://elephantandcastle.com/about-us/.

Elon, Amos. *Herzl*. New York: Holt, Rinehart & Winston, 1975.

———. *The Israelis: Founders and Sons*. Rev. ed. New York: Penguin, 1983.

Eskenazi, Tamara C. *In an Age of Prose: A Literary Approach to Ezra-Nehemiah*. SBL Monograph Series. Atlanta: SBL, 1988.

Fackenheim, Emil L. *The Jewish Return into History: Reflections in the Age of Auschwitz and a New Jerusalem*. New York: Schocken, 1978.

Farley, Maggie. "When a Name Won't Fit on the Tip of a Tongue." *Los Angeles Times*, Sept. 27, 2007. https://www.latimes.com/archives/la-xpm-2007-sep-27-fg-name27-story.html.

Faust, Abraham. *Judah in the Neo-Babylonian Period: The Archaeology of Desolation*. Atlanta: Society of Biblical Literature, 2012.

Fensham, F. Charles. *The Books of Ezra and Nehemiah*. Grand Rapids: Eerdmans, 1982.

Ferling, John E. *Winning Independence: The Decisive Years of the Revolutionary War, 1778–1781*. London: Bloomsbury, 2021.

Filstrup, Chris, and Jane Merrill. *The Turban: A History from East to West*. Chicago: University of Chicago Press, 2025.

Fishbane, Michael. *Biblical Interpretation in Ancient Israel*. New York: Oxford University Press, 1985.

———. *Garments of Torah: Essays in Biblical Hermeneutics*. Bloomington: Indiana University Press, 1989.

———, ed. *The Midrashic Imagination: Jewish Exegesis, Thought, and History*. Albany: State University of New York Press, 1993.

Freedman, Samuel G. *Into the Bright Sunshine: Young Hubert Humphrey and the Fight for Civil Rights*. New York: Oxford University Press, 2023.

Fried, Lisbeth. *Ezra: A Commentary*. Sheffield: Phoenix, 2015.

———. *Nehemiah: A Commentary*. Sheffield: Phoenix, 2021.

Friedman, David N. "The Spelling of the Name David in the Hebrew Bible" *Hebrew Annual Review* 7 (1983) 89–104.

Friedman, Richard Elliot. *Who Wrote the Bible?* San Francisco: HarperSanFrancisco, 1987.

Friedman, Samuel G. *Into the Bright Sunshine*. New York: Oxford University Press, 2023.

Garfinkle, Adam M. "On the Origin, Meaning, Use and Abuse of a Phrase." *Middle Eastern Studies* 27 (1991) 539–50.

Gesenius, William. *Hebrew and English Lexicon of the Old Testament*. Translated by Edward Robinson. Cambridge: Houghton, Mifflin, 1882.

Goffman, Daniel. *The Ottoman Empire and Early Modern Europe*. Cambridge: Cambridge University Press, 2002.

Graves, Michael. "The Public Reading of Scripture in Early Judaism." *Journal of the Evangelical Theological Society* 50 (2007) 467–87.

Guilfoile, William. "Why Cooperstown." *Road Trips: SABR Convention Journal Articles* (1989). https://sabr.org/journal/article/why-cooperstown/.

Gurkow, Lazer. "Hebrew Months – An Inspiring Explanation." Mizrachi World Movement. https://mizrachi.org/uncategorized/hebrew-months-inspiring-explanation/.

Hacker, J. R. "Jews in the Ottoman Empire 1580–1839." In *The Cambridge History of Judaism*, edited by Jonathan Karp and Adam Sutcliffe, 77–112. Cambridge: Cambridge University Press, 2017.

Hancock, Graham. *The Sign and the Seal: The Quest for the Lost Ark of the Covenant*. New York: Touchstone, 1993.

Hawks, Howard, dir. *His Girl Friday*. Culver City, CA: Columbia, 1940.

Heller, Joseph. *Catch-22*. New York: Simon & Schuster, 1961.

Hertzberg, Arthur. *The Zionist Idea: A Historical Analysis and Reader*. New York: Atheneum, 1959.

Herzl, Theodor. *The Complete Diaries of Theodor Herzl*. Edited by Raphael Patai. Translated by Harry Zohn. New York: Grosset & Dunlop, 1962.

Heschel, Abraham Joshua. *The Sabbath: Its Meaning for Modern Man*. New York: Farrar, Straus & Giroux, 1951.

Hickey, Andrew. "'Flying Home' by the Benny Goodman Sextet." Episode 1 of *A History of Rock Music in 500 Songs*, recorded Oct. 18, 2018. Podcast, transcript. https://500songs.com/podcast/flying-home-by-the-benny-goodman-sextet/.

———. *From Savoy Stompers to Clock Rockers*. Vol. 1 of *A History of Rock Music in 500 Songs*. Self-published, Lulu, 2019.

———. "'Respect' by Aretha Franklin." Episode 149 of *A History of Rock Music in 500 Songs*, recorded May 22, 2022. Podcast, transcript. https://500songs.com/podcast/episode-149-respect-by-aretha-franklin/.

———. "'Roll 'Em Pete' by Big Joe Turner and Pete Johnson." Episode 2 of *A History of Rock Music in 500 Songs*, recorded Oct. 25, 2018. Podcast, transcript. https://500songs.com/podcast/roll-em-pete-by-big-joe-turner-and-pete-johnson/.

History Editors. "Samuel Morse Demonstrates the Telegraph with the Message, 'What Hath God Wrought?'" History.com, last updated May 27, 2025. https://www.history.com/this-day-in-history/may-24/what-hath-god-wrought.

Hoffman, Joel. *A Short History of the Hebrew Language*. New York: New York University Press, 2006.

Hoffman, Lawrence A. *Beyond the Text: A Holistic Approach to Liturgy*. Bloomington: Indiana University Press, 1987.

———. *The Way into Jewish Prayer*. Woodstock, VT: Jewish Lights, 2000.

Horovitz, Saul. *Sifre on Deuteronomy*. New York: The Jewish Theological Seminary Press, 2014.

Huston, John, dir. *The Maltese Falcon*. Hollywood, CA: Warner Brothers, 1941.

Jack, Albert. *The Old Dog and Duck: The Secret Meanings of Pub Names*. London: Penguin, 2009.

Japhet, Sara. "Composition and Chronology in the Book of Ezra-Nehemiah." In *Temple and Community in the Persian Period*, edited by Tamara C. Eskenazi and Kent H. Richards, 189–216. Vol. 2 of *Second Temple Studies*. Sheffield: JSOT, 1994.

Javedanfar, Meir. "King Cyrus of Persia Rules Israel Streets OK!" Iran-Israel Observer, Jan. 22, 2014. https://iranisraelobserver.wordpress.com/2014/01/22/king-cyrus-of-persia-rules-israel-streets-ok/.

Johnson, Paul. *A History of the Jews*. New York: Harper Perennial, 1988.

Kalimi, Isaac. *An Ancient Israelite Historian: Studies in the Chronicler, His Time, Place and Writing*. Assen, Netherlands: Van Gorcum, 2005.

Kaplan, James. *Irving Berlin: The New York Genius*. New Haven: Yale University Press, 2019.

Kertzer, Morris, and Lawrence A. Hoffman. *What Is a Jew?* Rev. ed. New York: Touchstone, 1996.

Klein, Joe. *Woody Guthrie: A Life*. New York: Random House, 1999.

Koller, Aaron. *Esther in Ancient Jewish Thought*. New York: Cambridge University Press, 2014.

Kramer, Billy J., and Alyn Shipton. *Do You Want to Know a Secret? The Autobiography of Billy J. Kramer*. Sheffield: Equinox, 2016.

Krinsky, Carolyn Herselle. *Synagogues of Europe: Architecture, History, and Meaning*. New York: Dover, 1996.

Kurzman, Dan. *Genesis 1948*. Boston: Da Capo, 1992.

Lee, Nancy. *Hannevi'ah and Hannah: Hearing Women Biblical Prophets in a Women's Lyrical Tradition*. Eugene, OR: Cascade, 2015.

Levi, Gerson B., et al. "Ahasuerus." In *The Jewish Encyclopedia*, edited by Isidore Singer, 1:284–85. 12 vols. New York: Funk & Wagnalls, 1901–1906. https://www.jewishencyclopedia.com/articles/967-ahasuerus.

Levine, Amy-Jill, and Marc Zvi Brettler. *The Bible With and Without Jesus: How Jews and Christians Read the Same Stories Differently*. San Francisco: HarperOne, 2020.

Lim, Timothy H. *The Formation of the Jewish Canon*. New Haven: Yale University Press, 2013.

Lincoln, Abraham. *Collected Works of Abraham Lincoln*. Vol. 8. New Brunswick, NJ: Rutgers University Press, 1953. https://name.umdl.umich.edu/lincoln8.

Maimonides, Moses. *Mishneh Torah*. Haifa: Or Vishua, 2009.

May, Herbert, and Bruce Meztger, eds. *The New Oxford Annotated Bible with the Apocrypha, Revised Standard Version*. Oxford: Oxford University Press, 1977.

Marinkovic, Peter. "What Does Zechariah 1–8 Tell Us About the Second Temple?" In *Temple and Community in the Persian Period*, edited by Tamara C. Eskenazi and Kent H. Richards, 88–105. Vol. 2 of *Second Temple Studies*. Sheffield: JSOT, 1994.

Mariottini, Claude F. *Those Amazing Women of Ancient Israel*. Grand Rapids: Kregel Academics, 2024.

McLeod, Norman Z., dir. *Horse Feathers*. Hollywood, CA: Paramount, 1932.

Merkley, Paul Charles. "I Am Cyrus." *Christianity Today*, Aug. 8, 2008. https://www.christianitytoday.com/2008/08/i-am-cyrus/.

Meyers, Eric M. "The Vision of 6th Century Chanukah in Zechariah." TheTorah.com. https://www.thetorah.com/article/the-vision-of-6th-century-chanukah-in-zechariah.

Mikraot Gedolot. Jerusalem: Mesorah, 1986.

Milgrom, Jacob. *Leviticus 23–27*. Anchor Bible Commentaries. New Haven: Yale University Press, 2007.

Morris, Benny. *Righteous Victims: A History of the Zionist-Arab Conflict, 1881–2001*. New York: Vintage, 2001.

Myers, Jacob M. *Ezra-Nehemiah*. Anchor Bible Commentaries. New Haven: Yale University Press, 1965.

National Archives. "III. Jefferson's 'Original Rough Draught' of the Declaration of Independence, 11 June–4 July 1776." https://founders.archives.gov/documents/Jefferson/01-01-02-0176-0004#TSJN-01-01-0188-fn-0002.

Nisbet, Jeff. "Ancient Code of the Temple Builders." *Atlantis Rising*, July/August 2013. https://atlantisrisingmagazine.com/article/ancient-code-of-the-temple-builders/.

Noonan, Benjamin. *Non-Semitic Loanwords in the Hebrew Bible*. Winona Lake, IN: Eisenbrauns, 2019.

Oz, Amos, and Fania Oz-Salzberger. *Jews and Words*. New Haven: Yale University Press, 2012.

Pecise, Duane. "Baseball History Unpacked, April 2." Bleed Cubbie Blue, Apr. 2, 2025. https://www.bleedcubbieblue.com/2025/4/2/24398820/baseball-history-unpacked-april-2.

Plumer, Reinhard. *The Samaritans: A Profile*. Grand Rapids: Eerdmans, 2015.

Porten, Bezalel. "Did the Ark Stop at Elephantine?" *Biblical Archaeology Review*, May/June 1995. https://library.biblicalarchaeology.org/article/did-the-ark-stop-at-elephantine/.

———, ed. *The Elephantine Papyri in English: Three Millenia of Cross-Cultural Continuity and Change*. 2nd ed. Atlanta: Society of Biblical Literature, 2011.

Qataert, Donald. *The Ottoman Empire 1700–1922*. New York: Cambridge University Press, 2000.

Radosh, Ronald, and Allis Radosh. *A Safe Haven: Harry S. Truman and the Founding of Israel*. New York: HarperCollins, 2009.

Rainey, A. F. "The Satrapy 'Beyond the River.'" *Australian Journal of Biblical Archeology* 1.2 (1969) 51–78.

Remez, Gideon. "Alas, Poor El Al—My Granddad Name It." Times of Israel, May 16, 2020. https://blogs.timesofisrael.com/alas-poor-el-al-my-granddad-named-it/.

Rosen, Jeremy. *Minor Characters Have Their Day: Genre and the Contemporary Literary Marketplace*. New York: Columbia University Press, 2016.

Rosenberg, A. J. *The Books of Daniel, Ezra, Nehemiah: A New English Translation of the Text, Rashi and a Commentary Digest*. New York: Judaica, 1991.

Rosenberg, Stephen G. "The Jewish Temple at Elephantine." *Near Eastern Archaeology* 67 (2004). https://doi.org/10.2307/4149987.

Rubenstein, Jeffery L. *The History of Sukkot in the Second Temple and Rabbinic Periods*. Atlanta: Scholars, 1995.

Sipurei Givat Brenner. "Moshe Blaustein." https://tol.life/gbs__www/aurelia?fbclid=IwY2xjawQmonpleHRuA2FlbQIxMABicmlkETF1RjV6cHVTcjlaVlFoakY5c3JoYwZhcHBfaWQQMjIyMDM5MTc4ODIwMDg5MgABHjbQJ8Mk6RDLsJijEipe6LyntYXnwJKItlxk3hnKfwZ41HCDotEzyjRMyKzx_aem_1uUzsjGMzFUQDMGABVL-tA#/member-details/467/*

Scalf, Foy. "Persepolis: Images of an Empire." Institute for the Study of Ancient Cultures Museum. https://artsandculture.google.com/story/persepolis-isac-museum/KwVRKSxv_NfpLQ?hl=en.

Schniedewind, William. *How the Bible Became a Book: The Textualization of Ancient Israel*. Cambridge: Cambridge University Press, 2005.

Sears, Stephen W. *Chancellorsville*. Boston: Houghton Mifflin, 1996.

Segev, Tom. *One Palestine, Complete: Jews and Arabs Under the British Mandate*. London: Macmillan, 2000.

Shahbazi, Alireza Shapur. "Clothing II. In the Median and Achaemenid Periods." *Encyclopedia Iranica*, last updated Aug. 17, 2016. https://www.iranicaonline.org/articles/clothing-ii/#citation.

Shakespeare. *Hamlet*. Folger Shakespeare Library. https://www.folger.edu/explore/shakespeares-works/hamlet/read/.

Sharankshy, Natan. *Fear No Evil: The Classic Memoir of One Man's Triumph over a Police State*. New York: Random House, 1988.

Shinan, Avigdor. *Pirkei Avot: A New Israeli Commentary*. Rishon LeZion: Yediot Sefarim, 2009.

Simkovich, Malka Z. *Discovering Second Temple Literature*. Philadelphia: Jewish Publication Society, 2018.

Slotki, Judah J. *Daniel, Ezra and Nehemiah: Introduction and Commentary*. London: Soncino, 1951.

Steinsaltz, Adin, ed. *The Steinsaltz Talmud Bavli*. 42 vols. Jerusalem: Koren, 1990–2017.

Stern, Elsie R. "Esther and the Politics of Diaspora." *Jewish Quarterly Review* 100 (2010) 25–53.

———. "Megillat Esther: A Godless and Assimilated Diaspora." TheTorah.com. https://www.thetorah.com/article/megillat-esther-a-godless-and-assimilated-diaspora.

Sun Sentinel. "A Midnight Chat with Dylan." Last updated Sept. 25, 2021. https://www.sun-sentinel.com/1995/09/28/a-midnight-chat-with-dylan/.

Tec, Nechama. *When Light Pierced the Darkness: Christian Rescue of Jews in Nazi-Occupied Poland*. New York: Oxford University Press, 1987.

Thorn, John. "Debate over Baseball's Origins Spills into Another Century." *New York Times*, Mar. 12, 2011. https://www.nytimes.com/2011/03/13/sports/baseball/13thorn.html.

Throntveit, Mark A. *Ezra-Nehemiah*. Interpretation: A Bible Commentary for Teaching and Preaching. Louisville: Westminster John Knox Press, 1992.

Troy, Gil. *The Zionist Ideas: Visions for the Jewish Homeland - Then, Now, Tomorrow*. Philadelphia: Jewish Publication Society, 2018.

Tuchman, Barbara. *Bible and Sword: History of Britain in the Middle East*. London: Papermac, 1982.

Wheaton College. "I Have Plans for You: Jer 29:11 - With Dr. Michael Graves." Feb. 8, 2021, in *Exegetically Speaking*. Podcast, MP3 audio, 10:19. https://www.youtube.com/watch?v=AY4081Oobb8.

Wikipedia. "Anthony Ashley-Cooper, 7th Earl of Shaftesbury." Wikimedia Foundation, last updated Feb. 24, 2026. https://en.wikipedia.org/wiki/Anthony_Ashley-Cooper,_7th_Earl_of_Shaftesbury.

———. "The Laughing Cow." Wikimedia Foundation, last updated Feb. 6, 2026. https://en.wikipedia.org/wiki/The_Laughing_Cow.

Wilder, Laura Ingalls. *By the Shores of Silver Lake*. New York: Harper & Brothers, 1939.

Williamson, H. G. M. *Ezra-Nehemiah*. Word Biblical Commentary 16. Nashville: Nelson, 1985.

Wills, Garry. *Lincoln at Gettysburg: The Words That Remade America*. New York: Simon & Schuster, 1992.

Wimpfheimer, Barry Scott. *Narrating the Law: A Poetics of Talmudic Legal Stories*. Philadelphia: University of Pennsylvania Press, 2017.

Zangwill, Israel. "The Return to Palestine." *New Liberal Review*, December 1901.

Ziv, Otto Cohen. *Kibbutz: The Story of Givath-Brenner*. Los Angeles: Ziv, 1965.

www.ingramcontent.com/pod-product-compliance
Lightning Source LLC
LaVergne TN
LVHW050615100826
845148LV00011B/1597

* 9 7 9 8 3 8 5 2 7 1 2 3 8 *